To Mrs. M~
With ~~~
Bud Phillips
Nov. 25, 2002

Pioneers in Paradise

V. N. (Bud) Phillips

The Overmountain Press

JOHNSON CITY, TENNESSEE

Hardcover ISBN 1-57072-234-X
Trade Paper ISBN 1-57072-249-8
Copyright © 2002 by V. N. Phillips
Printed in the United States of America
All Rights Reserved

1 2 3 4 5 6 7 8 9 0

CONTENTS

INTRODUCTION

When Joseph R. Anderson founded Bristol, Tennessee/Virginia, he came close to naming his town Paradise, for such he hoped it would prove to be. The pioneer settlers of this new town found it to be a long way from the paradise its founder had envisioned. From near her beginning, Bristol was a wild and wooly, violent, grossly immoral, lawless town. And to you who think that Bristol has an overload of evil today, let it be said that our present times are as mild and harmless as a Sunday-school picnic when compared to the first few decades of her existence. Tragic and strange accidents, horrible murders, cunning thefts, robberies, shoot-outs, mayhem, fights (sometimes reaching free-for-all status), clever fraud, arson, thriving brothels, rape, incest, child neglect and abuse, even frequent sights and sounds of purported ghosts—all were part of pioneer life in the town that was almost called Paradise.

This writer is fortunate to have known many old-timers of this city who were loaded with tales of those early days. They gladly shared those tales with him, and he now feels an obligation to pass them on to you. As one old resident here expressed it: "They's been a sight of mighty quare thangs that's happened in this-here town." The writer fully agrees, and having heard about hundreds of those "quare thangs," he has concluded, "If it *can* happen, it *has* happened here in Bristol." If a thing is in range of human capability and experience—you name it—at some time and some place, it has been done in this city.

It is the opinion of this writer that in order for a city to have a complete history, some space must be devoted to her handed-down tales, legends, and lore. Such are part of any city's past and are worthy of preservation for this and coming generations. It should be explained that this work does not contain all the tales that have been shared with the author. It is rather a selection of those stories that, in his opinion, best represent what life was like for those Pioneers in Paradise, who seemingly accepted the strange and bizarre as a way of daily life.

This book, then, is an attempt to open the doors of the past and live again in those days when Bristol, as one old-timer expressed it, "was nearer to being hell than paradise." Yes, you can discover in this book that in those early days the town had a touch of both, and a lot in between. In spite of all that was negative about early Bristol, there was always much that was good, uplifting, inspiring, and heartwarming. Some of these more positive aspects of pioneer life did just about reach the borders of Anderson's envisioned Paradise, and there is a good portion included in this work. It is the hope of the author that what is read here will prove to be entertaining, informative, and enjoyable. To this end, the book was produced not only for the citizens of Bristol, but for all, near and far, who may now, or in the years to come, chance to read its pages.

V. N. (Bud) Phillips
Pleasant Hill
214 Johnson Street
Bristol, Virginia 24201-4132
276-466-6435

FOREWORD

Ice cream is available in a multitude of flavors. So also the writing of history comes in a wide variety of forms and modes. There is the sweeping survey, grandiose in its broad coverage of centuries and the formulation of general laws of civilization. There is the detailed political monograph, with a narrow concentration on the activities of legislative bodies and heads of state, and there is the economic analysis, which overwhelms the reader with a dazzling array of statistical data.

Equally important, and the forte of V. N. "Bud" Phillips, is the narrative story, a form which focuses upon the lives and activities of ordinary folks, how they lived and died and the concerns which were uppermost in their daily walk. In this volume, the fourth in his extended series on the history of Bristol, Mr. Phillips takes up several themes that amplify our knowledge of life in the Twin Cities: stagecoach travel in the early nineteenth century, local ghost stories, murder and violence and the administration of justice, and the state of moral standards in early Bristol.

Essential to any form of historical writing is the ability of the author to draw the reader into the narrative and to stimulate in his mind an intimate sense of the reality of the events that are related. And in this volume Mr. Phillips has excelled, displaying his usual fine hand for exacting detail. What reader would not find delight in the account of stagecoach "Number Five," freshly new from its maker in Abingdon and splendorous in its coat of royal purple trimmed in black and gold, making its maiden voyage to Bristol?

But like the famed *Titanic*, it was fated for an untimely destruction, although not by anything so immense as an iceberg. The culprit was an errant hornet whose random flight crossed paths with the great stage! One can well imagine that for years the story of "Number 5" must have been a favorite topic, retold many times over in country stores and at social gatherings. We are indebted to Mr. Phillips for including it in this volume and assuring permanence to the tale.

Many readers will be startled to learn that stagecoaches ran nighttime schedules. How drivers managed to find their way along rutted dirt tracks through dark forests strains the imagination. And although surely most drivers were male, Mr. Phillips introduces us to the story of "Old Moll Tate," who proved herself more than once equal to any occasion or unexpected circumstance that threatened her authority or ability to bring the stage through.

We tend to associate ghost stories and tales of the supernatural with cemeteries and abandoned houses that stand isolated on a lonely hill or are hidden in some dark crevice of a forbidding forest. The appearances of these apparitions come on those "dark and stormy nights" when shutters bang and stairs creak. But Mr. Phillips's tales of spectral beings demonstrate that Bristol's ghosts knew no such limitations. He has collected more than fifty stories which show ghosts and other unexplained phenomena appearing in virtually every quarter of Bristol, from the days of the Indians to the present. He leaves it to his readers to come to their own conclusions as to the truth or veracity of these tales, but surely there is in this volume more than ample material for any number of Halloween get-togethers for years into the future.

Mr. Phillips reminds his readers that Joseph Anderson, the founder of Bristol, once contemplated naming his newly established town "Paradise." Perhaps it is fortunate that he had second thoughts and changed his mind! This present volume details enough accounts of violence, law-breaking, and personal immorality to make it clear that Bristol was no paradise. His chapter "Hell on the Border" suggests that the Twin Cities might well have given any frontier town of the far West a run for the money when it came to acts of violence and lawlessness. And in his chapter "Morals of the Masses," Mr. Phillips takes, as he terms it, "a candid and fearless look . . . at the moral situation in early Bristol." Let the reader be warned! These stories of murder and mayhem, of prostitution, and of varying forms of sexual deviance display aspects of civic life not generally revealed in our more polite and genteel histories. But Mr. Phillips simply sets forth the facts as he as found them in the written and oral records, and his frankness can be compared to those Old Testament writers who also wrote with astonishing openness and a fearless honesty. Anyone who thinks that our present generation displays an unprecedented degree of immorality might well revise his opinion after perusing the accounts of deviance in the past that are collected in this volume. However, this section is also balanced with one entitled "Hearts of Gold," warm and loving stories of the basic goodness of countless numbers of Bristol's better citizens over the years.

All in all, there is much in this latest volume to entertain, to delight, and to instruct the reader. Once again, in giving these accounts the permanence of written publication, Mr. Phillips has performed a valuable service to the Twin Cities of Bristol, Tennessee/Virginia, and broadened our understanding of what life was actually like in those bygone days.

Dr. William J. Wade
Retired History Professor
King College

Tales of Stagecoach Days

If anyone living in Bristol forty-five years ago could make stagecoach days come alive, it was Old Daddy Thomas. Though then (1953) well into his nineties, his firsthand knowledge could not quite reach to that grand era, but his father had portrayed it vividly to him—so well that Daddy could clearly tell it to others. The elder Mr. Thomas, working with the construction crew of the Virginia and Tennessee Railroad as rails were laid into the new town of Bristol, arrived in the late summer of 1856.

The crew had first made camp on the site of the present Janie Hammitt home on a hill overlooking the Old Stagecoach Road. Later the crew moved the camp to about where Mary and Moore streets now intersect. This was within a short distance of where the stage passed down Flat Hollow and on to the stopping point on what is now known as Solar Hill. Evidently Mr. Thomas was fascinated with stage travel and often talked to his son about it. Often Daddy Thomas would begin his narration of stagecoach days in this manner:

Why, ye know, sir, I thank Pap could hear that stage a-comin' and a-passin' fer as long as he lived. He'd get to tellin' me about them fer-back times, a-settin' rat here on this very porch. He'd look yander towardge the gap [the little valley immediately north of Virginia Intermont College] and tell how the tootin' of that stage horn was his gettin' up call. Fer, ye see, one of them main stages from up the way got here soon afore daybreak about four o'clock, I thank. Old Moll Tate, that quare woman, were a drivin' that run then, and in spite of snow, storm, er high water she'd brang that stage a-rollin' through the gap jist about the same time ever' mornin'. Pap said the crackin' of her whip over the heads of them horses sounded lack the shootin' of a high-powered rifle. And when she done it, she'd call ever' one of them horses by name. Lack "Gitty up, Frank, Napo-

— 1 —

Daddy Thomas told of stagecoach days and of many other events in early Bristol.

leyon, Nicholas, and Big Dan." Pap 'membered ever' one of 'em. She'd allus [always] go through that crackin' and callin' as they got nigh that hainted graveyard in the Flat Hollow [present Rice Terrace], fer stage horses had been knowed to get to boogerin' and plumb balk there and woulden go by a'tall. But Old Moll could allus bring 'em through. Pap said that old woman [she was then in her late forties] could've drove that stage through the middle of hell and never get a scorch. Well, that buryin' ground was nigh to the places where Pap and 'em fellers camped, so they diden have any trouble a-hearin' their gettin' up call. They had to get up soon of a mornin' so's they could be at their work place by daylight. And Pap told a sight more about them stage days too.

The "sight more" that Pap, and others, told about those stagecoach days will be referred to throughout this chapter.

History

The claim has been made that stage services were operating in the late 1700s through the area where present Bristol is located. After careful research of the matter, this writer has come to the conclusion that the claim cannot be substantiated. He believes that stage service has been confused with mail delivery, which did begin in the area in 1794. The early mail route was called the Western Post and was serviced by riders on horseback. The route began in Philadelphia, extended through Southwest Virginia, crossed the state line near Bristol, passed through Sullivan and Hawkins counties in Tennessee, and continued on southwestward to Knoxville. By 1797, another route had also been established, running between Knoxville and Nashville. The early mail service—greatly dependent upon conditions of horse and rider, weather, flooding streams, and openness of narrow trails and primitive roads—was no doubt unpredictable.

It is virtually certain that stage service was operating in Southwest Virginia and East Tennessee by 1805, when Postmaster General Grainger awarded a stage mail contract to William Cocke, who was to deliver the mail from Blountville to Knoxville, Tennessee. It appears that the service operated on a rather irregular basis.

By June 1809, a Mr. Robert Hall had established a twice-weekly stage service over the same line. His service in Tennessee included regular stops at Christianville (now Kingsport), Rogersville, Bean Station, and Rutledge. It is evident that Blountville was being reached by a line that extended from Washington, D.C., to Nashville, via Abingdon, Virginia, and included the Blountville to Knoxville section as outlined above. The same records mention that four-horse coaches were being used and that, at some point in the period, this was a once-per-week service.

By 1810, the principal thoroughfare running through this section was called the Great Stagecoach Road. By 1817, a branch line had been established from Estillville (now Gate City) in Scott County, Virginia, to Christianville, to connect there with the northeast-southwest routes. The stage from Estillville arrived in Christianville on Sunday. By 1826, service through the area had been increased to three times per week, and some larger—and allegedly faster—stages, pulled by six-horse teams, were occasionally used on the principal routes.

Perhaps it should be mentioned here that stage service began about 1820 from Abingdon through Paperville, Union (present Bluff City), and on to Jonesborough. There it connected with another line leading on to Knoxville. The route taken by this line became known as the Old Jonesborough Road, a name still used. This writer has interviewed old-timers whose grandparents well remembered the stages which ran along that route.

One of them told of an incident his grandmother could never forget: One day the stage had to make an emergency stop at a wayside home that stood on the present Bristol Country Club property. It seems that a young passenger had become deathly ill. The parents and child were taken into the wayside home, where the child worsened and died during the night. The next morning, burial was made on the farm (somewhere on the country club grounds). A day or two later the parents caught another stage and journeyed on, never to visit the area again. The grave has long been lost.

It also seems that for a time stage service operated along the Watauga Road. This line began in or near Abingdon, passed down Holston Valley, and by some route went on to Elizabethton, where a connection could be made to Jonesborough and a main line to Knoxville.

In 1839, the Sapling Grove Post Office began operating in the home of Rev. James King, which stood at what is now 54 King Street in Bristol, Virginia. This apparently caused a rerouting of the line so that the new post office could be serviced. Prior to the change, the stagecoaches traveled along the Old Island Road, some distance from Bristol. Though the old King home was never set up as a wayside tavern, it was often used as such.

However, there is no record that relay horses were ever kept there, as was often the case with regular taverns.

In October 1853, the Sapling Grove Post Office was discontinued. A month later the mail was received and dispatched from the point where Sycamore Trail crossed the Old Stagecoach Road (present intersection of Sycamore Street and King's Alley). Nehemiah Strange, a slave who belonged to Joseph R. Anderson, always met the stage at that point for the purpose of the mail exchange, a practice which continued until the establishment of regular railroad passenger service to Bristol nearly three years later.

On October 1, 1856, the first passenger train came steaming toward Bristol. It caught up with and passed a stagecoach that was rolling along a dusty road, somewhere in the vicinity of Glade Spring, Virginia. A professor aboard the train made the wise observation that this passing foretold the end of stage service in the area. How right he was. Less than a month later, service had ceased from Lynchburg to Bristol.

Though main-line stage service ended in Bristol on October 28, 1856, the new town then became the point of origin for another line, which operated for several years. This line began in Bristol, then ran through Blountville, Kingsport, Rogersville, and on to Knoxville. At a later date, Henry Nave, a veteran stage driver, operated stage service from Bristol to Estillville. Connections could be made in Estillville for Jonesville and points west.

Until the East Tennessee and Virginia Railroad reached Bristol from Knoxville in 1858, there was still a need for stage service between those cities. Lewis Bachelor, a local drayman, picked up mail and passengers at the Bristol depot and transported them in a surrey to the old Hammer home in nearby Paperville, the stage stopping point along the Old Jonesborough Road.

An indication of the speed (or slowness) of stage travel of the period can be measured from an old timetable from the late 1820s. A stage left Blountville at 2:00 P.M. on Thursday and arrived at Bean Station at 11:00 Friday morning. Knoxville was reached twenty-four hours later (11:00 A.M Saturday). The forty-three miles from Blountville to Rogersville (considered to be a difficult stretch of road) took sixteen-and-one-half hours.

As were the later railroad and bus routes, the stage lines were made up of connecting divisions, usually owned by different individuals or companies. One early owner of a large section of the route was George Oury of

Christianville. With twelve coaches and fourteen four-horse teams (fifty-six horses), he had large stables in Christianville, but most of the horses were parceled out to relay stations, which were usually from ten to fifteen miles apart. Occasionally, as in the case of Mr. Oury, one person might own two, three, or even four connecting divisions.

Most divisions were from twenty-five to forty miles long. Bristol was on the Abingdon-Blountville Division, a distance of about twenty-five miles. It appears that this division at one time may have been owned by Henry Sinon (Simon) of Abingdon.

The Route

The old stage road, as rerouted in 1839, left the Old Island Road at West Point, the old Goodson homestead on Beaver Creek, about two miles above the newly established Sapling Grove Post Office. It followed Beaver Creek Valley through Long Bottom (now Mumpower Park), where it crossed the stream near the present railroad underpass southeast of the Janie Hammitt home. As late as the mid-1950s, a few old-timers referred to the crossing as the old stage ford. Beyond the ford, the road entered what was then known as Flat Gap (the little valley immediately north of Virginia Intermont College). At the end of this gap, the road descended down Flat Hollow along present Oakview Street.

At the head of the hollow is where the long tin horn was sounded by the assistant stage driver, advising of the approach to the Sapling Grove stopping point. The road passed directly by the Flat Hollow Cemetery at the corner of present Oakview and Buckner streets, then on through the present Rice Terrace area, crossing Piedmont at the point where it now intersects Oakview. From there it crossed the flat in front of the Bristol Steel building, then entered what is now known as King's Alley. It passed over what came to be known as Burn's Hill (the steep incline immediately south of Scott Street) and along King's Alley to the old King home, where Sapling Grove Post Office was located until 1853. (King's Alley now becomes King Street once Cumberland is crossed.) From the old King home, it swung around the high curve (now the corner of Sullins and King streets) from which there was a splendid view of the meadows and fields of the King plantation and the majestic mountains beyond. From this curve the road passed down what is now Sullins Street to the Little Creek Valley (earlier called Baker's Creek). A crossing of this creek was made between present State and Shelby streets. The route then angled into and followed what became Shelby Street to a point near Fourteenth Street, where it made a slow angle into what is now Broad Street and roughly passed along the present route of that street through Steele Creek Park and on toward Blountville. Remnants of the road between present Bristol and Blountville yet exist and are used today.

At Blountville the line split. One branch proceeded to Jonesborough, Greeneville, and on to Knoxville. The other went westward, rejoining the Old Island Road just before crossing Eaton's (later called Eden's and now Chestnut) Ridge to Exchange Place. Beyond Exchange Place the line passed on through Kingsport, Rogersville, Rutledge, and finally to Knoxville, where the two lines reconverged. Eventually another line was established from Kingsport to Estillville and westward to Jonesville and points beyond.

The Drivers

It has been said that a successful stagecoach driver had to be tough as a pine knot, healthy as a spring colt, wise as a serpent, and enduring as a granite mountain. Indeed, to endure the rigors of the road, he had to have an iron constitution; and certainly a great amount of discernment and wisdom was a necessity. A driver was always under pressure. One of the first requirements of employment was that he sign an agreement to have the coaches at certain stops by specified times. Otherwise he had to pay one dollar for every fifteen minutes that he was late. Only unavoidable incidents, such as when a wheel fell off or a coach turned over, would be accepted as an excuse for being late.

Too, he had to be an officer of the law. Almost invariably, a driver was deputized by the sheriffs of the counties through which the route passed. This enabled him to serve as the peace officer for the passengers he accompanied and to make arrests, if necessary. Occasionally such authority had to be exercised, not always under pleasant or safe conditions. At all times, the driver was charged with the safe delivery of his passengers, providing as much comfort for them as was possible. He also was obliged to keep his section of the stage road in good repair.

The latter challenge was not easily met. Most of the roads were nothing but ungraded, widened trails with no real means of adequate drainage. The rough and rocky paths usually followed the lines of least resistance, winding through woods, across streams, and up and down steep hills. Occasionally a fortunate driver had folks living along his route who were concerned enough with their own convenience that they did the road work for him.

Though charged with the comfort of his passengers, the driver had little comfort himself. He sat high on the top and front of his swinging, swaying, bouncing coach, trying to control and guide a usually high-spirited team of four horses. (At times, a special fast coach was pulled by six horses.) There he had to remain in all kinds of weather, because the stage had to continue on regardless of the elements. To be sure, there were many balmy, pleasant days and nights. But there were also times of violent storms with high winds, heavy driving rains, and sometimes the much-dreaded pelting hail. Some drivers had a sort of wooden shield, which they held over their heads when hail peppered down upon them. Nearly all of them carried long, supposedly waterproof capes, which offered a measure of protection from the rain. Mightily dreaded were thunderstorms. Being perched high atop a coach when lightning slashed all around was a harrowing experience.

It is said that on the run from Abingdon, Virginia, to Blountville, Tennessee, only one place offered some protection from such dangers. A large barn which stood near present Wyndale had a side shed under which a stagecoach could be driven. Rarely would a coach be in that area, however, when a violent storm struck, but fortunate drivers are known to have used the roadside refuge.

In connection with the storms, it was not uncommon for a stage to be stopped by a tree that had been blown across the narrow roadway. The drivers hoped that no trees or large limbs would fall upon the coach. On peaceful days, though, branches which frequently overlapped the long stretches of road did offer some protection from the sun.

Indeed, blazing summer sun was a problem. Broad-brimmed hats helped shield the drivers. Old Moll, the legendary woman stagecoach driver whose story is told in the following pages, chose a stovepipe-type bonnet which offered a little summer (and winter) relief. Drivers who did not easily tan wore gloves which reached to their elbows as protection against sunburn. Made of leather, the gloves heated up to the point that accumulated sweat almost scalded the drivers' hands, virtually giving them the choice between scald or sunburn.

Summer travel also brought dense, choking clouds of dust that swirled upward from pounding horse hooves and rolling wheels. Against it there was little, if any, defense. Driver and passengers often arrived at their destinations with sweat-soaked bodies caked in dust. One traveler who started out from Abingdon complained that by the time he reached Blountville his heavy black hair had turned yellow and was so dry that it would break.

Frigid winters were even more dreadful. The stage had to go through in spite of falling, often heavy, snow. The poor driver had but little protection against the elements, which also included blizzard-like sleet storms and long hours of cold rain. The overlapping trees which gave some relief from summer sun did not shield from the icy winds of winter, and their swaying bare limbs only served as reminders of the arctic blasts from the leaden skies. Sometimes on even cloudless days with shining sun, the temperature might hover around zero degrees.

The stage companies offered a little relief by filling metal boxes—a small one for the driver and a larger flat one for passengers—with fire coals. The boxes helped to some degree, but the coals had often cooled before another coaling station was reached. Because the box which was provided for the driver was exposed to the freezing wind, it often cooled quickly. The one provided for the passengers was set in the coach floor, and the tug-of-war to find places for numerous feet was not conducive to peace among cold, road-weary travelers.

One driver had his wife knit for him three pairs of heavy wool socks, each a little larger than the other, so that all could be worn at the same time. Perhaps he had the warmest feet on the line.

The foot-warming boxes were filled at the beginning of the run, then replenished at coaling stations along the line. The stations were not owned or maintained by the stage companies, but were simply hospitable homes which provided the services without financial remuneration.

According to the late Reveley and Hattie Owen and others, the old Goodson home (West Point) on Beaver Creek was such a station. An early traveler relayed an instance when the stage once stopped there between 3:00 A.M. and 4:00 A.M. A slave had risen sometime before the stage arrived, had stirred up the fires, and thus had plenty of hot coals to refill the foot warmers.

In spite of three pairs of woolen socks, foot-warming boxes, and passengers wrapped in numerous warm garments, winter stage travel at its best was a frosty ordeal—something to be avoided if possible. It is said that stage travel usually dropped fifty percent in winter, especially during the coldest months.

There was not much sleep for the drivers, who lived at one end of their divisions. In most cases when they drove that division, they had to drive back before any rest could be had. (There was a day's layover on some of the longer runs.) On the night run from Abingdon to Blountville, for example, the stage left Abingdon around 1:00 in the morning, and Blountville was reached about six hours later. The driver then waited until 9:30 A.M. before beginning the run back to Abingdon. It was not unusual for drivers, including Old Moll Tate, to snooze on the hard floors of the repair shop at Blountville while waiting to begin the up run. Once back in Abingdon, what sleep that could be had was wedged into those short hours before the Blountville run began again.

The drivers were under relentless pressure from the postal authorities—not only as to speed, but as to the safety of the all-important mail: It must be kept dry at all costs, even though most of the bags were not waterproof. Sometimes passenger comfort had to be sacrificed to fulfill this requirement. If rains were encountered, passengers might find themselves seated on the mailbags, which would be removed from the top of the coach and placed on the seats inside, or sometimes the bags were placed in the laps of the passengers.

Old Moll Tate, after suffering a mail robbery, always carried a dummy mailbag stuffed with cut-up newspapers. The real mailbag was kept hidden under the regular baggage.

This writer has many letters that were delivered into the area by stagecoach. Indeed, they appear to have been kept dry, and the fact that they did arrive is proof of their safety. Postage rates are marked on many of them, varying from ten to thirty cents, rather expensive for the period. In order to speed up the mail, drivers often tried to cut time from their schedules, even to the point of jeopardizing the safety of all concerned.

It is understandable that many drivers, who may have started their careers as jovial souls, soon become querulous, irritable, and outright cantankerous. Some of them seemed to want to take it out on the passengers. For example, a driver might announce before bedtime at a wayside stop that the stage would start again at 4:00 A.M. If that driver couldn't sleep because of indigestion, a bad bed, or whatever, he might jump out of bed at 2:00 A.M. and rudely wake the sleeping passengers with the announcement that the stage would be leaving in fifteen minutes.

Most runs also had an extra hand, an assistant driver of sorts, whose duty it was to help with the operation of the stage in any way needed. He was the horse changer at the relay stations, and he also did minor repairs. It was his privilege and duty to "sound the trumpet." A long tin horn was kept aboard, and it served a vital purpose. When the coach approached a stopping point, the horn would be sounded some distance from the expected stop. Many of the assistants prided themselves on their distance abilities, that is, sounding the horn to be heard at the greatest possible distance. Some of the men were excellent at long-distance trumpeting, able to make themselves heard for over a mile.

When approaching a tavern, the trumpeter sounded two or three long blasts to alert the inn and to let the passengers know that the stage was drawing close. He then blew shorter blasts (called "toots" by many people of the time), one for each passenger aboard, so the tavern hosts would know how many guests to prepare for.

The assistants received little pay. Their real purpose was to be trained as future stage drivers, and many of them went on to that goal. Others decided that because of the rigors of stage driving it was not the profession they wanted to take on, so they dropped out to pursue other vocations.

At first the stagecoaches traveled only during daylight hours, but by 1845 they were being driven on through the night. Thus the work of the drivers became more difficult. Traveling by night was much slower than by day, causing the work hours of the much-stressed drivers to be extended. Certainly any driver who worked during the nocturnal hours needed good night vision. However, according to travelers of the time, some of the teams just seemed to know the road and could safely pull the stage through the darkness.

The pay of a stage driver was very little. Charles Clemmons, a veteran driver, used to tell that his top earnings amounted to about five dollars per week. It is likely that other drivers received similar pay.

Some well-known early drivers (1820s) were A. M. Stanley, James Leedy, and his brother Horace Leedy. Another brother, Doss Leedy, was a horseback mail carrier through Southwest Virginia and East Tennessee.

Later stage drivers (1840s-1850s) included Henry Nave, Campbell Galliher, Charles Clemmons, and Henry Kerry. All these men drove for the Abingdon-Blountville Division, and all later settled in or near Bristol.

The story of another stage driver, the legendary Old Moll Tate, follows.

Old Moll Tate and Stage Number Nine

It may come as a surprise to learn that a woman driver once engineered

Old Moll Tate was the only woman known to have driven a stagecoach through Bristol.

the night stage run from Abingdon to Blountville. Indeed, she became a legend in her own time, and as late as the mid-twentieth century, a few elderly Bristolians still spoke of her. She was born into the Gragg family in the river hills somewhere in the vicinity of Greendale, Washington County, Virginia. She was named Mary Melzeeda Susan Elizabeth Cynthia Parnintha Sarah Adeline Rosey Daisy Laura Lucretia Louisa Jane for all the ladies who attended her birth, as well as two or three of her mother's sisters. Anyone with the name of Mary was often called Molly, so folks used the first of her fourteen names, which in time became Molly and then Moll. By the time she began driving a coach she was called Old Moll.

She was barely fourteen when she married thirty-seven-year-old Wilburn Tate, a twice-widowed neighbor. Soon after, they moved into the town of Abingdon, and several children were born to them. In the early 1850s a plague of some kind struck the town, and Mr. Tate and all the children, except one, died. The survivor was the oldest, a son, whose given name was Talbert. Old Moll was left alone with her son and no real means of support. Life became difficult for them.

In time she hired out to a family by the name of Clark, who lived a short distance west of Abingdon on the stage road. Working as a field hand, Moll often observed the passage of stagecoaches. One day as the field hands stopped to watch a coach go by, Mr. Clark, knowing Moll needed permanent employment, teasingly told her she ought to get a job as a stage driver. He knew how well she could handle a team, but in those days, of course, lady stage drivers were unheard of.

This set Moll to thinking. Looking ahead to a winter without a way to earn the bare necessities for existence was depressing and frightening.

She well knew the farm work would end in the fall and many long, cold, and hungry months would pass before such work would again be available. With bravery, perhaps born of sheer desperation, she walked to Abingdon and boldly asked for work on the stage line.

The story goes that an assistant was desperately needed on the Abingdon-Marion Division. The boss reluctantly agreed to let her try it— temporarily. Perhaps he too was acting on desperation. It soon became apparent that Moll Tate could handle the job with ease, indeed, far better than some of the regular drivers. With amazing rapidity she became an expert trumpeter. Shortly thereafter came her grand opportunity when the regular driver became ill and another driver was not available. It was left up to Moll to do it, and she did. She arrived in Marion a good half hour ahead of schedule, something no other driver had ever done.

She was put on as a regular driver on the Abingdon-Marion Division. In time, primarily because of her unusual night vision, she was given the night run from Abingdon to the new town of Bristol and on to Blountville. Even in darkness her steady speed was remarkable. Beyond Bristol, in daylight hours, folks gathered on their porches to see Old Moll and her coach (Number Nine) whiz by. An extra-tall woman, she always sat straight as a poker on the high seat. She seldom looked to the left or right; with her sharp, hawklike eyes she peered straight ahead as she guided the four horses over the rough and winding road.

Old Moll gave personalized service. Not only was she a capable stage driver, she was also willing to do about anything for the good of her passengers and for those who lived along her route. All up and down the line, her kind acts and generous helpfulness were well-known. She often delivered messages, presents, and supplies, all above and beyond her line of duty.

A new bride who was living near present Wallace, Virginia, wanted to send her mother some fresh gingerbread for Christmas. The mother lived near Blountville, Tennessee. The coach was halted before the new bride's front gate at about 3:00 A.M. A tired, sleepy young woman handed the spicy-smelling package up to Old Moll. Mother had gingerbread for her breakfast that morning.

Another young woman, perhaps of a poorer lot, stopped the coach in predawn hours, just above Bristol. She told Old Moll that she was "dying for some of Maw's good fresh eggs." About four miles west of Bristol, Number Nine stopped before a rather humble farmhouse. There, Old Moll and her drowsy passengers patiently waited while "Maw" sent a son to the barn to gather up a dozen or so fresh eggs. They were delivered to the hungry daughter by return stage later that day.

Messages of deaths, funeral notices, sicknesses, weddings, and bits of important news were all kindly delivered by Old Moll Tate. As her coach rolled along the rough roads, no one could be sure just what rolled with it. Whenever a death message was delivered, she always spent some time trying to console the bereaved, endearing herself to many a broken heart.

One traveler told of how one bright morning Old Moll stopped Number Nine at the entry of a narrow lane which led to a farmhouse some distance from the road. She left her assistant holding the reins while she walked about halfway up the lane. There, to someone standing on the porch, she called out, "Your Aunt Nan is improving fast. They gave her solid food last night." (Aunt Nan had been abed with typhoid and had long been on a liquid diet.) Doubtless, Old Moll's kind mission eased a few worried minds that morning.

Once, a little boy near Blountville was sick with measles. As often happens in such cases, he lost his appetite. He seemed to crave nothing. Eventually, he felt well enough to eat watermelon, and Moll heard about his desire. The next morning, before daylight, the stage was rolling along under a bright moonlit sky when Mulberry Grove was reached. (This was the large Frank Preston place above Wallace, Virginia. Though now gone, some readers may remember it as The Oaks, long the home of Bristol's noted H. P. King.) A stop was made, and Old Moll climbed a fence and walked far to the backside of the farm to a large watermelon patch. Shortly she returned with a nice fat watermelon under her arm. A sick little boy was made happy by the arrival of just what he wanted. No one would have called this stealing; there was not a farmer along the line who would not have gladly given a dozen melons to a sick and suffering child.

Old Moll made up for the unscheduled stops by "trottin'" the horses a little faster. Unscheduled stops or not, she always made it to her destination on time, often before she was expected.

While the driver on Number Nine, she delivered at least two babies. Once, somewhere in the vicinity of the old Goodson Place, two miles above Bristol, a distraught young man ran out from his cottage, entreating Old Moll to take word to Dr. R. M. Coleman to come quickly, for this young husband's wife was about to have a baby. Old Moll took time to go in and see for herself. She immediately realized that there was not time to get word to Dr. Coleman, and certainly not time for him to ride there. She told her passengers to take a stretch break, for she had a little job to do. She successfully delivered the baby and then drove right on along her line.

At another time a pregnant young passenger unexpectedly and suddenly went into labor. The coach was quickly stopped. Old Moll shooed the male passengers down the road a bit, then did what she had to do. A little later Number Nine was driven perhaps a mile from the usual route, and the weak mother and baby were safely ensconced at the young woman's paternal home in Blountville.

Old Moll was like that; her many acts of kindness were legendary. Though she was noted for her extreme thoughtfulness and kindness, she could be very firm. She discharged every duty as a stage driver and conductor, however unpleasant and demanding the task.

One night she left Abingdon, carrying only a couple and their child, a little girl about two years old. Such light loads were uncommon but occasionally did happen. She noticed that the parents seemed to be "at outs" when they entered the coach. In the vicinity of present Wyndale, their "at outs" erupted into a full-fledged battle, and they came to blows, as the old-timers used to say. Old Moll stopped the coach, pulled them out, flung them toward the bushes, slammed the door, crawled back upon her seat, and drove on. Perhaps a mile down the road, she suddenly remembered that the couple had a child with them when they boarded the coach in Abingdon. Again she stopped and found the lone child sleeping peacefully on a seat. She quickly turned her stage around and went back to the point where she had roughly discharged the fighting passengers.

They could not be found. The child was brought into Bristol and placed in the care of Mr. and Mrs. Jesse Aydlotte, who, Old Moll knew, would be very kind. The child grew up with the Aydlottes, never knowing who she really was. She married in Bristol (Daddy Thomas thought her husband's name was Williams), and the couple soon moved to Louisiana.

Old-timers long pondered over the mysterious disappearance of the girl's parents. Most of them believed that the husband murdered the wife— could have been vice versa—concealed the body, and then fled the area. To this day the mystery has never been solved.

Once, Number Nine had been crowded during a trip from Abingdon to Bristol. Upon arrival, all passengers got out, except two: a beautiful young widow and a middle-aged man. Old Moll, a rather wise judge of human nature, felt that there might be "complications" in such a situation, so she determined to keep an open ear for any sounds of distress from within the coach. As the stage rolled along through the predawn darkness, on what is now the general route of Broad Street, there was a scream in the coach, followed quickly by another. Actually, the stage had not gone far beyond the crossing of Little Beaver Creek (near the present site of Builders First Source), when the male passenger had moved across the center aisle to sit by the young widow. Then he moved closer and closer. Indeed, he took hold of her soon after that section of the Old Stagecoach Road which is now Broad Street was reached. Though she firmly resisted his advances, he would not let her go. It was then that the screaming began.

Old Moll knew what was happening. She brought the trotting horses to a halt. Whip in hand, she jumped down from her perch and quickly opened the door. Apparently the man was so intent on accomplishing his purpose that he did not realize that the coach had stopped; he still held the frightened young woman in his clutches.

Old Moll broke the clench. After jerking him loose from the widow, she dragged him from the coach, kicked him two or three times, then flung him into the brush at the roadside. She managed to give him a few lashes before he was beyond the reach of her whip. Assuring the young widow safe passage from there on, Moll closed the door and climbed back up to the driver's seat. With the usual roll call of her horses and the crack of the long whip over their backs, the stage lurched forward and rolled on toward Blountville. No one ever knew what became of the amorous male passenger.

So, for several years Old Moll expertly fulfilled her duties on her division of the great northeast-southwest stage line. Stories of those years are numerous—so numerous that they cannot all be included here. At first it was a means of earning a living, a challenging and unusual one for a woman. Before long it became a passion with her, a passion to surpass all others in the efficient and praiseworthy operation of a stagecoach service. From all accounts it appears that she did just that.

The Great Stage Robbery of 1855

Though there was usually not much, if any, cash inside the mail transported by stagecoach, most passengers carried money, occasionally in rather sizeable sums. Many wary passengers did not keep currency in the clothing they wore but hid it away in their satchels or bags. Some of them devised ingenious methods of concealing valuables, such as making pockets high up coat sleeves or under collars. One old veteran traveler told, long after his traveling days were over, that he always packed an extra pair of oversized boots with double insoles. Between those insoles he hid paper bills, often in large amounts.

It was not at all uncommon for male passengers, and often the females, to be armed in anticipation of a robbery attempt. Stage driver Old Moll Tate, known to be a crack shot when it came to using a firearm, always carried two pistols, and she kept a loaded rifle within handy reach. It was told that she could knock out a squirrel's eye at fifty yards.

Usually, month after month, year after year, the stage rolled along safely, each run being more or less uneventful. Things were a bit different on the morning of May 1, 1855.

Number Nine, the coach driven from Abingdon to Blountville by Old Moll, was running a bit late when a brief stop was made at Barker's Station, a few miles west of Bristol. (For years a post office that operated there was known as Stop, Tennessee. The old Barker home still stands on Old Stagecoach Road and, in recent years, was occupied by Mr. and Mrs. Brian Lewis.)

Old Moll, trying to make up lost time, left Barker's Station, pressing the horses hard. As was usual at such times, she was leaning forward, calling

This old house, known as Barker's Station still stands near Bristol

all the horses by name and cracking her long whip in the air over their backs. By the time Carden's Crossing (present Carden Hollow Road) was reached, early daylight was filtering through a moderately heavy fog. Beyond the crossing was Murphy's Lane, where timber and heavy brush crowded close to the narrow thoroughfare, making it even narrower. It was a rather dark and spooky stretch of road even in broad daylight.

One reason—perhaps the principal reason—that Old Moll had been given the night run was because of her remarkable night vision. She always claimed that she could see better in darkness than in daylight. Her good night vision was needed when she entered Murphy's Lane, for the little daylight which had penetrated the fog had not reached into that dark passage.

Leaning forward and intently peering over the horses' heads as if she were using their ears for rifle sights, she saw a fallen tree extending from thicket to thicket across the road. This was not a rare occurrence, especially after windstorms, and there had been one during the night. Old Moll set her assistant to sounding the emergency stop signal on his long tin horn. She quickly drew in the reins and yelled booming *whoa*'s to the horses, thus bringing Number Nine to a screeching halt.

A saw and two axes, kept on top of the coach for emergencies, were soon in the hands of some of the male travelers, and it appeared that the trip could be resumed shortly. Had anyone looked closely enough, it would have been discovered that the tree had been chopped down instead of being felled by a windstorm. This might have put the group on alert; but as it was, no one noticed.

Old Moll busied herself, overseeing the log removal by the passenger volunteers while other passengers dozed, yawned, and stretched to relieve travel fatigue or to wake up for the day ahead. Wake up they did! Suddenly, three masked bandits rose from the thicket with pistols drawn and cocked. It happened so fast that if arms were present—and they doubtless were—there was no time to draw them. Two robbers covered the passengers and crew while the other collected wallets and purses. Old Moll reluctantly handed over the mailbags but with the oath that she would see all three of them in hell or know the reason why. The outlaws then disappeared in the brush as quickly as they had come.

Later, the sleepy little hamlet of Blountville was startled by the emergency signal which sounded from the rapidly approaching stage. Old Moll was standing up, leaning forward and furiously cracking her whip over the backs of the racing horses. The late Rhea Anderson remembered an old Blountville resident had told of the excitement caused by the arrival of the robbed stagecoach. He remembered that townsmen came running, some leaving breakfast on the table, while late sleepers jumped from their beds and hastened to hear what had happened. In a short time the high sheriff and several deputies galloped off toward Murphy's Lane and Carden Hollow.

It is not known how much time elapsed before the bandits were apprehended, but eventually they were arrested and brought to the Blountville jail. It has been told that a merchant of Union (present Bluff City) became suspicious when certain locally known rogues suddenly had an unexplainable flush of money to spend. He contacted the sheriff, and the arrests were made.

An incident soon happened in Blountville that was long told and retold by those who were then living there. It seems that Old Moll had fumed much over the humiliation of being held up. She always felt personally responsible for the passengers who rode her stage and deeply regretted that they had been robbed of their valuables. Some of them were traveling long distances and had been left practically destitute far from home and in a strange land.

When she learned that the outlaws were in the Blountville jail, she told a friend that she would "tend to them" on her next run. Indeed, she did. As soon as she turned the reins of her coach over to the next section's driver, she, with the long horsewhip twirling in her hand, marched right over to the county jail. There she told the jailer and sheriff that she had come to "whip the breeches off them devils" who had robbed her passengers. Apparently, the sheriff agreed that her plan of punishment was worthy, for he stood by with gun in hand while the gnarled old stage driver proceeded to do just what she had promised. She very nearly did whip the breeches off the three bandits.

Unfortunately, the court records of Sullivan County were burned during the Civil War, so the final punishment of the robbers cannot be determined. One thing is virtually certain: They never forgot the morning when Moll Tate applied her form of frontier justice. As Old Daddy Thomas used to say, "That woman were a hellcat when she got riled."

The End of Stage Service in Bristol

When stage service ended on her line in 1856, Old Moll was again

Talbert Tate, Old Moll's son, became a railroad engineer.

without a job. For a few years she remained in Abingdon. Like many others, she was a widow with no certain means of making a living. She struggled valiantly, trying to provide for herself and Talbert, her only child. A neighbor family often had kept him during the years she worked, and he had become almost a son to that family. But they were also poor, so the real responsibility of his keep was upon Old Moll.

Finally, she turned to that last resort of widows: washing and ironing for her more fortunate neighbors. Old-timers remembered that a family living nearby allowed Old Moll to use their spring area as a wash place. She was often seen there, bending low over the pots and tubs, hour after long hour, in all kinds of weather. Always there were numerous garments hanging on clotheslines and fluttering in the breeze.

When the Civil War became a real threat, the family that had cared for Talbert decided to move to Texas, thinking it would keep their several young sons from having to fight in the war. They asked Old Moll to move with them. She always said she just couldn't live without her only child, so she readily agreed to the move.

The family, Old Moll, and Talbert settled near the little village of Joshua in Johnson County, Texas, a few miles directly south of Ft. Worth. There, for many years, she earned a living by working on the farm of the folks with whom she had moved from Abingdon. It was a hard life, laboring long hours under a broiling Texas sun. It is told that she continued this work until the last year of her life.

In time Old Moll's son became an engineer on the Texas and Pacific Railroad. As his mother had done on the stage line, Talbert became an efficient and faithful worker on the railroad. He married and became the father of eight children.

Mary Melzeeda Susan Elizabeth Cynthia Parnintha Sarah Adeline Rosey Daisy Laura Lucretia Louisa Jane Gragg Tate died in 1913. Old Moll is buried on a little cedar-shaded knoll, within sight of where she lived her Texas years. Few, if any, who pass by know that in the shade of those ancient cedars rests a woman who once was an expert stage driver long before and far away.

The Coaches

Many people think of stagecoaches as being drab, colorless, strictly utilitarian vehicles. Not so with those which ran through the Bristol area. According to Ann Bachelor, who arrived by stage in 1855, they were painted in bold, three-color schemes, with special decorations on the doors. The one that brought her to the area was green, gold, and white and had what appeared to be a family coat-of-arms on the side doors. Some coaches of the time bore the coat-of-arms of the family which owned the stage line, and that may well have been the case with the one she described.

She remembered another coach on the same stage line that was done in crimson, gold, and black, with pastoral scenes painted on the doors by hand. The coaches were well upholstered, some in fabrics that seemed to be a little too delicate for the wear they received. The better coaches had leather upholstery.

The back wheels, about five feet high, were taller than those in front, which measured only about three-and-one-half feet. The reason for the size difference is hard to determine. It may have helped when going uphill, but on downhill runs the passengers had to hold on for dear life or be thrown around.

The coaches were not mounted on springs; rather, they were suspended on heavy leather straps that were attached to iron braces on the front and rear axles. To say that those straps made ineffective shock absorbers is putting it mildly, because this type of suspension caused the coach to bob about like a cork on windblown waters. Forward, backward, and sidewise the coaches swayed and swung, so that passengers were well shaken, if not actually seasick, by the time their destinations were reached. Indeed, motion sickness was a common occurrence on stage runs, causing many unscheduled stops.

Small glass windows were in the side doors. The other windows or openings had curtains that could be rolled up or down, which often caused a fighting situation among the passengers. Some were always too hot or too cold. Of course, when the curtains were kept down, much of the view was cut off, which pleased some and irritated others. Many were the times that the peace of the coach was disrupted by a squabble over the curtained windows. Not a few times these quarrels heated to the point of necessary intervention by the driver. To say the least, the windows were not well designed for sightseeing.

Most coaches had a breast strap for the seats. This communal seatbelt of sorts stretched from side to side, supposedly keeping the passengers from being thrown around when the horses moved at a lively pace over rough roads, or when going down hills, and it may have compensated to a degree for the high wheels. Most of the coaches also had steps that dropped out and down when the doors were opened. If a coach did not have this convenience, the driver carried a small stool similar to those used by railroad conductors.

Baggage was carried on top of the coaches. Additionally, a storage compartment with an opening on the outside was built behind the rear seat. While the baggage had a supposedly waterproof leather cover, the coaches themselves were far from being waterproof. Water often came up through the floor when crossing streams, and passengers had to hold their feet high in order to keep their shoes dry.

The coaches were built to accommodate eight to ten inside passengers. Three persons could be wedged into the driver's seat; but after the driver and his assistant climbed aboard, only one place remained for a passenger. It was not uncommon for two or three brave passengers to ride in the baggage rack on top of the coach. Brave and strong they had to be, for they were constantly jostled by the rocking of the coach; they had to either hold steadily on to the rack or be tossed overboard. If the coach should overturn, as sometimes happened, a real tragedy could result.

Seating capacity inside was largely determined by body size. Ann Bachelor wrote that the backseat of the coach which brought her to Bristol was occupied by a woman so large that two other normal-sized people could barely squeeze in beside her. A man who traveled from Georgia lamented that all the way from Knoxville he was "pressed flat" between two women, whom he described as being the size of cotton bales.

In such cramped and often stifling, hot conditions, body odor could not be concealed, even if anyone wanted to. Most folks in those days were not much concerned about their own. One old man of the time boasted that he had never "tooken" a bath in his life. That was likely true of many who rode the stages at that time. Then there were the numerous passengers who were tobacco chewers and snuff dippers. When they spurted their foul juices out the coach windows, strong breezes often blew them back upon themselves and others who rode with them. Too, there were the occasional drunks who became obnoxious to the sober passengers. All these conditions made stage travel somewhat less than pleasant and perhaps a bit hazardous at times.

An early prominent citizen of Bristol arrived because of unpleasant and uncomfortable stagecoach travel. He started from Lynchburg, Virginia, intending to settle in Knoxville. By the time he arrived in Bristol, he vowed that he had endured all he could of jolting vehicles, rough roads, bad fare, hard and cold beds, dirty and uncivil attendants, and being crowded in the coach "like anchovies in a keg." So he alighted from the stage and remained the rest of his life. He who felt he had to find rest in Bristol now rests in the city's historic East Hill Cemetery.

Virtually all the coaches used on the stage line through Southwest Virginia and East Tennessee were built in Abingdon. Long before the Civil War began, Henry Sinon set up a wagon, buggy, carriage, and coach factory in Abingdon, not far from where the railroad depot was later built on the west side of town. High-quality vehicles were long made there, and the factory had such a good reputation that patrons came from a wide area to place orders. Some of the coaches built there were used on stage lines in such far places as Georgia, Alabama, the New England states, Texas, and other places westward.

Mr. Sinon's son, Henry J. Sinon, became a partner in the business as soon as he was grown. He became an expert upholsterer and long told that he did the upholstery in the last stagecoach ever built in the area.

It is generally acknowledged that the Sinons built superior coaches, but no matter how sturdily they were built, the rough roads over which they sped caused them to often be in need of mending. The Sinons maintained a large repair shop along with their manufacturing plant, and they kept a smaller shop in Blountville. For many years Abingdon was the great stage manufacturing and repair center of a large area.

From available records it appears that the cost of the coaches ranged from $300 to $375 per unit, largely dependent upon interior upholstery and exterior decoration. Size also made a difference. A vast majority of the vehicles made by the Sinons were for a four-horse team. Several were made to be pulled by six horses and cost about a hundred dollars more.

Most had fine, plush interiors, though they surely did not remain fine very long. What the boiling dust of the road did not do, the sweaty, unwashed bodies of many of the passengers did. In a short time the inside could only be called filthy. One lady traveler of the time described the interior of her coach as "being horribly dirty and stinking like a pig sty."

It is thought that the elder Mr. Sinon, a shrewd Jewish businessman, at one time owned the Marion-Abingdon Division of the line as well as the division from Abingdon to Blountville.

The Sinon factory burned

Henry J. Sinon of Abingdon and later Bristol, Virginia, partnered with his son to build stagecoaches.

in March 1856, and the family then moved to Bristol and set up a wagon works. They erected a building directly over Beaver Creek, east of the present intersection of State and Piedmont streets. Several years later a flood all but destroyed the factory, and it was never rebuilt.

After the move to Bristol, Henry J. Sinon became Henry J. Simon and was so called for the rest of his life, though no reason is known for the name change. He engaged in various business pursuits and, around 1904, built the fine home which yet stands at 211 Johnson Street in Bristol, Virginia.

Stage Fare

When compared to the cost of other goods and services at the time, stage fare was rather expensive. It varied from company to company and from division to division. Some companies based their charges upon the season; winter travel was usually the most expensive. On the average stage, fare ranged from five to seven cents per mile. Usually a passenger traveling a longer distance received the lowest rate.

The Great Stage Tragedy at Long Bottom

Probably the greatest stage tragedy that ever occurred in the Bristol area happened just before dawn on Tuesday, April 22, 1856. A heavy rain had fallen the previous day and continued until far into the night. A light rain was still falling when Number Nine left Abingdon for Bristol and Blountville. The coach was filled to capacity and carried an extra-heavy load of trunks and baggage.

Old Moll Tate was on the driver's seat that night, and she later said that she experienced "a mighty quare feeling about the whole thing" as the stage rolled away from the Abingdon station. The foreboding of impending disaster increased as the stage lurched through the dark, rainy night, causing Old Moll to keep a sharp watch ahead for fallen trees, always a hazard after heavy rains and windstorms.

Perhaps her strange foreboding was shared by the passengers. From the beginning of their journey, they joined their voices in well-known songs, even though it was usual—albeit near impossible—to try to sleep at that time of night. Sitting straight upright with the coach swinging, swaying, and bouncing was not conducive to peaceful slumber.

Number Nine made the routine stop at the Goodson place two miles up Beaver Creek from Bristol and found Col. Samuel E. Goodson himself waiting on the front porch of his home, which was unusual. The long practice had been for a slave to take care of the predawn stage duties, but Colonel Goodson said he had not been able to sleep because of great concern for the stage's crossing of the deep and swift Hoffman's Ford just below his home. He warned Old Moll that it would be dangerous, because Beaver Creek was in high flood and fast becoming worse.

But she—who sometimes allowed her zeal to exceed her wisdom—pressed right on. After all, she had the reputation of being able to drive her stage right through the middle of hell unscathed, so she wasn't about to let a "flooding little creek" bother her. Nevertheless, Colonel Goodson sent two slaves along to see if she made it across the treacherous Hoffman's Ford. It was a difficult crossing, but Old Moll made it, and the stage rattled on as the slaves returned back to report to the concerned colonel.

Farther down the creek the old stage road entered a long and fairly level stretch along what was then known as Long Bottom (now the site of Bristol's Mumpower Park). At that time the road skirted along the top of the creek bank and at places was perilously close to the floodwater.

Old Moll later recalled that the passengers had resumed their singing

after the dreaded Hoffman's Ford was cleared. They were singing an especially jovial song as the stage neared the midpoint of Long Bottom. Old
Moll was in anxious anticipation of the upcoming Flat Gap Ford (near the
present railroad underpass). Yet she knew that ford was wider and not as
deep as Hoffman's, which they had just passed through, so her anxiety was
a bit lessened.

Suddenly, the singing turned into yelling and screaming, as the road
beneath the passing stage gave way. The swirling waters of the flood had
eaten far back beneath the creek banks at a point about halfway through
Long Bottom, and the heavy vehicle, with horses, passengers, and baggage, fell into the deep, rushing waters.

Old Moll, seated high on the coach, was flung almost across the stream.
She somehow managed to kick off the heavy, men's, high-top boots she
always wore. Clinging to a floating trunk which had fallen from the baggage rack, she was carried swiftly downstream to a spot just above Flat
Gap Ford, where she grabbed a low-hanging branch of a sycamore tree and
scrambled safely to solid ground.

A group of railroad builders, camped about where the Janie Hammitt
home is now located, was just arising for an early breakfast when Old
Moll, wet and dripping, ran into camp with her sad tale of woe. Most—perhaps all—of the crew mounted the mules used in their roadbed construction and, with Old Moll riding double on one of them, quickly crossed
Flat Gap Ford and rushed to the scene.

Indeed, a large portion of the road was gone. No sound to suggest that
there had been survivors of the awful calamity was coming from the waters
or along the sodden banks. Suddenly, from the darkness, a little boy ran
into their midst.

Apparently stunned, he did not make a sound. He was slightly damp
from the light rain, but there was no indication that he had been in the
floodwater. He evidently had been thrown clear of the coach as it plunged
down the collapsing streambank. Old Moll remembered that the little boy
and his mother had been traveling from far up in Virginia to live with her
parents in Bristol.

Time did reveal that Old Moll and the little boy were the only survivors;
all the other passengers drowned, along with the horses. Most of the bodies had remained in the sunken coach, but two or three floated clear and
washed downstream. Strangely, one body, never identified or claimed,
drifted all the way into Bristol and was found in Buford's Mill Pond near

the present Goodson Street bridge. It has been told that the body of this man was buried on the bank of Beaver Creek just back of the present Athens Steak House.

The mother of the surviving little boy was first buried in the Shelby Cemetery (also called Oak Grove Cemetery) near the intersection of present Shelby and Fifth streets. She was later moved to East Hill Cemetery. Old Daddy Thomas once showed this writer her unmarked burial site, perhaps fifty feet north of and downhill from the John G. King family lot and monument. The grandparents took and reared the little boy. After he grew up, he married and moved to Paragould, Green County, Arkansas.

The road in Long Bottom was rebuilt farther back from the creek bank, and stages continued to run until soon after the coming of the railroad. Old Moll, case-hardened soul that she was, drove on, oftentimes through stormy, rainy nights with flooding streams. Whether in storm and flood, bright moonlight, or noonday sun, she always stopped her coach for a minute or so at the spot where the disaster had occurred. She always remembered.

The Wreck of Old Number Five

The run was called Old Number Five, but the coach which wrecked on that bright June day in 1856 was brand new. Indeed, it was her maiden run.

The Sinon coach makers of Abingdon had gone all out to produce what was purported to be the finest vehicle ever made by the company. The coach was rather showy, boasting a deep crimson, plush interior. Painted royal purple and trimmed in black and gold, the deeply paneled side doors were decorated with the Sinon family coat-of-arms. Gold fringe hung at the tops of the larger-than-usual windows. The suspension was said to be greatly improved, though it is not known how; perhaps the leather straps were a little tighter.

Number Five ran from Abingdon to Blountville, with veteran driver Henry Kerry at the reins. He had long driven a much-repaired, decrepit coach, so he was proud when a brand-new, first-class vehicle was manufactured to replace the wearisome older model. He anticipated that the first run would be long remembered. Indeed, it was, but not in the way he had supposed.

The new coach was loaded to capacity. The passengers included Henry Sinon and his son, who made it a practice to ride the maiden run of every coach produced by their factory. Another passenger that day may be a lit-

For many years Henry Kerry was a driver on the Abingdon-Blountville stage line.

tle better known; his name was Andrew Johnson.

Bristolians knew that the much vaunted coach was to arrive around noon. Many of them lined up along the lane fence in Rev. James King's big pasture on what is now Solar Hill. (The lane was actually the Old Stagecoach Road—now known as King's Alley and King Street.) The townsfolk waited and were thrilled when they heard the long blast of the tin horn as the stage emerged from Flat Gap and came sweeping down Flat Hollow, along what is now Oakview Street.

The four horses which had been purchased to pull the new coach were also making their maiden run along the route. The presence of so many people may have made the steeds nervous, contributing to the wreck. It was noted that Henry Kerry was having a harder and harder time keeping his team under control as the stage began rolling by the crowd. The crowd saw the coach—and also saw something much more exciting.

It is amazing that something tiny can often wreak great havoc, a fact certainly so in the wreck of Old Number Five. When the coach reached the point roughly behind the house now numbered 220 Johnson Street, a hornet flew into the passenger compartment through an open window. True to the nature of hornets, it promptly found someone to sting—right on the cheek. The passenger yelped and knocked wildly at the angry hornet; so did everyone else as it buzzed about from person to person. In desperation born of great fear, one of the female passengers threw open a door and jumped out, screaming all the while. Others quickly followed until only three were left within: Henry Sinon, his son, and Andrew Johnson.

The yelling, screaming, and running passengers so frightened the horses that within seconds the team was racing wildly and uncontrollably along the stage road. The sudden, unexpected excitement caused some of the assembled sightseers to race back toward town. Others remained to watch the show.

Nehemiah Strange, a slave who belonged to Joseph Anderson, was waiting to send and receive the Bristol mail. But there was to be no mail stop that day. It was at that point—near where the stage road crossed Sycamore Trail (now Sycamore Street)—that the assistant driver was shaken from the stage. He tumbled into a ditch at the roadside and fell directly on his tin horn, bending it just about double.

The horses became more frenzied, greatly increasing speed as they raced along. When they passed the old King home, at what is now 54 King Street, they were likely breaking the speed record for runaway teams. Just beyond that old hilltop mansion was a sharp curve in the road (where King and Sullins streets now intersect), long known as the high curve, because on the left was a high but gently sloping embankment. As the coach tore around that curve, it overturned and Henry Kerry was thrown from his lofty perch. He plunged down the embankment, still clutching his whip— he certainly hadn't needed his whip during the previous few moments. The horses broke free and raced down the road for another half mile or so. The coach had such momentum that it slid on its side for several feet before coming to a sudden halt.

The overturning, skidding, and sudden stopping made the coach unpleasant for the three men inside. Andrew Johnson came to rest on all fours in the shattered glass of the coach windows. Young Henry Sinon landed astride his back, and he loved to tell of that incident for years afterward, especially when Johnson was president. Old Henry Sinon was wedged headfirst between the backseat and the baggage compartment. Many who had waited to see the fine new coach pass by came running— but not as fast as the horses—to the aid of the injured.

Henry Kerry was badly "stoved up," as a familiar expression of the day so aptly described his condition, but he recovered to drive for as long as the stages operated. After the main-line service ceased a few months later, he drove the Bristol to Estillville (Gate City) run until ill health forced his retirement, around 1877. Well over eighty years old when he retired, he had been driving stagecoaches for more than fifty years.

The assistant driver received severe internal injuries from landing on his long tin horn. For weeks his life was despaired of, but he finally recovered—at least so it seemed. It was generally believed that his death two or three years later was caused by injuries received during the notable runaway.

Old Henry Sinon's neck was so severely hurt that from that time on it was painful for him to turn his head. He spent the rest of his life looking forward, so his son would always say. The younger Henry J. Sinon, having Andrew Johnson as a shock absorber of sorts, suffered no injuries at all. Johnson received a deep cut in the palm of his left hand from landing in the shattered glass, and he had minor cuts on his knees and right hand.

When Johnson was president, he was visited by longtime friend Maj. Z. L. Burson of Bristol. (Major Burson had actually helped put Johnson on the road to higher politics, leading eventually to the presidency.) During the visit, President Johnson talked of the great stage wreck in Bristol and showed him the scar on his left palm.

A possible death, a lifelong neck injury, a scarred hand which a future president carried to his grave, and a costly stagecoach damaged beyond repair all came about because of a little hornet that just struck and apparently flew away. As it has been said, "A little cause can bring on a great calamity."

Coming to Bristol by Stage, 1855

When it comes to history, nothing can compare with written and detailed personal memoirs. Bristol is fortunate to have had one of her earliest citizens do just that. At the age of 12 in the spring of 1855, Ann Bachelor came with her parents by stage from Fredericksburg, Virginia, to the new town of Bristol. When she was in her mid-nineties and living in central Georgia, she wrote a detailed account of that memorable journey.

Space does not permit the inclusion of all that she wrote of her trip, but enough will be repeated to give the reader a picture of some of the aspects of stagecoach travel in the mid-1850s. Doubtless this would apply to other periods as well. Quotations from her work will begin with the story of her not-so-pleasant-or-restful night spent in a wayside tavern somewhere between Big Lick (Roanoke) and Abingdon, Virginia, most likely in the vicinity of Wytheville:

> We had ridden through the previous night, and were very tired and sleepy when we arrived at this roadside tavern. Tired to the bone, that is. One can hardly imagine how exhausting it was to ride

for days on those swinging, swaying, bumping, jerking stages on real rough roads and that was the case with most of them. We were alternately thrown against each other or against the sides of the coach. We were always glad to have a packed coach that kept us from being tossed about so much. It was torture when the coach was near empty. We all were about as sore as if we had been in a real wreck. So we thought to stop over at this place and continue on next day. We had good visions of fine food, soft beds and hopefully good spring water. Rest, oh, we needed rest so bad.

The tavern, I don't remember the name, if it had one, many didn't or just where it was. It was in open country not in a village. It was a long two-story house with chimneys at both ends and one between them but not in the middle. I now think it was a house that had grown from a cabin to a sizeable house. I do remember that part of it was made of logs. Across the road was a creek or river along which was a long, sandy beach.

The coach on which we traveled was running late so that it was almost dark when we reached this place. The keeper was a most cranky old man and his dutchy wife. She may or may not have been pleasant for she never spoke a word so that we could determine her nature. They had a black woman, a slave, who seemed to be the cook, chambermaid and water carrier, whatever. She just about did everything that must be done. Supper was cold and sparse and was set in the kitchen. There was no dining room. The room was almost dark just had the dim light of one flickering candle. The fire had long died out causing us to think that the food had been cooked much earlier in the day.

As I recall the main dish was peas that seemingly a hog had never looked at. [Apparently, she meant that the peas had no seasoning, most often pork.] There was some molasses, and corn-hoe-cakes. They were tooth busting hard, Mama [Rosetta Bachelor] muttered that one could down a bull with one of them. I feared that the cook might hear and become angry. I think there was some buttermilk but it was well aged, about soured as I recall.

Only one other passenger had stopped with us for the night, a most unpleasant man the fatigue having soured his disposition it seemed. When the last bite was taken we all asked to be shown to bed. The room for the men was on the end of the house downstairs.

Our room was directly over the kitchen. It was reached by a narrow and steep stairway. There were three beds in that little room so close together that it was hard in the dark to tell where one ended and the other began. Ours and I suppose the others were of the old corded or rope type. There was a straw tick [mattress]. Seemingly the straw had been grown in ancient times for it was more powder than straw. It had settled in the middle of the much sagged bed. Indeed, the ropes had so sagged that the occupants were thrown together, whether desirable or not. There were no pillows and the bed stank from numerous former unwashed occupants. In a way we thought ourselves lucky for at the last stop we shared the bed with two others, four of us and most crowded and unpleasant. Here we started out at least with just us.

As soon as we cleared the stairs the old slave woman dropped the latch and we were locked in. [It is not clear why the door was locked.] I wondered what would happen if the place caught fire and no one to open the door. I later learned that the slave slept on a quilt in the kitchen so I should not have feared. We were too sleepy to long consider possible dangers.

Once in bed we were quickly drifting off when we found ourselves covered with bedbugs, just crawling and biting but being so bone tired we slept anyway. I learned next morning that the other man downstairs became angry at the situation, got up and spent the night on the sand along the creek. Papa [Lewis Bachelor] held his bed in spite of the little tormentors. As I write this some eighty and more years later I am made thankful for my clean, comfortable and warm bed which I much enjoy every night.

There were three or four big dogs at that place and I think it must have been about midnight when their ferocious barking awoke me. Mama slept on. I then heard a couple of wagons stopping and much pounding on the front door. Soon there was loud talking in the kitchen below and the clatter of pots, pans and dishes. I was about asleep again when I was startled to hear the latch lifted on the stair door and steps coming up. Suddenly, our room was invaded by four or five women and several children. They just began flopping down wherever they could find a space and that included our bed. They had a candle and just before they blew it out I saw that the big woman who fell down on Mama's side looked like an Indian.

Another woman flopped down by me and that bed rolling toward the middle caused their weight to bear down upon us. The one on my side immediately began to scratch after those bedbugs. Her arm was swinging like a woman sewing, only faster. That arm regularly bumped into my ribs. Even after she was snoring, she still continued to bump me, occasionally seemed to be scratching in her sleep.

The woman who had flopped down on Mama's side of the bed immediately went to sleep. After she had snored loudly for a few minutes she suddenly jerked awake, jumped up and excitedly called out: "Lord Gad, I'm about to do it, I've gotta git to the bresh quick." Then she lunged about in the dark room hunting for the stairway. While doing I heard her mutter, "I knowed I ort not to have et that big mess of polksallet back yander." She finally found the stairs and went stumbling, half falling downward. She yelled out as she went: "My Gad, I've gotta find the bresh quick, Lordy, I'm about to do it." Well, she found that door locked and she began banging on it, calling to the sleeping slave in the kitchen and after banging a time or two she began kicking that door and lunging against it. The slave awoke and said something. Then that woman blurted out: "Open this damn door, I've got to get to hell outta here and get to the bresh. I'm about to do it, oh Gad hit's purt nigh too late now. You dammed old wench open this cursed door quick. I tell ye I've got to get to the bresh!"

Well, that slave yelled back and told her to use the pot. That frantic woman yelled back that there was no time to find the pot. I guess that slave opened the door for the desperate woman running across the room and then she encountered another locked door. She had quite a swearing fit trying to get that slave to find the latch on that door. I then heard the great commotion among the dogs, which was I supposed, caused when she ran into the yard.

A little while later she came back up to our room, muttering and cussing about a dog nipping her shank and causing her "to do it" before she could get to the brush. Seems she had escaped the dogs by running into the smokehouse. I had never heard a woman swear before, didn't know any woman would talk that way. It would have so vexed the righteous soul of Mama, had she been awake.

In spite of that woman's excited and angry condition she was snoring again soon after she got back in bed. I could no longer sleep.

It seems that the bedbugs had gained reinforcements and were renewing the attack. Four or five women loudly snoring made the roof rattle. Maybe an hour later Mama 'roused and feeling a big body against her whispered and asked me who it was. I made the mistake of whispering back that I thought it was a big Indian. I had forgotten that Mama truly thought that western Virginia was still infested with savage Indians who might attack and scalp one. She was mortally afraid of Indians and was hard against moving to Bristol.

Land, at the mention of an Indian, Mama leapt up out of that bed, right over the woman who was then rolling to the middle and landed across the short space into a bed full of children. One of those older children, maybe he was having a nightmare, screamed out to his Mama that a bear was in his bed and on top of him. Mama was big and heavy. By that time she had grabbed me and went stumbling down the stairs. Mama kept excitedly whispering to me that she had left her pistol and knife in her baggage and it was in the kitchen. There we sat silently on that lower step, Mama listening intently for any sound of the Indian coming down upon us. Fortunately, all that we heard in the room above was that great chorus of snoring. I firmly believe that Mama would have knocked that door from its hinges had she heard the slightest sound of someone up and about to come at us.

I was so glad when I heard that old slave up and stirring the fire so as to make breakfast. Luckily, except for the one man who had spent most of the night on the sandy beach, we had breakfast to ourselves. If those other folks had come down I don't believe that Mama could have stayed civil.

Once on that early stage, I heard her say to Papa that there would be no more stopping at inns, even if it were a thousand more miles to Bristol. I don't remember much about the country that we passed through before reaching the next place to change coaches. I do recall seeing a big brick house at a place called Seven Mile Ford. There was a big yard around it and full of early spring blossoms. Mama thought we were coming to a ford in the river that was seven miles wide. She said to Papa that the rivers must be awful big in the West. How well I remember such little incidents of that trip so long ago.

After a long and wearisome journey we arrived in the old town of Abingdon but it was far into the night and there was a considerable wait for a connection. I remember an old man, all ancient, stooped and with a beard down to his waist, who talked with us as we waited. Someone told us that he was a veteran of the War of 1812, that he had no family and that he never slept, but spent most of his time around the stage stop seeking someone to talk to. He told us much about the country, indeed, assured Mama that all the savages were long gone. He did strike terror in her heart when he told of a spot almost in Bristol where a ghost sometimes stopped the stage. Mama lived in mortal fear of hants, as she called them.

When the man saw that Old Moll Tate, as they called her, was to be the driver on our run into Bristol, he assured Mama that Moll could drive a stagecoach through a nest of hants. "Why, I believe that old worman could take a stage through the middle of hell, a-spittin' in the devil's eyes and come through without a scratch," the old man added. I guess that helped to relieve Mama a bit.

I never shall forget my first sight of Old Moll whom I saw many times after we had settled in Bristol. She was tall, raw boned, lanky, and as quick motioned as a cat. She wore a long black dress and wore a black stovepipe bonnet. She came to the stage stop with a long leather whip wrapped around her with the handle in her dress pocket. Folks told us she went to bed at four in the afternoon, then got up near midnight, all fresh and ready for her run.

Mama instantly liked her. Somehow she always had great admiration for women who did men's work. We boarded her coach long after midnight. That gnarled old driver mounted the driver's seat, then went through her noted roll call of the horses, as she prodded them forward. The stage left the Abingdon stop with a great lurch that set it to swaying and swinging thus making it so that we couldn't become sleepy. I know we came down the main street of Abingdon but after that all was lost in the dark. After leaving Abingdon the road became rough and was pocked with mud holes some of great depth. Other than the rattling rumbling of the coach and the clopping of horses hoofs the only sound was the frequent shouting of Old Moll as she cracked the whip over the horses.

Somewhere perhaps about halfway between Abingdon and Bristol we had what some referred to as a brush stop. There was a big spring there where those that were thirsty might drink from a gourd dipper that hung on a big tree near the spring. On either side of the road were dark brush thickets. Old Moll called out that the left thicket was for the men, while the right was for the ladies. I recall one timid little lady was afraid to go into the bushes, saying that there might be snakes out there "big enough to swallow a person." Old Moll went before her beating the ground with that long whip so the little woman followed her. Now Mama didn't mention snakes but she allowed there might be hants in those bushes. It was no help that a woman on the coach, who apparently was a local, blurted out: "Might be, fer they's plenty of 'em in these parts. Lots of them been seed rat 'round here." That precluded a rest stop for Mama. She just stayed in the coach and hoped Bristol would come up before long.

The next stop was at the home of old Colonel Goodson who later became such a good friend to us. He was not then home. We later learned he was staying in Bristol, Virginia, while he sold lots in his Goodsonville. An old slave man stood on the Goodson porch with a lighted candle. It seems this was a place where folks left letters and packages or whatever to be sent out on the stage. I think passengers sometimes waited there. The stage picked up passengers anywhere. I well remember that somewhere just below the Goodson place we were hailed by a man waiting in the dark. He was the last person that could have been wedged into that coach.

I got so tired that I was dozing when suddenly I was jolted awake by the long blast of the stage horn that announced our approach to Bristol. Actually we were nearing that hanted graveyard but we didn't know. That night the stage passed that place without incident.

I remember coming to a halt where the stage road crossed Sycamore Trail [present Sycamore Street and King's Alley]. There, a black man, a slave of Joseph Anderson [Nehemiah Strange], was waiting with a little leather bag that contained the outgoing Bristol mail. He emptied that into a larger bag held by Old Moll. Then she placed the Bristol incoming mail in his leather bag. I recall that the black man was showing his heels, barefoot as he was, back toward Bristol before the stage could start again. Actually he more loped than ran.

It seemed no time until we drew up before a huge brick house and here our journey by stage to Bristol ended. [This was the old James King house at what is now 54 King Street, Bristol, Virginia. At that time it was operated as a rooming boardinghouse by Drs.

Hammer and Wiloughby.] I recall that when Papa alighted he asked Dr. Hammer, who always met every stage, if we were in Bristol. I shall never forget his answer: "Well, sir, there are actually three towns down yonder along Beaver Creek, Bristol, Tennessee, Bristol, Virginia and Goodsonville, but we here are not in any of them. They are all mighty close. Take your pick." This Dr. Hammer was the first person we met in this area and he was our doctor later.

Dr. Hammer told us later that if we wanted lots in Bristol, Tennessee or Bristol, Virginia, we needed to see Joe Anderson. If we wanted lots in Goodsonville we'd have to see old Col. Goodson and he added that he thought the Colonel was staying at the new Columbia Hotel which we later found that he was.

I do not know the hour we arrived here but I do know that it was rooster crowing time. Several were heralding the coming morning, both at the house where we stopped and down in the valley below. I suppose the town folks were arising but we could not discern a light anywhere. Though we were not sure of it at the time we were at home and in a short while day would dawn over the distant mountains to show us how beautiful was the spring blossom bedecked valley where we were so long to dwell.

We were served the best breakfast at Hammer's that we had enjoyed in many a day and the best we would have for many days in the future. The breakfast was cooked and served in a yard kitchen by the largest black woman slave I ever saw. They called her Aunt Fornia, and good and kind she was. She dropped dead in that kitchen, as she stood stirring a kettle of soup, not many weeks after we arrived here.

Soon after daylight we made our way down to the town to which Papa had so long desired to see, why I do not know. Town, it was not. Was then just an oversized village. We passed a store operated by a man named Moore. [This would have been John Moore, whose store stood on the northwest corner of what is now State and Lee streets.] Mr. Moore came out and welcomed us to the "town." He was cheerful and friendly and made us feel so good. There was a big garden just beyond his place in which an extra-tall and big slave man was working. He was preparing the garden for spring planting. Just beyond it was a little office building and beyond that was the finest house in the village. We were told that it had been the first house erected in Bristol, Virginia. [She is describing the former setup of Dr. B. F. Zimmerman, Bristol's first doctor. The slave working in the garden was Big Elbert, whose little cabin stood about where the drive-up booth of the Blue Ridge Bank is now located.]

Up and across the street was the home and business place of Joseph R. Anderson. There was a store, bank, and post office in his home. Mr. Anderson later proved to be so kind to us. Mama, an absolute Presbyterian, was so glad to learn from him that services of her faith were being held in the town.

Up beyond where the railroad would come was the hotel of A.T. Wilson [the Columbia]. This we learned was in Bristol, Virginia, the state line running near it. We went there and so spent our first days in the new town. An old man whom we learned was Col. Goodson was staying there and was most kind to us. He sought to sell us lots in his Goodsonville across and north of Beaver Creek hard by the town of Bristol. He had built some rent houses not far back of the hotel but there were no business houses there. At that time all business was in Bristol, Virginia, and Bristol, Tennessee. Papa felt that our future was best served there so did not buy of Col. Goodson. I must say that he [Goodson] was so very gracious and kind, a real Virginia gentleman. We often ate at his table in the hotel.

It took us many nights on the good beds at that hotel to overcome the weariness that had come upon us by stage travel. One who has never so traveled cannot imagine how such rides wear one out. As I write this there is a new Packard in the old carriage house, just waiting to carry me in great comfort wherever I wish to go. How different it is than the stagecoaches that I rode from Fredericksburg to Bristol, Virginia, some eighty-five years ago.

Coming to Bristol with virtually nothing, the Bachelors in time became rather wealthy, probably ranking as one of the three richest families in town. Lewis Bachelor died in 1876 and is buried near the old gate in East Hill Cemetery. Rosetta, eccentric to the nth degree, became the best known of the town's many odd characters. She died in the summer of 1903 at the home of a niece in Catonsville, Maryland, and is buried there.

Ann operated the town's first brothel. In 1870, she married into an elite family and moved to Georgia, where she became a respected and beloved citizen of her area. She and her husband owned a large and prosperous plantation. As she neared the century mark she wrote her memoirs. She died in the late fall of 1944 as she sat on the veranda of her palatial home, having reached the age of 102 years. She is buried in the family cemetery on her Georgia plantation.

The Last Stagecoach Run

Because of a certain girl's birthday, we know the date of the last main-line stagecoach run through Bristol. Ann Bachelor was born October 28, 1842, and on her fourteenth birthday the last run was made on the Abingdon-Blountville Division. The fall of 1856 was very late. Ann wrote in her memoirs that her birthday "was as warm as summer, under a cloud-less deep blue sky" and that the trees were in "great" color.

Everyone knew far ahead of time that the last Blountville-to-Abingdon stage would come through Bristol on the noon run. Ann Bachelor joined other town citizens who had gathered along the fence in King's pasture (Solar Hill) to watch the historic event. They were pleased that the legendary Moll Tate, who had endeared herself to many, would "drive the last stage into history," as J. B. Palmer so aptly termed it in his priceless diary.

Old Moll's custom was to have her assistant driver sound the approach horn at about where present Tenth Street crosses Shelby Street. That day he began early and continued to give frequent blasts as the brightly painted coach swept down what is now Shelby Street Hill, across Baker's Creek Bottom (now generally called Little Creek), up what is now Sullins Street, and into sight around the high curve just beyond the old King home. At about the same time, an approaching passenger train began to blow for the depot in Bristol. Ironically, the sounds of an ending epoch and the beginning of a new one blended together that day. Old-timers talked of this strange coincidence for years.

The swiftly moving stage rolled past the old mail stop at what is now Sycamore and Cumberland. The mail had been switched to the railroad, but Nehemiah Strange, who had long met the stage there with his mail-bag, ran over and stood far down the hill to watch.

Old Moll, who was not averse to a little showmanship now and then, two or three times while within hearing of the crowd cracked her long whip and went through her noted roll call of the horses: "Up Frank, up Napoleon Bonaparte, up Nicholas, and on Big Dan." It all sounded so familiar but would never be heard again. The stage swept down the north side of the hill and on up Flat Hollow before disappearing into Flat Gap. An era had ended.

A Parting Word

The grinding of hastening wheels over rocky roads, the rattle of chains, the cracking of the whip, the ofttimes profane shouts of stressed drivers (even the euphemistic oaths of a lady driver), the raspy wail of a long tin horn, the clip-clopping of trotting horses—all these once-familiar sounds are no longer heard resounding through the hills and valleys of Southwest Virginia and East Tennessee. There are no longer the anxious faces of waiting travelers, the crying of road-weary babies and children, or the wild scramble from overcrowded wayside taverns to claim almost nonexistent coach seats.

No longer do candles flicker or small oil lamps glow in tavern or station windows while sleepy hosts and managers prepare for the coming of strangers from afar, most of them to appear briefly at widely scattered meccas, never to pass through again.

Soldiers, sailors, doctors, lawyers, professors, drunks, cutthroat outlaws, thieves, preachers, widows, orphans, prostitutes, and gamblers— young or old, famous or obscure, saint or sinner, civil or uncivil, sick or healthy—all rode the high wheels together along the peaceful valleys, across dangerous waters, through tranquil, flower-strewn woods, or beside leafless, wind-tossed trees. They traveled along in the best mode available at the time, through sunshine or rain, in summer heat or bitter cold. Some were rich, some were poor; many were in between. Some had great estates, while others carried all their worldly goods on their backs, in pockets, or in bags. Some moved from one great house to another, while others came from hovels or humble cottages and would have no better at journey's end. Some had lives of ease; others knew nothing but burdensome toil. Fears, hopes, high ambition, despondency, despair, joyous anticipation, grief, remorse, grinding and guilty consciences, free and happy spirits, such and more—all were part of the lives of those who rode the stages long ago.

Just as the colorful and sturdy coaches no longer exist, the passengers who rode them no longer live; not one remains. Whether they traveled on to fame and fortune or to futility and obscurity, somewhere across this vast land they all now sleep; some on high, windy hills, some in valleys low. Some of them rest under towering marble shafts, some under crude fieldstones, and others in graves that are lost.

The era of the stagecoach was glorious, but it ended and will never come again.

Bristol Boogers

This writer grew up in an area where any tale of a strange, unexplainable, and fearful happening was called a "booger tale." To a lesser degree he has found the same to be true in Bristol and the vicinity. Thus comes the title for this chapter.

It seems that fearful ghostly appearances and sounds have always been a part of Bristol life. There are tales of such happenings in the area long before the town came into existence. The author is convinced that many, if not most, of Bristol's pioneer settlers firmly believed in ghosts. Certainly many of them were given to sharing stories of mysterious and fearful sights and sounds that they or others had seen and heard.

It is becoming more apparent that not only were Bristol's pioneer citizens believers in ghosts, but that a large percentage of today's residents also believe in the same type of phenomenon. Many of them can tell lots of firsthand scary tales, and one begins to think while listening to their many booger tales that the city can claim more ghosts per square block than any place in America. Perhaps the spirits have read the sign BRISTOL, A GOOD PLACE TO LIVE and have acted accordingly!

These ghost stories come from a great cross section of the city residents, ranging from the poor and unlearned to the elite and best educated, even including some of the locally famous. This writer well remembers when those who believed in ghosts were considered to be ignorant and superstitious, and most of them were ashamed to acknowledge that they held such beliefs. No more, for there indeed has been a marked change. The strongest believers now are usually found in high schools or colleges, and most of them are not ashamed to openly admit and defend their beliefs.

Seldom does a week pass but that this writer receives one or more calls, usually from college or high school students who wish to be directed to houses or places where they may encounter a "real live" ghost. It seems that they wish to tempt the ghosts to appear, perhaps for faith strengthening. One wonders what would happen if the wish came true!

The reader is advised that this chapter is not to be construed as necessarily being an endorsement by the author. Rather, it is written so that a bit of local lore and legend might be preserved, as well to entertain those who delight in reading of such purported strange happenings. It is a retelling of what was told him nearly fifty years ago by several aged Bristolians. To many—yes, most of them—such things were beyond dispute.

PRE-BRISTOL GHOSTS

Strange Light at the Grave of General Shelby

In December 1794, Gen. Evan Shelby died at his fort, which stood in the general vicinity of the present Weaver Funeral Home (Locust and Seventh streets). He was buried on a little knoll a short distance northeast of the fort, near what is now the intersection of Fifth and Shelby streets. Those who remained at the fort began to see a ghostly pulsating light that seemed to rise up from the newly made grave. The light would rise up to about head height and then float around among the giant oaks that towered over the small cemetery. Afterward, it would start toward the fort but would suddenly disappear. On a few occasions, however, the ghostly light changed its routine a bit.

A hunter from the fort had gone far, and darkness overtook him long before he reached home. The night was very dark and a light rain was falling. His path went by the little graveyard where the noted general had recently been buried. As the hunter was passing the cemetery gate, an eerie light appeared. But instead of moving slowly around among the giant oaks, it suddenly made a beeline toward the hunter, who in turn made a beeline toward the fort, with the pulsating light in hot pursuit. Somehow the hunter missed the fort's gate, and around and around the stronghold he ran, still swiftly pursued by the ghostly light. Finally, overcome by sheer exhaustion, he fell to the ground in a swoon or faint. When he finally came to, the light had disappeared. One may be certain that after his frightful chase, the hunter was careful to be inside the fort before nightfall. The strange light near Shelby's grave continued to appear on various occasions well beyond the founding of Bristol.

The restless spirit of General Shelby was not confined to an eerie light. Soon after James King moved to his new home in 1817, on what is now Solar Hill overlooking present downtown Bristol, a frightened slave rushed up from the spring with a fearful tale. On that bright, late-summer morning the old slave had gone down to the big spring that gushed forth where the Robert Boswell Insurance Agency building now stands. He was dipping his wooden pail into the crystal-clear water when he heard the splashing of a horse as it crossed nearby Beaver Creek. The slave looked up to see General Shelby approaching, sitting straight and with great dignity astride his extra-large white horse. He had long lived on the King plantation (Holly Bend), only four miles from Fort Shelby, and well knew General Shelby, who often visited there. Even Shelby's favorite horse, White Mockingbird, was recognized by this aged slave. Remembering the manners that the Kings had instilled in his mind, he was just raising his hat in salute and was about to say, "Good morning, General Shelby," when suddenly the chilling realization swept over him that the general had been dead for over twenty years. By then the horse and rider were—using the expression of the greatly frightened slave—within three hoe-handle lengths of him, but not for long. The old slave dropped his bucket and bolted like a frightened deer back up the hill to the King house. Once his fearful tale was told, some of the King family went out to the edge of the yard and looked down upon the meadow that surrounded the spring. No horse and rider could be seen; they seemed to have vanished as quickly as they had appeared. This was the first appearance of the deceased general upon the King plantation, but it would by no means be the last.

It seems, however, that the old general was not always privileged to requisition his favorite horse from the heavenly stables. In the spring of 1818, he was seen strolling around King's big meadow (site of present Cumberland Square Park). A little later he was seen sitting under one of the huge shade trees near the Beaver Creek side of that meadow.

Later that year, several King slaves were hoeing corn in the Broad Bottom (general vicinity of the present courthouse in Bristol, Tennessee). Suddenly, General Shelby appeared, standing in the rows ahead of them. The old slave who knew him well was in the crew. At his yell of, "Hit's General Shelby's hant," the slaves threw down their hoes and fled in all directions. The overseer had a hard time getting them rounded up and back to work. It was noted that the overseer was a bit nervous about continuing to work in the Broad Bottom.

The old home of General Shelby stood until long after the fort's walls were gone. Sometimes, in the darkness of night, a lighted candle could be seen moving around in that old dwelling. Was the general roaming through his old home again? Everyone thought so.

The last known ghostly appearance of General Shelby was in 1839. (The date was remembered because it happened within a week or two of the opening of the Sapling Grove Post Office.) At that time the old fort area had been made into a sheep pasture. One of the field hands who had been with the corn hoers when the unexpected meeting with the general occurred had been promoted to the chief keeper and shearer of the sheep. One day he was shearing sheep in a little barn that stood near the eastern edge of the pasture. (Because of this structure a street that was graded through this pasture was called Barn Street. It is now known as Locust Street.)

As the man was working on the third or fourth sheep, he slowly realized that the animal had become far too easy to hold. Puzzled, he looked around to find that General Shelby had appeared and was helping with the shearing. The startled and greatly frightened slave gladly turned the entire job over to Shelby and quickly fled toward home.

Later, he marveled at how he had made such a sudden exit from the barn. He remembered that General Shelby's apparition had been between him and the door, and he knew that he would not have gone in that direction. Two or three days later, when he finally ventured back to the shearing barn, he discovered that several shakes had been knocked from the low roof over the area where he had been working. He concluded that—as he put it—when his mind left him, he must have leaped through the roof and made his hasty escape. A few days later the old sheep keeper and shearer was found dead in the same barn where he had met Shelby's ghost. The Kings often wondered if the ghost had appeared again and literally scared the man to death.

The Ghost of an Indian Warrior

Though no known spectral appearances of General Shelby occurred after 1839, the King Plantation was still not completely free of ghosts. It seems that the King slaves were especially plagued by "hants," as the slaves called them. The biggest problem overseers had with the slaves was keeping them in the fields when a hant scare was on.

Not long after Shelby made his final appearance on the plantation, the phantom of an Indian warrior soon took his place. The first sighting was made by a crew of King slaves while they were working in a hay field which spread around the Shelby burying ground. The apparition, painted and dressed for battle, waved a tomahawk and filled the air with blood-curdling battle yells while running circles around the startled and frightened slaves. The slaves were soon running and yelling also, but not in circles—they were running madly toward home.

Over the following years, the phantom Indian was seen again. On one notable occasion, he appeared in King's Meadow and put on his act among the cattle. This caused the herd to wildly stampede, tearing down fences and scattering far down Beaver Creek and into the surrounding hills.

The Indian may have appeared one more time a few years after the founding of Bristol, the story of which will be told a little later.

Goodson's Ghost

Did Col. Samuel E. Goodson, one of the better known, prominent citizens of the Bristol area, believe in ghosts? He once said that he didn't want to believe in such things but he had to. Now, just why did he have to?

Long before Bristol became a town, Colonel Goodson was living at his old family home, West Point, about two miles up Beaver Creek from present downtown Bristol. West Point was long a well-known and patronized tavern on the old stage road.

Late one afternoon a young family traveling to Kentucky stopped at the tavern to seek shelter for the night. The parents and their four-year-old son were assigned a room on the second floor, near the head of a long narrow stairway. During the night the little boy woke his mother, asking for a drink of water. She told him that there was none in the room and that he would have to wait until morning. Exhausted from long hours of hard travel, she immediately went back to sleep. The little boy evidently began to wander around in the dark, most likely hoping to find water. He opened the bedroom door, stepped out into the hall, and fell down the long flight of stairs to his death.

His body was found before daylight by a servant who started to go upstairs to awaken the guests. The sad accident happened on Colonel Goodson's birthday—he had been born October 7, 1793—and the day would never be forgotten.

On October 7 one year later, Colonel Goodson was home alone. Whenever no guests were in the tavern, he would light a couple of candles and read late into the night, usually until the candles were consumed. As he sat in his parlor, reading on that particular night, he was startled to hear a door open near the head of the long stairway. Almost immediately, something came bumping down the stairs and landed with a dull thud in the hall just outside the parlor door. Then a child began crying. In great alarm, Colonel Goodson hastened to investigate, but the hallway was empty. All was quiet and so remained the rest of the night, indeed, for another full year. On the evening of the colonel's next birthday, there was a repeat of the ghostly performance.

On the third birthday night following the child's death, guests staying at the tavern were seated in the parlor, enjoying lively conversation with Colonel Goodson. Perhaps he thought that with guests present the ghost would not play to a full house. Near bedtime the ghost did play to a full house—in a louder manner than the previous times.

Colonel Goodson later admitted that he found the strange experiences a bit unnerving, and after the third appearance of the ghost, he always managed to be away from the tavern on his birthday. It was years later when he made the statement, "I didn't want to believe in ghosts but I had to."

Finally, the colonel came to Bristol to live. Apparently, the ghost remained. Tenants who later occupied West Point reported the same strange, ghostly happening. In fact, more than one tenant family quickly left the place, explaining that they could not live in the same house with a hant.

Many years later, West Point was sold to Dr. W. H. Teeter, whose wife greatly added to the existing building and renamed it The Crossing. An aged neighbor who knew of the ghost asked the good doctor if he had heard anything strange in the house. Dr. Teeter more or less brushed the question aside but did shyly comment, "There are things there which cannot be explained."

BRISTOL GHOSTS

The Ghost Children in East Hill Cemetery

In 1857, three children were buried on Round Hill in what would become Bristol's East Hill Cemetery. In those early days local citizens usually referred to the area as Cemetery Hill. It was then heavily wooded, including a lot of underbrush. Old-timers told of having to cut a trail through the heavy growth to reach the burial site of little Nellie Gaines, the first person to be buried there. It was also necessary to do likewise when two more children were buried there later in the year. As one early Bristol pioneer put it "the place sure did look mighty hanty in those days." It did become "hanty" for several unfortunate persons through the following years. The first ghostly incident happened soon after the third child was buried.

Christmas week, 1857, was frigid. Snow had been on the ground for nearly a month, and more was falling every few days. The high day itself was clear but very cold, near zero degrees, as night descended over Bristol. The extremely cold weather did not deter a love-struck young man, who lived near Paperville, from spending Christmas Day with his sweetheart in the little village of Bristol. In fact, he stayed on until around midnight before beginning the long walk home through the bitterly cold night. The stars twinkled bright in the clear skies, and a waning moon hung low in the west.

The ghost children were heard near this imposing monument in Bristol's East HIll Cemetery.

The young man was well aware of the little burying ground high on the hill above the village and was feeling some apprehension as he neared the place. He was trying to walk as fast as he could along the snow-and-ice-covered road. As many late travelers have done when passing cemeteries at night, he began to whistle and sing, in an effort to keep from hearing "things." Though he was trying to look away from the cemetery as he passed by, from the corner of an eye he caught sight of little flashes of light among the trees and brush that covered the top of the hill. He later described the lights as being like that of dozens of fireflies (called "lightning bugs" by many Southerners), flying around through the brush. Knowing that no such insects were out at that time of the year, he froze in fear, "neither being able to go forward nor backward," as he described his horrible plight.

Then he heard a sound which frightened him; little children were gleefully shouting and chattering as if they were playing about over the crest of Cemetery Hill. Of course, the young man knew that no children should be there at that time of night—or likely anytime in such frigid weather. Standing there unable to move, he perceived that the sound was moving toward him. Then, as if the ghostly children had seen him, three little white figures emerged from the woods and swiftly moved down the hill toward where he stood. It was then that, with a new jolt of fear, he regained his mobility. Swift as a fleeing deer, he raced over the icy road toward home. He slipped and almost fell several times, but was always up and running before he hit the ground. He made it to Paperville in record time.

Over the next few years others reported similar experiences. It seems that the ghostly children would only perform on clear, frigid nights when snow lay white upon the ground. No less a person than W. W. James, a prominent Bristol merchant, was riding by the cemetery on such a night, when his horse became greatly frightened, began running, and could not be brought under control before he was in downtown Bristol. Though Mr. James was "too enlightened to believe in such things," he once stated, "I heard and saw a-plenty" as the horse raced from the site. He added that for once he was glad that his horse ran away.

The Ring-of-Fire Ghost

In early Bristol, there was a pike leading to the Holston Valley country. In the earliest years of the town it left Fifth Street (then the main road to Bluff City) about a block beyond the old campus of King College (present site of King Pharmaceuticals). The Valley Pike then crossed the railroad tracks and angled into what is now Pennsylvania Avenue and thence southward to the great valley beyond. The route lay through the dense Fairmount Forest, which was a part of Linwood Plantation, property of James King III.

Shortly before the Civil War, a band of highwaymen set upon a peddler who was traveling through the forest at twilight. He evidently was armed and tried to defend himself but was soon overpowered and dragged from his wagon. His throat was slit from ear to ear, and the robbers quickly grabbed his money and fled.

While bleeding to death, he had run in a circle around and around his wagon. Travelers who found him early the next morning told that a distinct circle of blood drew in closer and closer to the wagon as the peddler had made his final and frenzied run for life.

There was no indication of who he was or where he had come from. He was buried in the Whittaker Cemetery near the present campus of King College. His wagon and remaining merchandise passed to G. H. Mattox, local undertaker, for payment of the funeral bill.

Soon after, a terrifying ghost appeared at the spot where the unknown peddler had been murdered. (The location is near the present intersection of Pennsylvania Avenue with Spruce Street.) It seems that a traveler, riding on horseback along the pike, was suddenly surrounded by a whirling band of fire. At first the circle was wide but began drawing inward, closer and closer to the terrorized traveler. The horse lunged forward and backward, left and right, but could not seem to run free of the closing circle of fire. The whirling band of fire closed in until it seemed that it would consume both horse and rider, then it suddenly vanished. The frightened horse then lurched forward and could not be brought under control for two miles or more.

Over the following years, many travelers found themselves suddenly surrounded by the mysterious band of fire. Like the horse, no one could run free of it until it finally disappeared. One old-timer described it as being about a foot wide and about knee high above the ground. Several said it was accompanied by a weird whirring sound. Always it closed in until almost touching the victim, then suddenly ceased. The reader may be sure that those in the know avoided the pike at night, and many were fearful of day travel through that area; more than one traveler claimed to have encountered the ring of fire in broad daylight.

Never did the ghost appear to more than one person at a time. For that reason many fearful travelers went to great lengths to make sure that someone traveled with them. It seems that the ring-of-fire ghost gave up about the time the Fairmount section of Bristol began to develop, circa 1890.

Little Sammy Comes to Supper

In the early days of Bristol, J. H. Buford built a fine house in a grove of huge oaks that stood on the present site of the Athens Steak House (Buford Street across from the northern end of Short Street). His rather pretentious estate, at least by early Bristol standards, was known as Buford's Grove. It was later known as Campbell's Grove and finally as

Hobson's Grove.

Near the present northwest corner of Buford and Lottie streets, he erected a small cottage to house his chief workman, Julian Handsford, who had five children ranging in age from two to ten years, including four-year-old Sammy. The town was small then, so almost every resident knew and loved little Sammy.

Shortly after the Civil War, an epidemic of whooping cough hit Bristol, and several children died of complications from the disease. Among them was the much-loved Sammy Handsford. He was buried in the then-new cemetery, now known as East Hill Cemetery. The grave was within sight of the Handsford cottage.

The remaining Handsford children often romped on the slope of the hill between their home and the cemetery. They sometimes went on up to linger a while at the grave of their brother. Occasionally, they played games around his burial site, pretending in their childish way that he was again frolicking with them.

Late one day as twilight settled over the town, Mrs. Handsford stepped out on the front porch to call the children to supper. She found that they were in the cemetery, so she just called a little louder to them. They heard and came running down the hill toward home. Mrs. Handsford returned to the kitchen but glanced through the window as she worked over her stove. She turned toward the kitchen table, and it slowly dawned on her that something was just not right. She looked closer at her fast-approaching children, then she gasped in shock and unbelief.

Not four, but five children were running home for supper. No, it could not be, but it was. Little Sammy, dead since the past October (it was then April), was running along with his brothers and sisters, seemingly just as healthy, happy, and joyful as they were. The other children did not seem to be aware that Sammy was with them.

Weak with shock, staggered to the front porch just as the children ran through the gate and into the yard. Little Sammy came no farther. He was wearing the little white suit in which he had been buried, and there seemed to be a light around him. He smiled ever so sweetly at his mother, turned, ran back up the hill, and disappeared through the cemetery gate.

Mrs. Handsford did not tell the other children of Sammy's strange appearance. After they were seated at the table, she felt an irresistible urge to go out on the front porch and look toward the cemetery again. She saw little Sammy standing in the cemetery gate and looking down toward home. He waved to her, then just seemed to fade away.

Though the Handsfords continued to live on the Buford place for several more years, little Sammy was never seen again.

The Jailhouse Ghost

Earlier in this work, the story was told of the strange light that was seen in the Shelby burying ground. Soon after the founding of Bristol, the light was again observed by several people. Perhaps its most dramatic appearance was to Marcus Blevins, who had the misfortune to be incarcerated in the first town jail.

It may be remembered by those who have read the first volume of this historical work that Joseph R. Anderson, founder of Bristol, sought and succeeded in having the town's first jail erected at the edge of the Shelby Cemetery. His stated purpose was that being so located, it might cause prisoners kept there to think upon their certain mortality, in that symbols (gravestones) of man's certain demise would be in clear view from the only window in the crude jail. It seems that the Shelby ghost, on at least one occasion, cooperated in the effort to reform a prisoner.

Marcus Blevins, a laborer in early Bristol, was caught stealing from his employer. He was placed in jail, awaiting trial before the circuit court in Blountville. One dark, misty night he was lying on his crude prison bed (a plank platform upon which straw had been spread). Unable to sleep because of remorse for his crime and fear of an uncertain future, he suddenly became aware that the jail was being lit up by what appeared to be the coming of daylight. He well knew that this could not be, for darkness had been over the town for only three or four hours. Startled, he sprang from his bed and peered out the little window.

He saw a strange, pulsating white light which he described as being about the size of a pumpkin. Hovering over General Shelby's grave, the light did not stay put. It slowly moved toward the jail, circled it three times, then returned to hover near the small window. Suddenly, it sailed through the window and began moving around and around the cell. All the while, there was the sound of heavy breathing much like the final gasps of a dying man.

Blevins would later tell that he thought he would surely die of extreme fright. Mercifully, he did faint. When he came to, the light was gone, and he said all was "black dark" outside. Only the soft patter of an incessant light rain broke the stillness of what must have been a very long night for the quaking prisoner inside the tiny Bristol jail.

It seems that Anderson accomplished his purpose; the Shelby ghost evidently caused Marcus Blevins to think much upon mortality and the need to change his erring ways. He always ascribed his amazing reformation to that "soul-shaking experience," as he described it.

He served six months in the county jail at Blountville, then returned to Bristol, where he soon joined what is now the State Street Methodist Church. A little later he moved to Central Alabama, where he became a well-known

John Marcus Blevins of Alabama was "brought to the light" by the jailhouse ghost. He later became a minister in Central Alabama.

traveling Methodist evangelist. He often told of his ghostly experience and would sometimes add that he had been brought to the Light by a light.

Another prisoner in the tiny Bristol jail may have also had a visitation from the Shelby ghost. When the jailer brought breakfast early one morning, he found that the prisoner—a large and strong man—had fled. The well-secured jail door had been knocked off its hinges from within, "as if an elephant had lunged against it." There were tracks in the mud outside which seemed to indicate that the fleeing prisoner had left in long leaps rather than by a regular run. It was generally supposed that the Shelby ghost had so frightened the prisoner that he had gained super strength, knocked the door open in a mighty surge, and then fled with deer-like leaps. He must have leaped a long way, for no trace of him was ever found.

The Ghost That Changed the Old Stage Road

For years the Old Stagecoach Road followed the approximate course of present Oakview Street through what is now known as Rice Terrace. Near the present corner of Oakview and Buckner streets was Flat Hollow Cemetery, and a stagecoach from Abingdon usually passed by around 4:00 A.M.

On a late August morning in 1855, the coach was approaching the graveyard when the horses suddenly began to "booger." (It is generally believed that animals can see or hear ghosts before people can.) The horses snorted, bucked, and tried to back up; by no means could they be made to go forward. About that time the air became stiflingly warm. Then the driver and his assistant saw something which looked like a large white pillow. It was sailing rapidly around and around the old burying ground, and it was getting higher with each round. By then the passengers were disembarking, and they too witnessed the frightful sight. In moments the driver and assistant were left alone with the coach—the frightened passengers had fled down Flat Hollow toward Bristol. The driver (a man named Nave) later shyly admitted that "me and my man" were soon right behind them.

At daybreak Nave and "his man" ventured back up and found the coach and horses exactly where they had been abandoned. With no further problem, the coach was brought to the old King house on what is now Solar Hill. The passengers were picked up, and the stage, far behind schedule, continued toward Blountville.

The stopping of the stage by the ghost at Flat Hollow Cemetery reoccurred several other mornings. Sometimes almost a week of unhampered passage might be had, and then, without warning, the ghost would appear and again stop the stage. Only Old Moll Tate, the legendary female stage driver, could get the horses to run by the haunted cemetery.

Finally, an arrangement was made with the Susong family to reroute the line though a large wheat field that was part of the vast Susong plantation. (The field encompassed about half of that area now traversed by Euclid, Fairmount, and Highland avenues.)

Of all the ghost tales heard by this writer, this is the only one concerning a ghost that caused a change to be made in a public road.

Cold Reception at Flat Hollow Cemetery

The news of the frightful happenings at Flat Hollow Cemetery quickly spread through the town and around the local area. A young man living near Paperville (the writer was told that his name was Carmack) who said he wasn't afraid of the pure old devil got together with two or three Bristol youths and planned a late-night visit to the haunted graveyard.

On a hot, mid-September night, the party ventured up Flat Hollow, intending, as they said, to spend the night there—if it took that long to cause the ghost to appear. As they neared the overgrown cemetery, the air suddenly became frigid. Young Carmack later described it as being like a zero-degree winter night. They did not see the sailing white pillow but told that the ground began to quake.

Carmack and his companions may have not been afraid of the devil, but they were apparently afraid of the "hanty" happenings at Flat Hollow Cemetery. Receiving such a cold reception, they had no trouble in deciding to go back to town—in a rather hasty manner!

CIVIL WAR GHOSTS

There were several supposed ghosts in early Bristol that were connected to events or places pertaining to the Civil War period. Several will be shared with the reader, in much the manner as they were told to the author many years ago.

Nickels House Ghosts

The Exchange Hotel, which was later and better known as the Nickels House, was used as the main Confederate hospital in Bristol. Two or three other nearby buildings were also used to treat desperately sick and horribly wounded soldiers, many of whom died. After the war ended, at least two of the buildings were said to be haunted.

In the late 1860s, a guest at the Nickels House occupied a room that had been used for some of the worst cases, and in which many soldiers had died. Of course, the guest was unaware of all this. At about two o'clock one morning, he was awakened by a flickering blue light that slowly moved around the room, near the ceiling. Finally, it stopped over his bed and began to lower toward his face. He was not his bed long; he sprang from it, grabbed his suitcase, and spent the rest of the night in the lobby.

Another time, a man and his wife quickly fled the hotel in the wee hours of the morning. All they said to the night clerk was, "There's something mighty strange up there."

On other occasions, guests reported being awakened by groans and moans or heavy breathing coming from darkened corners of their rooms. As long as the Nickels House stood (it was demolished about 1900), fully uniformed Confederate soldiers were occasional sighted striding along the dimly lighted halls.

Another building used for a Confederate hospital was the old Bristol-Goodson Male Academy that stood on Virginia Street, immediately north of the First Baptist Church (then known as Bristol Baptist). Soon after the war, it was sold to the Masonic Order. The Masons renovated the badly abused building and set up their lodge in the upstairs rooms while renting the downstairs for school use.

Though the staid old members of the Masonic Order were reluctant to talk about it, reports leaked out that on occasion strange groanings and moans seemingly came from nowhere and sometimes seemed to be just floating around in the air. Once, when the brethren were engaged in a meeting, blood began dripping from the ceiling, and a hasty adjournment was called.

Downstairs one sultry summer afternoon, a ghost became a little more explicit—indeed horribly explicit—so much so that students had nightmares of the event, some for as long as they lived. Near the close of the last class period, the professor stood up to lay out the studies for the following day. All eyes turned toward the professor. Without a sound, a Confederate soldier with a badly mangled, bloody face suddenly appeared at his side, rolling his head from side to side as if in terrible pain. The professor, who always said he did not see the apparition, doubtless was greatly startled when screams and yells arose from the pupils, who fled as one from the building. Indeed, it must have been a nervous student body that met in the old academy building for the rest of the summer.

Among the students was the late James King Brewer, whose old home yet stands at 220 Johnson Street, Bristol, Virginia (next door to the home of this author). Though he a time or two talked of the matter to close friends, he would never mention it to his family.

The Big-Boom Ghost

The most notable of Civil War-related ghosts was manifested in sound rather than sight. It was heard by virtually everyone in Bristol and for miles throughout the surrounding area. In this respect it was different, for ghosts usually prefer to make themselves known to only one or a few eyewitnesses at a time. In this case hundreds of people became earwitnesses.

Sunday, June 6, 1869, was an unusually hot and muggy day, more like midsummer than late spring. When folks came home from church that evening, some sat down on their porches to cool a while, rather than going straight to bed as was the usual practice of most Bristolians in those days. However, many of the town had already retired and were soundly sleeping when, suddenly, the stillness was shattered by a dreadful, thunderous noise.

Col. N. M. Taylor would always remember the exact time of the horrendous sound. He owned an old wooden-movement, weight-driven clock that he wound every night, just before going to bed. He long boasted that the clock would not vary two minutes per week from his fine pocket watch. On Sunday nights, he always set the clock to match his watch, and he had just adjusted the time to 8:57 when the reverberation began.

To the many Confederate veterans of the town, the sound was unmistakable. A mighty cannonade had begun, seemingly upon the western slope of Cemetery Hill, where so many casualties of the war had been buried. Most folks, if they took time to think, knew that no real cannons could be found within miles of Bristol.

The ground shook, buildings trembled, windows rattled, the very air vibrated. Sleeping folks were shaken awake. Confederate veterans, half asleep but awake enough to think they were again in the midst of battle, sprang from their beds, wildly grabbing for their rifles. Farther from town, other veterans, hearing the familiar sound of distant cannonading, thought Bristol was under attack.

The nearest witness was Confederate veteran Jacob Susong Carmack, who had been in town and was riding his horse toward home (High Point). He had just passed Cemetery Hill when the earsplitting roar broke forth right behind him. Greatly startled, he whirled his horse around and, for a moment, the present gave way to the past. He again was charging into battle; he saw streaks of fire slashing among the trees that covered the hill. In seconds the frightened horse turned in the other direction and, totally unmanageable, raced toward home.

Capt. J. H. Wood, who then lived on East Main (now State) Street about four blocks from Cemetery Hill and had been in the thick of many a battle, ran from his house and looked intently toward the hill. Capt. John F. Terry, who had been at the train depot when the ghostly cannonade began, raced up Main Street toward the hill. Captain Wood joined him. The two intrepid veterans were about halfway there when the strange sound ceased. They raced on. When they reached the Confederate portion of the cemetery, all was quiet. A heavy cloud of strange white smoke drifted low among the trees, and the men smelled the unmistakable odor of gunpowder.

Later that evening, several men rode into town from nearby areas to see if war had broken out again in Bristol. There was not much sleep in the town that night. Folks were frightened and puzzled. Many thought the strange occurrence was a warning that the country would soon be engaged in another war.

That event was made part of at least one sermon on the following Sunday. While preaching to his church, a minister vowed that the "divine warning" meant that a mighty war would soon rend the land asunder—in a greater measure than had just been experienced.

Captain Wood later said that it sounded as if at least fifty cannons were roaring forth at what he termed "full blast." He wrote to his father about the matter, stating that he did not want to believe that such a thing had happened, but that he was certain it had. (Apparently his father had heard about the ghostly cannonade and had written a letter of inquiry about it.)

Over the years following, there were many tales of ghosts, both seen and heard, in what is now East Hill Cemetery, but none made a greater impression or was so much talked of as what many later termed "the big-boom ghost."

This writer is fortunate to have talked to one person who remembered hearing the mysterious noise. Born in 1860, she was nine years old when the event occurred. Asleep when it began, she awoke to much consternation in the household and ran out on the porch, where her parents were looking toward Cemetery Hill. She recalled that the reverberation was deafening, and she also remembered that when a thunderstorm later rumbled near the town, folks thought the unearthly cannonade was beginning again and cringed in fear.

Old Daddy Thomas, who told this writer so much about early Bristol, was away visiting his grandparents and did not hear it. He always said that he hated he had missed "the worst hant that ever was in Bristol." Far more than a century has past since that loud evening in 1869, but that "worst hant" has never troubled the town again.

The Hanging-Tree Ghost

By late 1864, the need for doctors in Bristol's Confederate hospitals had become critical. At that time a Dr. Butterfield arrived, supposedly from Nashville, Tennessee. He offered his services and soon was put to work at the branch of the hospital in the old Bristol-Goodson Male Academy building on Virginia Street.

Virtually all the soldiers placed in his care died, however. Details are scarce, but in some manner it was determined that Dr. Butterfield—if he were indeed a doctor—was actually a Union sympathizer and was aiding the cause by poisoning the sick and wounded soldiers in his care. He was turned over to the local authorities, who immediately arrested him. Though arrested in Virginia by Virginia officers, for some reason he was placed in jail in Bristol, Tennessee.

News spread rapidly of the shocking situation. One can well imagine what a furor was soon whipped up among the many Confederates who lived in Bristol. As all expected, and probably hoped, an enraged mob soon gathered with the intent of meting out a bit of frontier justice. It is said that a local enforcement officer or two, as well as several staff members of the local Confederate hospitals, were in the crowd.

Soon after nightfall, the jail was surrounded by the ever-enlarging throng. Without the least resistance from local officers, the jail was broken open. Butterfield was seized and bound in a long white feather bag from a local mercantile establishment. He was then carried across town to the top of what is now known as Solar Hill.

At that time, most of Solar Hill was covered by the long-unused pasture of Rev. James King. (The land was formerly owned by Joseph Johnston, who was holding it for speculative purposes.) When King's slaves had cleared the area fifty years earlier, they were directed to leave a grove of large old oaks on what is now the northwest corner of Solar and Cumberland streets, so that the slaves and livestock might have a shady resting place. (There were several such groves scattered about over the vast King plantation.) Because the cows tended to gather there about noon on hot summer days, the place was called Noon Grove.

One of the big oaks at Noon Grove stood a little apart and to the south of the others. It was from a low limb of this tree that Butterfield was hanged, still bound in the long white feather bag. The mob finally dispersed, leaving the body dangling from the tree.

Joseph B. Palmer, a prominent Bristol lawyer, wrote of the event in his diary:

About 9:00 P.M. news reached me concerning the event. I hastened up to Noon Grove to see what had really happened. A bright full moon had just arisen over East Hill giving much light. The crowd was gone, but the body was still there, swinging gently back and forth, clearly visible in the bright moonlight. I did not long tarry. I thought much on the matter throughout that night.

For the next six or seven years, the area around Noon Grove remained unused pasture. During that time, two or three young men of the town, including Marion Faidley, went coon hunting in the vicinity. A full harvest moon was shining overhead, making the hill almost as bright as day. About midnight, the young men decided to quit the hunt. Their path homeward passed Noon Grove. Near there, their dogs "boogered," began to whine, and ran back to their masters. The young men looked toward the grove. In the bright moonlight something white could be seen, swinging slowly back and forth from a low limb of the old hanging tree. This writer strongly suspects that the sight hastened their journey home!

Soon after, a road leading to the Susong settlement on Baker's Creek was graded across Solar Hill. (Present Cumberland Street follows the old road.) The road passed under the outermost branches of the old hanging tree, including the limb from which Butterfield was hanged.

One dark, misty night, Dr. James A. Templeton was called by a messenger to see a sick person who lived near the Susong settlement. He quickly saddled his horse and was soon galloping across Solar Hill. As he neared Noon Grove, his horse suddenly went crazy, snorting and whirling about and kicking wildly, and could not be made to continue on. Then Dr. Templeton saw something white swinging back and forth from the old hanging tree. The good doctor had to retreat back to town and journey around the south end of Solar Hill in order to reach his patient.

Around that time, the former King home, which stood within sight of Noon Grove, was turned into a boarding school for girls. When it was rumored that the grove was haunted, the girls became afraid to look in that direction at night. Once, a girl who was wakeful became brave and decided to look toward the grove from her upstairs window. She was not disappointed. A blue light was moving slowly around the old hanging tree. Though she didn't sleep during the rest of that night, she did stay in bed, with her head covered!

Perhaps the most frightful experience of all came to W. A. Rader, Sr., a prominent area resident. He had married Louise Susong, and the couple lived on Baker's Creek near her family home. One night, he visited until around 11:00 with friends in Bristol. He then mounted his horse and started homeward. As he rode under the overhanging limbs of the tree, there came the distinct sound of a man moaning, struggling, and gasping. Then, something suddenly sprang from the limbs and landed on the horse, right behind Mr. Rader. It clutched him tight, then began to rub icy hands over his face. The horse went wild, kicking and jumping about, and then dashed down the road toward Baker's Creek.

Later, Mr. Rader was asked how long the ghost with the icy hands stayed with him. He replied that he remembered no more until the horse stopped at his home gate, and by then the ghost was no longer with him.

Soon after Mr. Rader's harrowing experience, Baker's Creek Road became Cumberland Street. At that time the old roadway was regraded and widened, which necessitated the felling of the old hanging tree. The tree was given to Lemuel Strait, the town woodcutter. He cut the tree into fireplace-sized pieces and sold the lot to a family on Moore Street.

It seems that Butterfield's ghost was determined to have one last fling. The family on Moore Street built a roaring fire of the oak wood the night after it was delivered. Family members then sat down to enjoy what they expected to be a nice warm room. The room may well have been warmed, but the family did not remain to enjoy it. Soon after the fire was lighted, there suddenly came loud moans, groans, and wild gasps from the leaping blaze. The family jumped up and quickly abandoned the place.

Did the hanging-tree ghost become an arsonist? The house went up in flames within two hours after the family left it.

The Uninvited Guest

The modest cottage home of young widow June Ann Strother stood on the east side of Fourth Street, immediately south of where S. P. Rutherford Transfer and Storage is now located. On a bright, late-spring morning in 1867, June Ann was in the side yard of her home, gathering fresh, colorful flowers. The previous day she had shined up the little parlor of the modest cottage, and the flowers would add the touch of color and fragrance she so much desired. She had also baked a cake and prepared what other delicacies were available in those lean years immediately following the Civil War. Her best dress was starched and ironed and ironed again until it met her stringent approval. June Ann Strother, whose late husband was a casualty of one of the last battles of the Civil War, was about to be married again.

Her husband-to-be, Jason Bland, was a young widower from near

Blountville. The wedding was set for noon and was to be performed by Rev. Asa Routh (spelled Ruth by many persons at the time). Several close friends of the bride-to-be and her late husband were to be the guests.

The day was bright and balmy. By noon, the flowers were in place, the reception table was spread, and guests were seated in the little parlor. The bride and groom were standing near the fireplace, and Rev. Routh had taken his place before them. The

The Widow Strother had her wedding stopped by the ghost of her late husband.

venerable Reverend had been acquainted with June Ann's late husband, and he was pleased that the young widow was getting a man whom he knew to be able to provide for her.

Just as Rev. Routh straightened himself in his usual dignified manner and made the standard query, "Are you now ready?" he suddenly gasped and fainted.

At the same moment, several of the guests showed various signs of consternation. Women screamed, two or three swooned or fainted, strong men yelled out, and some of both sexes took the nearest exits—in a rather brisk manner. One man, who had been a close friend of the deceased husband, stiffened in his chair and bawled out, "Great Gawd a'mighty, hit's shore him." He not only stiffened in his chair, he froze there. The bride, at first greatly puzzled at what was happening, suddenly looked to the right, screamed a time or two, then just fainted away.

Perhaps there was a good reason for fainting, fleeing, or freezing in one's chair. For just as Rev. Routh had started the ceremony, the deceased husband suddenly appeared, standing at the right side of the bride. He was just as he had died, a bullet hole in his throat and blood flowing down his gray uniform.

The poor bridegroom, apparently not seeing the specter but extremely puzzled by the strange action of the others, blurted out, "What happened?"

Immediately the ghost, in an unearthly but easily understood voice, triumphantly replied, "It's what *didn't* happen that pleases me!" The image and voice then just seemed to fade away.

Not many had remained to hear his parting words. It seems that the ghost accomplished his purpose. Once Jason Bland realized he was within touching distance of June Ann's deceased husband—and a ghostly husband, at that—he left the room, not running, but in wild jumps. Outside he made another jump, onto the back of his horse, and raced toward Blountville. Never again did he show any interest in marrying the young widow Strother.

The appearance of the ghost not only stopped the wedding but almost caused a real tragedy. A woman, said to have been the first who tore out of the room when the apparition appeared, sailed out the back door into the garden. From there she ran into the railroad yard and jumped across the main track just a few feet in front of a rapidly approaching passenger train, so close that it "fanned her dress tail," as one observer stated it. No one seemed to know where she went from there. It is certain that she, as well as others present, never forgot the wedding that was stopped by a ghost!

Crying for the Christmas Cake

On a cool rainy day in early November 1868, Betsey Clanton, a destitute war widow, came to the house on Moore Street built by Madison Jones but then occupied by the Dr. R. M. Coleman family. In the twilight, she appeared at the door with her two rain-dampened and cold children; the youngest was a five-year-old doll of a girl named Betts. Mrs. Clanton begged for food and shelter for the night, which was common in the years immediately after the close of the war.

It so happened that the Colemans were looking for live-in help, so they gave the worried mother the job of housekeeper and cook. The fatherless family was assigned the room adjoining the kitchen, where they were warm and comfortable in their new and much-appreciated home. Dr. Coleman, a very understanding person, and Mrs. Coleman, one of the kindest of women, did all they could to make the former wanderers feel at home and saw that their needs were fully met.

The weeks quickly passed toward the Christmas season. As the high day neared, plans were made for a large gathering of family and friends for a great holiday feast.

On December 23rd, Mrs. Clanton baked a huge cake. Little Betts was playing in the front hall, but as the tantalizing aroma from the oven drifted throughout the house, the curious girl trotted into the kitchen and asked what smelled so good. The mother pointed toward the oven and told her that a fine Christmas cake was about done. Betts stood by until the cake was removed from the oven, then hungrily asked for a piece. The mother told her that she would have to wait until Christmas Day.

The disappointed child began softly sobbing and turned to go to their room. At the door she suddenly turned and looked steadily at her mother as she softly and sadly said, "But, I won't be here at Christmastime." Mrs. Clanton, busy with the preparation of the current meal, thought little of what the child had said. Little Betts went on to their room, climbed into bed, and cried herself to sleep.

When supper was finally called, the youngster did not respond. After another unheeded call or two, Mrs. Clanton went to investigate. The child was found lying prostrate with a high fever. The sudden onset of so high a fever puzzled the well-trained Dr. Coleman. When it became evident that the condition was worsening, he called in another doctor or two, all to no avail.

Little Betts Clanton died at three on Christmas Eve morning. At about the time the Christmas dinner would have been spread the next day, the child was buried in the Coleman Square in East Hill Cemetery.

Mrs. Clanton could never recover her tranquility. Within weeks her sanity began to waver. All she could hear deep in her troubled mind were the last words of her young daughter: "But I won't be here at Christmastime." If a little sleep came, then the child appeared in her dreams, repeating over and over those agonizing words. Finally, all sanity was gone, and Mrs. Clanton was admitted to the Western State Hospital at Staunton, Virginia. The remaining Clanton child was reared by the L. F. Johnson family.

A year later, on December 23, 1869, Mrs. Coleman was alone in her home. In the late afternoon, she slowly became aware of the strong odor of baking cake. Knowing that no one was cooking at that time, she went into the kitchen to investigate. The fires were cold, no one was around, but from the empty servant's room came the sound of a crying little girl. Recognizing the weeping as being that of little Betts, Mrs. Coleman ran to a neighbor's house and stayed there until her husband came home.

The crying ghost continued through the years. Each December 23rd, at about 5:00 P.M., the strong smell of baking cake and the crying of a little girl came to haunt the house. Dr. Coleman died in 1870. Mrs. Coleman married a Mr. Head and moved to Illinois. Later, the Jeremiah Bunting family bought and moved into the house. The Buntings also had the annual visitation of the ghost of little Betts.

Many years later, the house at 308 Moore Street was enlarged and became the Grigsby Maternity Hospital. Apparently, the disappointed spirit of Little Betts did not leave. A former Bristol lady who now lives in Tuscumbia, Alabama, was a patient in the hospital on December 23, 1947. Late in the afternoon, her roommate remarked that cake would be served for dessert at suppertime. The tantalizing aroma drifting up from the kitchen did seem to indicate such a probability. When a nurse came into the room, the two patients voiced their eager expectations. The nurse somberly stated that she thought dessert was to be peaches and ice cream. Then, before she left the room, she mentioned that if they were near a certain room downstairs they could hear a ghost crying. But it was not until many years later that the Alabama resident would know what the nervous nurse had meant by the strange statement. It is told that one of the hospital cooks, knowing what would happen, never worked on December 23rd.

Over the years, news of the faithful appearance of the ghost every December 23rd caused many brave persons to come at that time to hear for themselves. They were never disappointed. Some stood their ground while others fled in terror, never to return. One extra-brave woman, who vowed that she was not afraid of the worst ghost that ever was, walked right into the room from whence the ghostly sobbing came. She did stand her ground and finally came out to report that nothing could be seen, but that the crying seemed to be everywhere around her.

As long as the old house stood, Betts Clanton cried for the Christmas cake. The Jones-Coleman-Bunting house was torn down in the 1960s, apparently ending what many called "the Christmas ghost."

The Fiddling Ghost on Fourth Street

In his youthful days, long before he became a Presbyterian minister, James King was what old-timers called an "overhanded" (very capable) fiddler. He was often called upon to play for frolics (dances or parties) in the area and was delighted to do so.

He learned the art of fiddling on an old instrument owned by his father. The fiddle, to put it mildly, was not quite up to par—noticeably so. Once, when young James was playing for a frolic near Blountville, a skilled wood craftsman in the crowd came forward and promised to make a much finer fiddle for him. A large apple tree which had long stood in the craftsman's orchard had recently been toppled in a storm, and it was with wood from this old tree that the promised fiddle was created. Indeed, it was a fine instrument.

James King was fond of one of the craftsman's daughters, Betsey, so he named his prized fiddle "Beautiful Betsey." His pride and joy, it became much better as it aged and mellowed. Music from his applewood fiddle delighted and thrilled many a crowd. By the time King became a devout Presbyterian, in 1819, Beautiful Betsey was considered to be the finest fiddle in the area.

For a short while after his conversion, he continued to play his fiddle. He soon became aware that most Presbyterians of the time strongly condemned dancing. Many of them thought the fiddle was an instrument of the Devil. So, in deference to his church, he laid Beautiful Betsey away in his attic, where it gathered dust for more than thirty years.

When Rev. King and his family moved from what is now Solar Hill to their new home on Beaver Creek, in 1853, the almost-forgotten fiddle was brought down from the attic. The Susong family owned a large plantation adjoining King's, and one of their slaves, Caesar Susong, was a skilled fiddler. Caesar had not much to play on, just a battered old fiddle that someone had given him. James King, acting on what he called a strange impulse, decided to give Beautiful Betsey to the talented slave.

Caesar was thrilled beyond measure. Through the years leading up to the beginning of the Civil War, he delighted and cheered his fellow slaves, the Susongs, and occasional visitors with his expert playing of the applewood fiddle.

When the slaves were freed, Caesar, like so many of his fellow bondmen, became a displaced person with no means of livelihood. He came into Bristol with barely more than the clothes on his back and his much-prized fiddle. He soon became a street fiddler and daily strolled along the streets and played lively tunes for nickels and dimes. Sometimes, but rarely, a generous soul might give him a quarter, which made him feel like he had made a day's wages from one person. He was thus able to earn a meager living for himself and his never-quite-well wife. The couple had no children.

Perhaps his best-known listener was the affluent and prominent Maj. Z. L. Burson, who usually did give him a quarter. Once, when Caesar was "really getting with it" playing "Fire on the Mountain," the major became young again and got the joy in his feet. He cut the Tennessee back-step around and around the fiddler and up and down the sidewalk, waving his tall silk hat in the air as he did his lively dance.

Major Burson was a Baptist minister and a member of the local Baptist church. Someone reported to his church that the major had been seen dancing a jig—in public, right on Main (State) Street. This became one of the charges that caused him to be excluded from the membership of his church. No matter, Major Burson just used some of his great wealth to build the finest church in town, where he preached right on. He still sought out his favorite fiddler and kept on dancing.

During his church trial, Major Burson had declared that he believed Caesar Susong could make any preacher dance when he got his applewood fiddle "warmed up right good." Caesar became a legend in his own time. For many years he was perhaps the best-known figure on Bristol's Main Street.

Not only was he given nickels, dimes, and the occasional quarter, but kind merchants often gave him a bit of produce or perhaps a few staples to carry home. W. W. James, an early merchant prince, occasionally gave him a new suit of clothes. Caesar, who had come to Bristol in rags, could now dress like he was "somebody." Across the street, Joseph Anderson always provided new fiddle strings when needed.

Beautiful Betsey continued to become better with the passing years. The well-practiced musician was probably not excelled by anyone in Southwest Virginia or East Tennessee. His fame spread far. Folks came from great distances just to hear Caesar play. Sometimes travelers left their trains and stayed over a day or two for a sampling of what some called the best fiddling in a hundred miles. A railroad conductor once delayed a train so the passengers could lean out the windows of the coaches to hear the legendary fiddler, standing on the platform, give a foot-tapping version of "Riding a Bucking Mule Through Cumberland Gap." The street fiddler often strolled up to the depot to play for incoming or departing travelers. It was one of his best-paying stands.

On rainy or cold days, Caesar took refuge in Jimmy Yost's blacksmith shop on the east side of Fourth Street (now Edgemont Avenue, near the northern edge of the Salvation Army property). For hours he played lively breakdowns for Yost and others who might gather around. The busy blacksmith often said his labor was made lighter by his friend's music. As was his practice on the streets, Caesar always stood as he played, even though there was a crude bench or two in the shop, upon which he could have been more at rest. When he really got into his music, he always leaned forward over the applewood fiddle.

It was not uncommon for a thrilled bystander to "stir up the dust" on the dirt floor of the shop when Caesar got to "burning the strings," as one old-timer expressed it. Among the better known jiggers were Dr. H. T. Berry, W. W. James, and Col. D. F. Bailey, a prominent early Bristol lawyer. It was said that Colonel Bailey, who was a little on the corpulent side, would bounce like a rubber ball at such times. Occasionally a passerby would pause on the sidewalk and cut a few steps.

Late one muggy afternoon in August (some old-timers thought the year was 1888), Caesar appeared at Yost's shop, carrying his treasured, oilcloth-wrapped fiddle. He seemed to be in an especially jovial mood. Only Jimmy Yost was in the shop at the time, but Caesar began to play. After warming up, he began a lively rendition of "Catfish A-Floppin' in the Forked Deer," a popular breakdown of the time. (Forked Deer is a river in West Tennessee.)

Yost's back was turned as he worked over his brightly flaming forge. Suddenly the music stopped, and he looked around to see his friend fall forward. The fine old fiddle was crushed as he fell to the dirt floor upon it. Caesar Susong and Beautiful Betsey perished together.

Shortly after Caesar's abrupt demise, late passersby began to hear the lively notes of a fiddle issuing forth from the darkened blacksmith shop. The tune was always the one Caesar had been playing when he dropped dead. The ghost was not always confined to darkness; some claimed to have heard the ghostly music in broad daylight.

Perhaps there is no connection, but Jimmy Yost soon moved his blacksmith operation to another location. The old shop building stood vacant for years; apparently no one wanted to rent a building where a fiddling ghost was a cotenant.

A lady who was living on lower Fourth Street when this writer came to Bristol in 1953 often told of her father's experience with Caesar Susong's ghost. (She called it his "hant.") Her story goes like this:

I know it was in 1891, for that's the year that my brother, Boone, was born, and Mama was expecting him when this strange thing happened. Papa had gone with a neighbor man to town to get some supplies. They got their stuff and were on the way home and needed to pass that old blacksmith shop. We had just moved here and didn't know about that fiddling hant. When they were passing that old shop, they heard the liveliest fiddling ever one could hear.

Now Papa just loved fiddling and dancing. He began to knocking the back-step right there on the sidewalk. Now that neighbor man didn't seem interested in dancing. He yelled out to Papa that he was dancing for a fiddling hant, then took off running up the street. He had lived here all his life and knew all about that hant in the blacksmith shop.

Henry Steele danced for a ghost on Fourth Street.

Papa got the message and started using his feet a little livelier, but not in dancing. He split out for home right behind the fast-fleeing neighbor.

A little later the old Yost blacksmith shop was demolished, which seems to have ended the run of the fiddling ghost on Fourth Street.

Whipped by a Ghost

Chad Barwick was only ten years old when his father, a Confederate soldier, was killed in the Battle of Shiloh. Even at that tender age, Chad was already a problem child. His mother, a weak, sickly woman, soon found that she could not successfully control her son, so she asked her aged, widowed father to move into her home.

Her father was a large man and, though well up in years, was still rather strong. He was a strict disciplinarian, and that is putting it mildly. He had raised a family of thirteen children and, by frequent application of the hickory switch, had made upright and law-abiding citizens of them all. One may be sure that he lost no time in applying the same formula to his young grandson.

Chad only grew more resentful and rebellious, but being afraid of his stern grandfather, he tried to outwardly obey his rules and regulations. When the lad was barely fourteen, an epidemic of typhoid fever developed in Bristol. He and his mother were not affected, but the white-haired grandfather came down with a severe case. For weeks he was attended by Dr. Richard M. Coleman, reputed to be one of the most-skilled physicians in the town, but to no avail.

The old man grew steadily weaker. Near the end he called Chad to his bedside and made him promise to obey his mother and not bring sorrow upon her. The lad gave halfhearted, insincere assent. Even then, with the grandfather disabled, he was already delighting in rebellious independence. Though he would not dare admit it, he was likely glad and relieved when the old man died.

With his last and only restraint gone, Chad Barwick soon became what the town called "red-dog mean." He began running with a crowd of the town's wild youth, became increasingly resentful of and mean to his mother, and soon found himself in trouble with the law. He and two companions were caught shoplifting in the mercantile establishment of W. W. James. They were arrested and taken before the town mayor, who then served as juvenile judge. They were fined and sternly warned not to become involved in crime again, or the penalty would be much greater.

Soon afterward, Chad began to turn to strong drink. There were several saloons in the town at that time, strictly forbidden, of course, to sell to minors. However, a few saloonkeepers would slip a drink out the back door to anyone who had the money.

One cool, bright, moonlit night, Chad indulged in a drink or two, but he had no money for more. He remembered that his mother had some coins stashed away in an old teapot, which sat high on a kitchen shelf. He reasoned that she would already be in bed and he could slip and get the money without being detected.

He hastened over to their Broad Street home, quietly opened the back gate, and started toward the kitchen door. Then he saw it. From the shadows of a side-yard tree, a tall, white-haired figure emerged and quickly stepped toward him. He froze in horror as he realized that it was unmistakably his deceased grandfather, who was carrying a long switch. The ghost silently seized Chad and, swinging him around and around, applied the whip in greater fury than he ever had when alive. The greatly shaken lad was then released. He started to run but was grabbed again and given an even more

This old grandfather came back from the dead to discipline his erring grandson.

severe whipping. Then the ghost simply vanished. Instead of continuing his thieving mission, the lad huddled in the house, shivering in fear for the rest of the night.

For a while, Chad did nothing to provoke another appearance of his dead grandfather. However, he did ultimately venture back out to rejoin his wild companions. Again he was caught in a crime and was placed in the Bristol, Tennessee, jail.

The walls of that jail, though holding its prisoners in, did not stop the entry from without of the "whipping ghost." He appeared in the prison cell and three times in one night administered thrashings never to be forgotten.

When released, Chad, in desperation, decided to catch a freight train and leave Bristol far behind. Soon after dark one night, he slipped away from his home and hastened to the railroad yard, where a freight train was preparing for a trip south. Just as Chad entered the yard, he heard heavy footsteps behind him. Whirling around, he came face-to-face with his grandfather again. The troubled old spirit apparently just could not rest and had come down from the Round Hill (now East Hill) Cemetery to make another effort at straightening out his wayward grandson. This time he almost literally whipped the trousers off the terrorized boy; they were actually split into shreds. The ghostly grandfather then escorted him back home before disappearing into the darkness of the night.

Chad would later tell that as he lay suffering on his bed that night he came to a great conclusion: It was apparent that he could not escape his grandfather's ghost, for not even thick prison walls had stopped the spirit. He decided that the only thing to do was to reform and live in the manner desired by his mother and grandfather.

This he did. A few years later, Chad Barwick married, and he remained in the area until after his mother's death. He then moved his family to Indiana, where descendants live today. As far as can be determined, the stern old grandfather ever after rested in peace.

The Ghost That Stopped a Train

A light snow covered the ground one night in late February 1876. The skies had cleared just before dark, giving way to a full moon. The bright moonlight, combined with the newly fallen snow, made the evening almost as light as day. Brooks Menifee was at the throttle of a passenger train which was due in Bristol from Lynchburg at 1:00 A.M. The run had been uneventful, and the road-weary engineer looked forward to his reserved bed in the Virginia House Hotel.

The train was rolling at a fairly good clip as it swept into the outermost reaches of the Virginia rail yard. Then Menifee saw him. In the middle of the tracks, a few yards ahead, stood a man frantically waving his arms over his head. Menifee thought it strange. He was sure that, just moments before, the track had been completely clear for a great distance ahead; yet all of a sudden this man had appeared, waving the danger signal. Menifee was too busy trying to stop the train to think much on that.

He noticed that the man waving the signal was dressed in a bright red shirt—very red. Red shirts had been popular in the 1850s but were seldom seen in the late 1870s. Again, there was no time to think on that.

Just as the train ground to a screeching halt, Menifee realized that the man with the red shirt had suddenly disappeared. The night was so bright that he could see for a great distance around where the man had stood just moments before but was now nowhere to be seen.

A brakeman rushed forward to examine the tracks. Just back of where the strange man had stood, a length of rail had been loosened and turned over, an action which was sometimes done by those with grudges against the railroad company. A local man had just lost a damage suit against the company, and most people thought it was he who had tried to derail the passenger train that night, but no proof was ever obtained against him.

The point where the derailment had almost occurred was close to a high embankment that dropped sharply down to Beaver Creek. Had the plan succeeded, the train might have rolled down the embankment with disastrous results.

What of the disappearing phantom who saved the train? Of course, no one really knows, but the father of Old Daddy Thomas thought he had the explanation. Thomas had helped construct the rail line into Bristol in 1856 and quickly recalled that one of his fellow workers had been murdered "rat square plumb," as he put it, where the mysterious flagman had appeared. And, yes, he had been wearing a bright red shirt the day he was murdered. Thomas had no doubt that the long-dead workman had appeared to do one more good deed for the railroad which he had loyally served so long.

The Persistent Ghost of Old Henry Kimes

Young Holly Tidwell had worked for a few years in a notorious Bristol brothel. When she left there and married old man Henry Kimes, folks thought she had reformed and intended to live a new life. Actually, she married the frequent visitor to the brothel because she thought he had money. But she was sadly mistaken.

He did have a little cottage on Virginia Street, and there she went to live. Her husband was still spry enough to walk downtown about every day. He would sit for hours on a long bench in front of Seneker's Store, whittling and swapping stories with other loafers of the town.

Holly, left alone at home, made good use of the time by rummaging through her new husband's personal effects. She found no money, but, after a day or two of intensive plundering, she managed by use of a flattened nail to unlock a small trunk which he always kept under the head of his bed. (Virtually all the old-style trunks could be unlocked with a screwdriver or a flattened nail.) The trunk was filled with old Henry's business papers, including a life insurance policy made out for a staggering $500.

Immediately, ideas began to click in her covetous mind—ideas which she hoped would bring her a great sum of money and would prove fatal to her unsuspecting husband.

Knowing that Henry dearly loved onion soup, she hastened out to Emmert's produce stand (northeast corner of Washington and Main streets) and bought the makings of that much-desired dish. One of her former visitors at the brothel, who was yet slipping over to see her, worked at Bunting's drugstore. She asked him to bring an order of carbolic acid, explaining that she wished to do away with a mangy old dog that had been hanging around her yard.

The ghost of Henry Kimes would not be quieted.

That night, Henry Kimes was delighted to find a big pot of savory onion soup simmering on the kitchen stove. Holly claimed she was not feeling well and so excused herself from the table. Onion soup has a way of disguising any "special" spices that have been added to it, and old Henry enjoyed a double helping of the much-loved soup.

For most of his long life, Henry had a habit of going straight to bed after finishing his supper. With a stomach full of onion soup, he felt especially drowsy that night, so he stretched out on his feather bed, expecting to have a long and peaceful rest. Holly sat down in the parlor, which adjoined the bedroom, and began to read—or to wait—by the flickering light of an oil lamp.

In a few minutes Henry arose, came to the connecting doorway, and there in the shadows, with a quivering voice, piteously moaned out, "Help me, Holly, I'm so sick." Then he staggered back to his bed, fell upon it, and within minutes was in that land where onion soup—if it is available there—is served by angels and contains no carbolic acid. Indeed he would have a long and peaceful rest, but not in the manner he had expected.

Dead from old age and heart failure—or so it was generally believed—Henry Kimes was buried in what is now called East Hill Cemetery. The night following the burial, Holly's Aunt Bess came to spend the night with the "lonely and disconsolate" young widow. The two had supper (not the leftover onion soup), then sat down in the little parlor to quietly rest.

Quiet rest was not to be theirs. A rustling sound came from the adjoining bedroom, then old Henry appeared in the shadowy doorway, dressed in the suit in which he had been buried. Then in that ghostly, quavering voice, he again moaned out, "Help me, Holly, I'm so sick."

The women didn't offer to help. Instead they quickly vacated the cottage and raced across town to Aunt Bess's house, where, badly shaken, they spent a restless night.

That first night with Aunt Bess proved to be uneventful. It was not so the following night. The women ate their supper at twilight, then retired to the living room. Hardly had they been comfortably seated when a rustle came from near the bedroom door. Old Henry appeared and again moaned out his piteous appeal, "Help me, Holly, I'm so sick."

If he said more, the women did not hear it. They flew out the front door. Over the next several days, Holly fled from place to place trying to elude the ghost of her murdered husband. Everywhere she went the ghost seemed to go with her. No matter where she was during the time between twilight and complete darkness, the ghost of old Henry always appeared, repeating his appeal for help.

Holly finally went to the Virginia House Hotel, where she thought surely in such a public place she would at last escape what she called "that horrible hant." Escape she could not; the hant found her there. On the second night in the hotel, she completely lost her mind.

When old Henry again appeared, she went into a kicking, flailing, screaming fit and had to be dragged from the room by local authorities. She was transferred to the Western State Hospital at Staunton, Virginia. On the way there, in what seemed to be a partially lucid state of mind, she confessed the entire murder in minute detail, then slipped back into complete insanity.

The ghost of old Henry Kimes had no mercy upon her. Even at the hospital he appeared at her bedside and moaned out his message: "Help me, Holly, I'm so sick." Holly immediately went into another screaming, writhing fit and could not be quieted. In tortured agony the fit continued until near midnight when she suddenly died.

Alas, it was later found that the insurance policy that brought all this about was not valid. It had long before lapsed because of nonpayment of premiums.

The Ghost Children of High Ridge

Towering over the western end of Windsor Avenue is High Ridge, a place known well by that name long before Bristol was founded. When the area was still far out in the country, two or three youths from Bristol went out to the Beaver Creek Knobs for a possum hunt. The night was cold and frosty, under a clear and star-filled sky. As they ascended the eastern slope of High Ridge, they froze in their tracks. From up on the ridge came the distinct sound of a crying child. Shortly, another child joined in the crying, and then a third. After the initial shock the youths advanced a little and peered up the ridge but could see nothing. The crying seemed to just come from the ground. Shaken, they hastened back to town and spread word that some children were lost on High Ridge. The Bristol, Tennessee, constable was alerted. He soon had a large company of local men hastening toward the ridge.

Though the constable and his men searched throughout the remainder of that long cold night, no children could be found. Joined by several other searchers at daybreak, they combed the coves and hollows around High Ridge, without success.

About midmorning a lady then living on Anderson Street sent word to the constable that he might as well call off the search, for they "were hunting hant children."

Though old and poor, she was still living when this writer came to Bristol in 1953. Her home was then in Crumley's Alley, a slum section of Bristol, Tennessee (it ran parallel with State and Shelby streets between Ninth and Tenth streets). Let us have the rest of the story of the ghost children on High Ridge from her:

> When I was young—that's been a long time ago [she was eighty-six in 1953]—we lived in a little valley up behind High Ridge.

Another family lived up near the ridge. They were awfully quare folks, especially the man. No one could get acquainted with them—they didn't seem to want to be neighborly. I think they lived awful hard. The man just hunted and dug roots for a living, and he may have had a little truck patch or two.

During an awful cold winter, one of those children died. No one knew about it for the longest time. Him and his wife buried the child on the ridge, not far from the eastern slope it was. You know, another one died real soon and they buried it up by the other one. You know, I don't think they even had coffins to put them in. It was an awful cold time, and their shack was not much to keep out the weather, so we allowed they probably died of pneumonia. Another family that lived closer to them than we did told that after those two were buried, the other one—oldest one, I think—would go up there and cry over their graves for hours. She was lonesome for them, I think. Well, along in the spring that one took something and died too.

That man didn't believe in religion. He wouldn't tell anybody about them dying. They wasn't any singing or preaching over them. He didn't put up rocks to mark the graves. Just smoothed over the dirt and put leaves back over them.

Not long after that last one died, that man and his wife just disappeared. No one knew where they went. Just left their stuff, what little they had, in the shack.

That next winter after they left, my brothers were up there hunting, and they heard those hant children crying. We thought they were lonely for their parents. And other folks heard them several times after that.

Now way back when the constable and several men were up there hunting for lost children, I sent them word that they might as well come in, for they were hunting for hant children. They came back to town soon after that.

Well, who knows, maybe if you were to go up on High Ridge on a cold, starry night, you might even yet have an encounter with the ghost children.

The Reformation of Whiskey John Wolford

The stretch of East State Street (old Main Street) from the railroad crossing to Pennsylvania Avenue was long known as "Loafer's Glory." It

Whiskey John Wolford - The ghost of his dead child caused his reformation.

was the haunt of prostitutes, bootleggers, petty criminals, beggars, and a wide assortment or ne'er-do-wells. A couple of blocks along the west side of Second Street was a section known as "Little Hell" during the 1880s and 1890s. It was considered to be a bit worse than Loafer's Glory.

"Whiskey" John Wolford earned his nickname not only because he was the leading bootlegger east of the tracks, but also because he was a heavy consumer of his own products. He was about half drunk most of the time, and was completely out of it on frequent occasions. He "imported" most of his illicit whiskey from moonshiners who operated in the mountains south of town, but he also made some of it using a little still he kept in the cellar of his home.

As a sideline, he did a bit of pimping for the numerous freelance prostitutes who infested both Loafer's Glory and Little Hell. Often, when he sold a man a pint or quart of liquor, he tried to include (for an extra fee) a visit to one of the area ladies of the evening, in what might well be called a package deal! More often than not, he was able to swing such an accord.

Whiskey John had a large family; some say ten or twelve children. His wife—a weak, sickly, timid soul—bore a lot of verbal and physical abuse from him, as did the children from time to time. All suffered for the want of the bare necessities of life. What money Whiskey John made seldom benefited the family. He squandered most of it on strong drink, wild women, or gambling. The latter finally became more and more a consuming passion with him.

Among the children, Whiskey John did seem to have a favorite. Little Monroe, then about five years old, seemed to be his pet of the lot. If any one child received any affection, special attention, or favor, it was Little Monroe.

There was a long and severely cold winter in the late 1880s. (The informant could not remember the exact year.) The Wolford family suffered much through that time, not having sufficient food, heat, or clothing to give even a meager amount of comfort. About midwinter, Little Monroe came down with a severe cold, which rapidly developed into pneumonia.

Dr. H. T. Berry came, diagnosed the case, and prescribed medicine which he said must be had at once. This noted early Bristol doctor, in his usual abrupt and imperious manner, told Whiskey John to go immediately to Bunting's drugstore for the remedy and to return as soon as possible.

Whiskey John started for the medicine just as darkness of a very cold night settled over the snow-covered town. Somewhere near the depot, he ran into one of his drinking and gambling buddies. Noticing that Whiskey John was wrought up about the serious illness of his favorite child, the friend offered him a drink "just to settle your nerves." That drink led to another, and that to another. Whiskey John could never remember what happened next.

About daylight of the dreary, bitterly cold morning, he arrived back home without the medicine—indeed, he could not remember going for it. There was no need for it then; Little Monroe had died shortly after midnight. The child was buried near the northwest corner of what is now the East Hill Cemetery.

By the time spring arrived, Whiskey John, perhaps trying to soothe his grief and assuage his guilt, had become far more given to drink. By then he rarely saw a sober moment and had become much more abusive of his family. He never spent a night at home; he always drank the night away, usually with his buddies over in Little Hell. The destitution of his long-suffering family had become critical.

One balmy spring evening, after much verbal abuse of his hungry and ill-clad family, he stepped out onto the side porch of his home, heading for Little Hell. A big bright full moon had just risen over East Hill, making the night almost as bright as day. Just as he reached the bottom of the porch steps, he looked toward the yard gate, which he had heard open, then froze in shock and horror.

Through that open gate came Little Monroe, dressed all in white. Smiling and with his head lifted, he ran up the walk toward Whiskey John. Clutching his father's legs, he looked up into his face and begged him to never drink again and to be good to Mommy and the brothers and sisters. Then, calling out, "I love you, Daddy, I love you," he ran back down the walk toward the open gate. He vanished before he reached it.

Whiskey John later told that he must have stood for close to an hour before he could move at all. He finally was able to stagger back into the house, much to the surprise of his family, and fall upon a bed. For about three days he could not speak, sleep, or eat.

From then on, Whiskey John was a different man. He never took another drink; he never again gambled nor associated with the numerous prostitutes of Loafer's Glory and Little Hell. He began to engage in honest labor and provide for his large family.

At that time, a new building for the Bristol Baptist Church (now First Baptist) was being erected by McCrary Brothers Builders at the northeast corner of Main (State) and Virginia streets. He was given a job on that project and continued to work for the firm for several years afterward. In time, he worked on some of the finest structures erected by McCrary Brothers, including the E. W. King house, still standing on the southwest corner of Anderson and Seventh streets, and the Samuel McCrary house on Taylor Street.

The wonderful reformation of Whiskey John Wolford came about by just one visit from a ghost.

Rooster Ghosts

The crowing of roosters is no unusual occurrence where such fowls are kept. But when a chorus of them crows where none are visibly present and where hundreds have died, it becomes a bit creepy.

In the earliest days of Bristol's existence, the high knob in which the oldest portion of East Hill Cemetery is located was called Rooster Hill. It received its name because well-attended rooster fights were often held there. Old-timers told that the ground was often red with blood and littered with dead roosters at the conclusion of these fights. The principal supporter and promoter of this brutal sport was Webb Sykes, a former convict who had early settled in the new town.

Webb died near-penniless and friendless in early 1874. By then, his rooster battleground had become a cemetery, and there he was buried. By the charity of the town and the generosity of early undertaker A. H. Bickley, a decent coffin was provided for him. The funeral sermon was preached by Maj. Z. L. Burson, who frequently was called upon to say the final words over the outcasts of early Bristol society. The funeral was conducted and the burial took place in about the center of where Webb had directed numerous bloody rooster fights.

A small crowd was present, mostly made up of Webb's former associates from the shadier parts of town, as well as a few curious citizens and two or three persons who always attended every funeral in town. Among the latter was Old Daddy Thomas, then a youth of some seventeen summers. He will be quoted for the rest of the story:

Old Zack Burson had jist said his piece [preached the funeral sermon], and they wuz a ropin' old Webb's coffin down [lowering the casket by use of ropes], when all of a sudden roosters begin crowing right loud like all around us. Ye couldn't see nary a one. Land, they seemed to be everywhere—rat under us, rat over us, and all out in the bushes around that place. And lawsy, they wuz a-gettin' louder and more uv 'em. We all knowed it wuz hants, and thought them old slaughtered roosters wuz rejoicin' that old Webb was a-gettin' his due.

And blessed Becky, them ropin' men dropped that coffin. They said that they wuz crowin' all down in that grave jist like it was full of roosters. And I don't rightly know what happened after that, fer I wuzn't there no more! I tore outta that graveyard and run down the hill towardge town, and they wuz plenty of folks a-runnin' with me. Land, ye could hear them roosters a-crowin' up there on the hill plumb down past the depot. They wuz extra loud, fer they weren' rail [real]. They wuz hant roosters. Folks up that way said that some of them wuz still crowin' at dark. You know, sir, it was one of the quarest kinds of hants that ever wuz in this town.

Indeed, it is one of the strangest ghost stories that has ever been told to this writer.

NOTE: Old Daddy Thomas further told that the grave of Webb Sykes was left open for a day or two until, finally, the town constable, who said he wasn't afraid of "all the hants this side of Jericho," went up and filled the grave.

The Ghost of a Jealous Husband

In the mid-1870s, there lived far out on what is now East State Street (it was then Paperville Road), young Jeremiah Strouth and his wife, Lucy. Married for only two or three years, they had no children. Jeremiah was learning carpentry under John M. Crowell, an early Bristol builder. The great Johnston land sale in 1871 had created a need for much new building in the fast-developing town, so the apprentice carpenter and his employer were seldom idle.

Shortly before daylight on a misty, foggy morning, Jeremiah was riding horseback to his work in Bristol. Apparently he did not see a rapidly approaching passenger train at the Main (State) Street crossing, for he rode directly into its path. Both he and the horse were instantly killed. He was buried in what is now known as East Hill Cemetery. His grave was within a few feet of the old Paperville Road (now East State Street).

Before her marriage to Jeremiah, Lucy had been engaged to Luther Meeks. Shortly after she was widowed, the romance was renewed between the two; barely two weeks had passed when Luther began to make frequent courting trips to the home of the recently bereaved widow. One night he had tarried long with her before starting the long trek back toward town. The night

Luther Meeks was ridden by the ghost of his girlfriend's deceased husband.

was misty and foggy, very much like the time when Jeremiah Strouth had been killed.

It was well past midnight when Luther neared the town cemetery where Jeremiah was buried. Just when he was about even with the newly made grave, the recently deceased husband, framed in shimmering light, appeared standing in the road "not more than a bedstead length away" as Luther later expressed it.

Terrified, Luther whirled to run back up the road. Alas, the ghost blocked his way in that direction. Then he lunged to the right, and, behold, the ghost stood before him. He lunged to the left, and again his way was blocked. He tried jumping around the dreadful apparition. It was then that the ghost jumped onto his back.

Luther tore down the hill toward the town with that "awful thing" hanging on to him. He was not released until he reached the point on the railroad tracks where the tragic, fatal accident had recently occurred.

Later, when he was asked if the "thing" was heavy, he replied that with a dead man holding on to him, his mind had sort of left him, and he couldn't remember whether there was heaviness or not.

The courting urge was mighty strong in Luther, so he soon ventured back out to see Lucy. He was determined to return home by a roundabout road that did not pass the cemetery. Perhaps the ghost of the jealous husband read his mind. For hardly had Luther and Lucy seated themselves in the front room of her little cottage, when the ghost of Jeremiah, again framed in shimmering light, floated through the closed front door.

Lucy screamed, fled out the back door, and ran up the road toward Paperville. No one knows what ever became of her. Luther jumped through a window and tore back toward town. Almost instantly, he heard heavy and fast-falling footsteps right behind him. He glanced backward and, sure enough, the ghost was following him. Again the ghost landed on Luther's back. As before, it did not release him until the site of the fatal accident was reached.

It was more than a week before Luther became brave enough to go back out to Lucy's cottage. Even then, he had not become courageous enough for night travel. Instead, he went in broad daylight. Alas, Lucy's house was all he saw.

The doors stood wide open; Lucy and her belongings were gone. He spent several hours making inquiries among the neighbors, but no one could give him the slightest clue as to where she had gone. In fact, his inquiries consumed so much time that night was fast coming on as he neared the town cemetery on his way home. The gathering darkness was hastened by a fast-approaching thunderstorm from the west.

As Luther came within sight of Jeremiah Strouth's grave, no ghost appeared as he expected. From the vicinity of the grave came the sound of loud laughter. Perhaps the jealous husband was rejoicing because he had broken up the escalating courtship. Lightning flashed, and heavy thunder drowned out the ghostly laughter. It didn't matter. By that time, Luther was racing down the hill toward town!

Though Luther Meeks lived in Bristol until he was an old man, it is said that he was never on Cemetery Hill again.

Ghost and Horse Thief, Too

Old Daddy Thomas, venerable citizen of Bristol, could tell much of the ghostly experiences of others. Once while he was doing so, this writer asked him "flat out," as he would say, if he had ever seen or heard a ghost. The reply is best told in his own words:

Dog take it right, I've had two or three run-ins with rail [real] hants in my time. Bad ones too. I shore can't fergit 'em. Sometimes have bad dreams about 'em yet.

When I were about nineteen, I think [around 1876], I got to courtin' old man Baz Shreve's daughter. They lived up here off the end of Big Buck Ridge [vicinity of the Mountain View Cemetery]. She shore were a purty gal, and we soon wuz courtin' rail strong. Old man Baz didn't like me a bit. Fact, he wuz dead set against me comin' there. He finally told me to go square home and never be seen on his place again. He were rather a savage old man, so I tuck him at his word. But me and Biney—that were her name—kept slippin' notes to each other.

Then 'long in early fall, that old man tuck bad sick and died right off. They buried him rat up here in Cherry Hill graveyard. [Though long known as the Sharrett Cemetery by the time Daddy Thomas told this story, he always called it by the original name.]

Right off I rode up to see Biney, and she shore were glad to see me. Her stepmammy didn't care fer me to come around there. Fact is, she tried to take me away from the daughter later on.

Now, we courted until way past midnight that first time I went back up there. I guess it wuz nigh on to two in the mornin' when I left and started ridin' towardge home.

I wuz a little juberous [nervous] about passin' that graveyard where Old Man Shreve had been buried. The main road ran jist below it, so I jist rode along that way. It were a bright moonlight night. You could purt-nigh read a paper outside.

Long afore I got there, I decided I wouldn't look towardge that graveyard a'tall. When I got pine blank afore [just at] the lower gate, my horse started to boogerin' and lookin' to the left towardge old Cherry Hill. He wuz a-snortin' as he looked.

I looked too. And, land, there wuz a tall man in a dark suit, a-makin' fer us. He didn't seem to be a-walkin' but jist a skimmin' over that ground. Now, he didn't open the gate but jist seemed to float rat through hit.

I whipped that horse and tried to get him to run, but he couldn't seem to get started. That man came on and grabbed ahold of the bits and looked rat up at me, not sayin' a word but jist a shakin' his head and blowin' like a mad goose.

Law, and when he looked rat up at me, I saw it were Old Man Baz Shreve. Without havin' to think, I jumped off that horse backward, rat over his tail, and I hit the groun' a-runnin'. I's stooped over when I hit the groun' and didn't take time to straighten up till I's guess a quarter of a mile back up the road.

I run plumb past the Shreve place and wuz in front of old John Worley's house afore I could stop. [It was at that time the Sam Millard place and is now occupied by Ed and Linda Stout.] I guess I'd kept on runnin', fer I thought old Baz might be rat ahind me. I couldn't take time to look around, but I was done plumb run out. After I got my breath I took a long way around to get home. I shore didn't want to pass that graveyard agin.

Next day I ventured back up to see iffen I could find my horse. You know, sir, I found his tracks where he'd stopped rat afore that graveyard gate, but they wuz no more tracks leading off anywhere. Seems that horse done been taken by that hant. Never did find him. I reckon I had met a hant and a horse thief too!

Never would go back up there a-courtin' at night. Jist went in daylight time. Finally Biney got to courtin' me in daytime and some other man at night.

You know, they soon run off an' married. Hadn't been fer that hant, I think I'da got her, shore.

Though Daddy Thomas lost Biney, he was privileged to marry three other women in his long lifetime. He was a widower when this writer first met him in 1953.

The Indian Warrior Ghost

The reader may remember the story of the ghostly appearance of a lone Indian warrior that used to terrorize the slaves of Rev. James King as they labored in the vast fields of his plantation. It appears that the same ghost made a dramatic appearance a few years after the founding of Bristol.

Soon after the end of the Civil War, Col. Abram Fulkerson, a former officer in the Confederate Army, settled in Bristol and soon opened an office for the practice of law. Within a few years he entered the field of politics. He was well liked and respected by local citizens. His remarkable intelligence and ability to influence those around him were well-known to all. Thus, when he ran for public office he usually got a hefty share of the votes in Bristol and Washington County, Virginia. In one of his runs for office, he and his opponent scheduled a public speaking event to be held on a vacant lot on what is now the northwest corner of State and Piedmont streets. The location was then an unused corner of John M. Crowell's brickyard.

On one of this writer's last visits to Old Daddy Thomas, a highly valued informant, he gave the story of the strange occurrence. Let us hear it in his own words:

I went there along with my pap, who always liked to hear the old Colonel get steamed up—and he knowed he would that day. The talkin' was being done in the edge of Crowell's big brickyard and rat about Old Pokey's [Pocahontas Hale] ginny barn [local slang term for a brothel]. I recollect how the gals there wuz a-lookin' out the winders and Pokey was a-standin' rat out on the front porch. Old Col. Fulkerson always drawed a big crowd, and they shore wuz a biggun there that day. Oh, it were a powerful large gatherin'.

Now, lack everybody expected, old Colonel Fulkerson got all riled up good and proper in no time. Land, he charged about, left and right, a-wavin' his arms and bellowin' out a mighty powerful speech. That crowd wuz with him. They was givin' attention to ever' word and agging [egging] him on. He went on fer nearly a hour.

He finally got to windin' down and wuz about ready to let the man that wuz runnin' against him start his say. You know, sir, all of a sudden the air was split by a bloodcurdlin' whoop that seemed to be comin' rat out of the air over our heads, and seems like rat out of the air jumped a big Indian. He's all dressed and painted for war, he wuz. Yessir, I wuz rat there not more than two fence-rail lengths away, and I seed 'im with these own eyes, I did.

Now, that Indian hant—I knowed what he wuz—began runnin' in a circle rat around the Colonel, a-wavin' his hatchet in the air and yellin' to high heaven ever' time he hit the ground. Land, you could hear that yellin' fer a long mile. Lawsy, hit was the awfulest sound I ever heared.

Most of the crowd scattered lack scalded dogs, but some jist froze in their tracks and couldn't move a bit. And a few women, and maybe a man or two, jist died off [swooned or fainted]. Now, old Rosetta Bachelor wuz in that crowd, and she wuz scared stiff of Indians. Allus had been since she come out here from way east some place. Hadn't been no bad Indians around fer years, but I don't reckon she knew that. I reckon she thought that Indian wuz rail, or maybe she didn't think. Anyhow, she drawed out one of them pistols she allus carried, and, you know, sir, she emptied that pistol at that hant, and then drawed out the other and emptied hit too. Course, hit didn't bother that hant none. Anyone with a good mind knows you can't kill a hant.

Now, folks aroun' here was about as afeared uv Rosetta as they wuz Indian hants, so that added to the excitement a bit. So when she started shootin', most of 'em that hadn't run did then. And, you know, when that old gal emptied her last pistol and seed it didn't do no good, she whirled and tore down the street. The last I seed uv her, she was a-takin' cover behind Old Pokey's ginny barn.

I guess I jist couldn't run, and I recollect that old Col. Fulkerson wuz still jist a-standin' where he wuz when that hant got among us. And about that time, that hanty Indian jist got to jumpin' higher in the air, and jist a-gettin' higher in the air. Now, that man that were a-runnin' against the Colonel weren't there anymore. I don't rightly know where he went.

Col. Abram Fulkerson, who had been in the midst of many a bloody battle during the Civil War, later declared that the appearance of that phantom Indian was the most "unnerving experience" he ever had. In writing to a fellow lawyer in Abingdon (Daniel Trigg), he described the strange happening: "But whatever it was, it was of great benefit to me, for my opponent never got to speak at all."

Shall we say that the ghostly Indian was a political activist! This seems to have been the last appearance of the ancient Indian warrior. Beware! Ghosts are not bound by time and space, you know. That "hanty" Indian may just jump out of the air in downtown Bristol again sometime!

The Official Ghost

The appearance of a ghost is recorded in official chancery court papers in Washington County, Virginia. It is doubtful that such exists in any other court records in America. The very unusual occurrence came about in this manner:

In the early 1880s there lived a certain man in a little cottage that stood on Railroad Street in Bristol, Virginia. (Railroad was later known as Spencer Street.) There he lived happily with his wife and four small children. Though a humble, laboring man, he was well-known to most of the residents of the town.

During the spring of 1882, an epidemic of diphtheria hit Bristol. One of the first to die of this dreaded disease was little Rachel, the much-adored baby of this family. About a month later the father became ill with typhoid fever, lingered for several weeks, and then he too died.

The young widow made every effort to provide for the remaining family and, in doing so, became heavily indebted to a local merchant. Her needs were greater than her means, and much of her indebtedness to the merchant remained unpaid. In time he sued for his bill. Eventually, the chancery court of Washington County ruled in his favor and decreed that the widow's home must be sold to satisfy her creditor. (There were numerous such sad cases in early Bristol.)

Col. David F. Bailey, an early Bristol lawyer, was appointed a Commissioner in Chancery to conduct the sale. The property was duly advertised in the *Bristol News,* with sale time set. This sale was to be held in front of the mayor's office, on Lee Street in Bristol-Goodson, Virginia. The destitute widow begged and pleaded with several noted local property owners to buy the house and rent it back to her, even offering to do hard work for them as payment of rent, but none would promise to do so. As sale day approached, she became almost frantic with extreme anxiety as to the future welfare of her little family. Though none in the town would heed her pleas, perhaps somewhere in the unknown Great Beyond, her late husband heard and heeded, as will be indicated later.

As was usual on such occasions, a large crowd of the curious and bargain seekers gathered in front of the mayor's office for the commissioner's sale. Colonel Bailey, dressed as always in his black scissor-tail coat and tall silk hat, appeared. He quieted the crowd, read the judge's orders, explained the terms of the sale, then opened for bids.

Let us now hear what happened, as told by the late Tom Faidley:

I tell you, sir, I saw it. I was right there and I'll never forget it if I live to be a hundred years old. I couldn't believe my eyes, but I had to. That's been around sixty-five years ago, but there's never been a day but what I thought of that strange happening, and I've had several bad dreams about the thing.

Just as Col. Bailey opened for bids, that dead man suddenly appeared at his left side, and he was holding little Rachel in his arms. I knew them well. I was there when both of them died. I helped to lay him out. I lived up there near them and I knew them well. He [the deceased husband] said not a word but just looked that crowd right in the eye. That little baby [Rachel] smiled just like she used to do so much when she was living.

I'll never forget what effect it had on that crowd. Nearly all the folks there knew well who they were. Instead of wildly scattering like a bunch of chickens that a hawk's landed among, as usually happens when a hant's around, those people just froze in awe of what was happening.

Now, that broke up the sale. Col. Bailey, not knowing at first that the hant was standing by him, begged for bids. Then he realized that no one was looking at him, but was looking at something near him. When he finally saw that man and child, he knew them both, he went dumb and just couldn't seem to say another word. Why, you couldn't have got old Zack Burson, who was always looking to buy a house cheap, to have made one bid then. Then that man and his child just slowly faded away. I tell you now, I never saw the beat of it.

In a few days Colonel Bailey submitted a paper to Judge Kelly, explaining why his duties had not been completed. Along with that paper he submitted his resignation as commissioner. He stated that he supposed his honor had heard of the matter, in that much notoriety had been given to it. He called it a mystical happening, which he could hardly believe but certainly could not deny. He further stated that in light of such strange developments, he doubted that a successful sale could ever be had, "for everyone here believes that if it is ever tried, the ghost will appear again."

There the matter ends; there is no further mention of the case in the chancery court records of Washington County, Virginia.

The Ghost Quilt

The much-dreaded typhoid fever was an ever-present threat in early Bristol, and the late summer of 1882 saw an unusually severe epidemic of the often-fatal disease. A young man and his wife, then residing on Fourth Street in Bristol, Tennessee, became its victims, dying within a week of one another. Their passing left three little orphan boys, all less than six years old.

The deceased husband's mother, a widow, was then living nearby, and she took her grandsons into her home. They were beautiful children. All had light blond hair and bright blue eyes. Winter was coming on, so the kind grandmother went to J. M. Barker's store, where she bought wool suits for each of them.

Late in the following spring, a diphtheria epidemic hit the town. The oldest of the three boys was the first to be stricken by the often-fatal malady. The other two took it from him. They all suffered much and lingered long, but, sadly, all three eventually died.

The following autumn, the still-sorrowing grandmother made a patchwork quilt of their little wool suits. After it was completed, she could not bear to look at it or use it. She soon gave it to her younger sister, who operated a boardinghouse in downtown Bristol.

The sister used the quilt on her bed for two or three nights but would not use it longer. She never explained why. She then put the quilt on a bed in one of her rented rooms. That first night, she lost her roomer. He told that he'd had the most-vivid dream of three little blond-haired, blue-eyed boys. He then awoke to find the same youngsters in his room, slowly pulling the cover from his bed. In moments they "just vanished" into thin air. He said he "knowed they were hants" and he just would not stay another night in a room "where hants had been." It should be noted that he had no prior knowledge of the three deceased boys.

The quilt was then moved to another room, where the same thing happened—the vivid dream, followed by an appear-

These sisters quickly got rid of a haunted quilt.

ance of the little boys. Another roomer was lost. Then the quilt was moved to a third room, where there was a repeat of the ghostly performance.

Finally, it was given to a poor family that badly needed bedcovers. Badly needed or not, the quilt was used only two nights, with that many visitations of the ghostly little boys. Without telling what had happened, the family sold it to a middle-aged spinster, who lived in a slightly more elite part of Bristol.

She thought it was a unique bit of handiwork, was pleased with it, but her pleasure was not for long. At first, she put it in a blanket chest that was kept in a small room immediately behind her bedroom.

One night she retired early and was drifting into peaceful sleep, when she was suddenly jolted back to wakefulness by what sounded like children's voices coming from the back room. She quickly sprang up and, with lighted lamp in hand, went to the open doorway of that room. There around the chest, trying to lift the lid, were three little blond-headed boys. After a moment they just faded away.

It was a disturbing experience, and she hardly slept through that long night. There was no reoccurrence of the ghostly appearance over the next several months, so she lost her nervousness about the matter. At the time, she did not connect the three boys with her recently purchased quilt.

When fall came on, she put the woolen quilt on her bed. During the wee hours of the next morning, she had a vivid dream in which she saw the little boys who had so strangely appeared around the blanket chest in her back room. Awaking in great fright, she was horrified to find the same youngsters pulling the quilt from her bed.

She didn't wait for them to vanish. It was she who vanished from the room! She spent the rest of the night with the family that lived next door.

The next morning, acting on the advice of local psychic Pocahontas Hale, she ventured back to her house, gingerly picked up the "hanted" quilt, and carried it to the backside of her garden. There she poured a gallon of kerosene over it and set it afire. For fear that ghosts might appear again, she did not stay to watch it burn.

Perhaps the advice of the local psychic was well given; after the burning of the ghost quilt, the three little blond-headed, blue-eyed boys never appeared again.

The Phantom Stagecoach

"Wild" Peter Jefferson was long the stable boy, carriage driver, gardener, and general handyman for Capt. J. H. Wood at Pleasant Hill, 214 Johnson Street, in Bristol, Virginia. He lived in a room on the second floor of Captain Wood's carriage house, a long frame building, always painted red, which stood at the back of the home and fronted on the Old Stagecoach Road (now known as King's Alley).

In the lower part of the building was the carriage room, feed room, and stalls for three horses—one for Captain Wood's riding horse and two for the carriage horses. A narrow stairway led up from the carriage room to the hayloft at the north end, where Peter's small bedroom was. One window on the roadside (west) was his only outlook on the world.

Though Wild Peter had well earned his nickname, he nevertheless was an industrious, hardworking, honest, and truthful young man. His reputation for truthfulness caused many in the town to take note when he told one day of seeing a phantom stagecoach.

Peter always awoke about 4:00 A.M. He had no clock, but he was one of those fortunate persons with a built-in alarm. He could just "set his head"

The ghost stagecoach appeared in King's Alley, forefront of this picture. The author's home is the center house.

to wake up at a certain time, and he would. Strangely, after he awoke he always "rested in bed," as he put it, until 5:00 A.M. Then he would hop up, dress, and go down to the kitchen door, where his mother would have his breakfast ready. (His mother, "Aunt" Sadie Jefferson, was long the cook, housekeeper, and nursemaid at Pleasant Hill.) When breakfast was finished, the day's duties began.

In the earlier days, the Old Stagecoach Road was a busy thoroughfare. For years a stage ran from Abingdon to Blountville, usually arriving in Bristol at about 4:00 A.M. One of the drivers on that run was Henry Kerry, who had finally come to Bristol to live.

Captain Wood had done some legal work for Mr. Kerry, and in the course of time they became good friends. In February 1887, Henry Kerry became very ill. Late one afternoon, Captain Wood had Peter hook up the horses to the carriage and drive him across town to see his old friend. Mr. Kerry was found to be critically ill, sinking fast, and not expected to live through the night.

The next morning, Peter awoke at the usual 4:00 A.M. Immediately, he noticed that the morning wasn't "heavy quiet," as he called it. From down toward Scott Street came the sound of wheels grinding, multiple hoofbeats, the cracking of a whip, and the yell of a driver urging horses up Burn's Hill. Peter knew that things just didn't sound right.

He quickly jumped from his bed and ran over to his little window. He leaned far out and peered up the Old Stagecoach Road. The early morning was brightened by a full moon, hanging low in the west. Then at the top of Burn's Hill he saw it; a white stagecoach, pulled by four white horses, was sweeping up the road toward him.

A stagecoach had not traveled that road in well over a quarter of a century. Peter somehow knew that what he saw was not real. He froze in both fear and fascination. As the stage rolled past his window, he noticed that it was empty. No passengers were inside, no baggage was on top. The usual driver's helper was missing. He really froze in his bones when he saw that the driver was old Henry Kerry, whom he had seen lying deathly ill only a few hours earlier. Old Henry was blending well with the stage and horses, for he was fully dressed in pure white. The ghostly coach and driver passed Peter's window and swiftly rolled down the long slope toward Sycamore Street. He had no recollection of the next hour. He said his mind just "sort of faded out."

By daylight, he was excitedly telling Captain Wood about the passing of the phantom stagecoach and that it was driven by Henry Kerry. Now, Captain Wood prided himself on being too intelligent to believe in such things, but he did immediately send his oldest son to see about the critically ill ex-stage driver. The son soon returned to report that Mr. Kerry had died at 4:00 A.M., the exact time that Wild Peter Jefferson had seen the passage of the ghostly coach and driver. Indeed, the old stage driver had made a journey alone into the great beyond.

After that ghostly appearance, Peter would never again sleep in the carriage house. In winter he slept on a pallet in the Pleasant Hill kitchen, and in summer he slept on the adjoining back porch.

The Black Shadow of Death

That high day, in early October 1889, was cloudless under an azure blue sky. It was so comfortably warm that the Highnite family gathered on the front porch of their Moore Street home in anticipation of a pleasant and leisurely afternoon. Even old Granny Highnite, while somewhat feeble and a bit puny—but what can one expect at 94—hobbled out to spend a while with her family.

Before long, a young lady who lived next door came over for a congenial visit with her much-loved neighbors. That pleasant visit turned into a hanty happening which that young lady vividly remembered into extreme

The black shadow of death appeared at this house.

old age. She told it to this writer in the autumn of 1953. Let us hear it in her own words:

We were sitting there enjoying that bright afternoon when, all of a sudden, two or three of us noticed a large black shadow that just seemed to flow over the front gate like a waterfall. It then moved ever so slowly across the front yard, toward the house. At first we thought it was the shadow of a low cloud or a big bird or something. Some of the family stepped into the yard and looked up, and there was nothing up there. The sky was bright and clear. That shadow moved right on until it came up on the porch and stopped directly in front of Granny Highnite's feet. It stayed there about a minute, then just ever so slowly faded away. Several of us thought it was a warning hant for Granny, but we didn't say so at the time.

We all stayed there kind of quiet-like. About an hour later that big black shadow came back just like before. Only this time it didn't stop at Granny's feet but just seemed to cover her. Granny just got real serious and didn't speak no more that afternoon. I think she knew what it meant. We were all shaken up. The family went back into the house, and I came on back home.

At suppertime that night, just after sundown it was, they all got in the kitchen and were sitting down. Mrs. Highnite got Granny seated and was putting food on her plate when that old lady just gasped right loud-like and gasped a time or two more then just died right there in the kitchen at the table. Doc Berry said her old heart just quit. We all knew we were right about what that hanty shadow meant. I never heard of it around here again.

NOTE: Tales of "warning" ghosts were very common in the area of northern Arkansas where this author grew up. Strangely he has encountered very few in the Bristol area. While there seem to be more ghosts here, few of them seem to be of the warning variety. There were many persons, including his own mother, who admitted to be believers in warnings, but not in the regular variety of supernatural appearances.

The Ghost Dog in East Hill Cemetery

Isaac DePrato, a railroad brakeman, died in his Bristol home around Christmastime 1890. His funeral and burial took place in the old section of the East Hill Cemetery. About halfway through the funeral service, the family dog came running from home, which was over a mile away. He entered the cemetery gate howling and barking, and through the remainder of the service he slowly circled the crowd, still barking, whining, and howling. Indeed, the minister shortened the service because of this touching display of grief by the faithful family dog.

Once Mr. DePrato was buried, the dog lay down atop the grave and would not move from the site. As darkness settled over Cemetery Hill, he began a piteous howling that continued through the night. The next day he remained quiet. Members of the family returned to the cemetery and tried every way they knew to get him to leave the grave and return home with them, but all efforts were in vain. Kind folks living near the graveyard took food and drink, as did the DePrato family, but the dog refused to partake of it. After several days he died, still faithfully guarding his master's grave.

After the dog's death, folks living around the cemetery thought that their nights would then be peaceful. It was not to be so. At midnight of the first full moon, a ghostly howling began on Cemetery Hill. It continued for about an hour, then began again shortly before daylight. This was the pattern every time there was a full moon. One old lady living nearby said she always dreaded the fulling of the moon because she "knowed that hant would commence in the graveyard." A couple of brave men who lived in the vicinity ventured into the moon-bathed cemetery to investigate. The howling became louder as they neared the grave, yet nothing could be seen.

Over the years which followed, the ghost dog was heard less and less frequently. At last, it seemed that the piteous howling had ceased forever. In recent years, however, there have been reports that the ghost dog has been heard again. It seems that the faithful companion of Isaac DePrato still grieves over the grave of his master.

Converted by a Ghost

In the early 1890s, there came to Bristol from Lynchburg a young, cultured, and well-educated lawyer, M. D. L. Clarke. He became a partner with Col. D. F. Bailey. All looked promising, and he did attain a mild degree of success. That success might have been greater had he not been an avowed atheist, a fact that did not set well in a town where fundamental Christianity reigned supreme. Many viewed him with a bit of suspicion, and that did somewhat hinder the advancement of his career.

M. D. L. Clarke was converted by a ghost.

In spite of his open atheism, he was able to marry a beautiful young daughter of a prominent and devout Christian family of the town. (She was a member of the Bristol Methodist Church, now known as State Street Methodist.)

The marriage horrified many members of the church, causing one of them to publicly state that she had "made her bed in hell." The love-stricken couple paid little attention to family and friends. They settled down in a little rented cottage on Goodson Street and began what they expected to be a happy and fulfilling life. To the credit of both of them, she continued to faithfully attend her church and he did not oppose her.

Perhaps their time together was happy and fulfilling, but it proved to be tragically short. A little over a year later the beautiful bride died during the birth of their first child. The baby also died within a few hours, and they were buried together in East Hill Cemetery.

The young atheist husband was devastated by the tragic death of his wife and baby. Every night he hastened from his office up to East Hill Cemetery, usually without stopping at home for a bite of supper. Late travelers on the Paperville Road (now East State Street) told of hearing his piteous wails as he grieved over the newly made grave. Indeed, one passerby, not knowing of the situation, thought he was hearing a ghost and made a faster journey to Paperville than he had planned.

Finally, Mr. Clarke confided to a friend that he actually hoped to see the ghost of his wife and that if he did, he would then know that there is something beyond this life. On a moon-bathed night a little later, he made his usual trip to the cemetery. As he later told, he had wept until he could weep no more and was just sitting silently on the stone curb that surrounded his wife's family lot. Sitting there in the silence alone, he slowly became aware of a familiar sound: a woman was softly humming a soothing lullaby. He well knew the voice and the cradlesong. A few weeks before her death, his wife had gone about the cottage, humming and singing that "sweet song," as he called it. She told him that she had learned it from her mother and grandmother and that she was going to sing it to their baby. Now he was hearing it again.

Then he saw her. Along the path that led up from the cemetery gate, his wife, dressed in shining white, was slowly moving toward him. She was sweetly crooning the familiar lullaby to the baby she held in her arms.

Amazed, so glad, and yet a bit fearful, he sat transfixed as she approached him. When she was within a few steps of him, she began to rise up slowly, higher and higher up above the treetops, and higher until she disappeared into the heavens.

The message to him was clear: there was something beyond this life. He had seen his wife alive, and he had seen her ascend into heaven.

Almost instantly his grief subsided. He stopped his nightly visits to the cemetery. He professed his faith and joined the Bristol Methodist Church, much to the delight of many who had so vehemently opposed his marriage to one of their own. He was a faithful member and heavy supporter of that church for as long as he remained in Bristol.

After about a year of being a widower, he married his deceased wife's sister. They had two children before leaving Bristol.

About 1898, he was persuaded by a former law school classmate to join him in a law firm in East Central Texas. There he greatly prospered, first as a lawyer, then as a lawyer and rancher. He died in 1944 and is buried in a large, well-kept rural cemetery near his ranch.

His substantial monument, towering nearly twenty feet over his grave, bears an interesting and unusual inscription:

> M. D. L. Clarke
> Born – August 21, 1866
> Died – October 15, 1944
>
> A former unbeliever, he was suddenly brought to the gospel light in Bristol, Tennessee, May 28, 1894. He lived an exemplary Christian life and was a member of the Methodist Church for over fifty years.

Likely, those who read that inscription today do not know that he was suddenly brought to the gospel light by a ghost.

Self-Winding Clock

Old Granddad Reeves long lived on Third Street Hill. For the last fifteen years of his life he was a widower. A few years of that time were spent alone, but after he became feeble, his son and family moved in with him.

The humble cottage contained the most common of furnishings. As in many poorer homes, there was one fine and treasured article, an old striking clock. A Seth Thomas OG model finished in burled mahogany, it sat on the mantel, where it was the focal point of the room. On the lower glass was a colorful scene, an egg-filled bird's nest with one bird sitting on the edge of the nest and another flying to it.

The clock was weight driven and ran only thirty hours on one winding. A man for whom Granddad Reeves long worked had bought a finer eight-day model for his family, and then passed the old clock on to his faithful employee. Every night just after the clock struck nine, Granddad Reeves arose from his fireside chair to wind his highly valued timepiece.

This was the signal that the day had ended and bedtime had come.

On a cold, snowy night in January 1888, Granddad Reeves fell dead upon the hearth just after he had finished winding the old Seth Thomas weight-driven clock. He was buried late the next day in East Hill Cemetery, as wind-tossed snow swirled around the funeral party.

That night, while the howling snowstorm intensified outside, the sad son and family huddled around the fireside. Exactly at 9:00 P.M., the door of the old clock slowly swung open, the key was lifted into place, and, seemingly by an unseen hand, the clock was slowly wound. Of course, this ghostly happening stunned and frightened the family. One may be sure that sleep, if it came at all that night, was light and fitful. The next night, just after the clock finished striking nine, there was a repeat of the ghostly performance. When this happened again the third night, the somewhat sleepy son vowed that, come morning, he would do something with that "hanted clock."

Do something he did—he gave it to his mother-in-law, thinking that once it left the family home, the hant would also leave the clock. Alas, he was mistaken; the ghost of Granddad Reeves did not miss one night of winding the treasured clock.

One night was enough for the mother-in-law! It is said that she was always "scared stiff by anything hanty." She immediately sold it to a neighbor for two dollars. (Seems that, being a practical woman, she thought she might as well make a little money while ridding her home of a ghost.)

Now, this neighbor, a little on the elite side, had a formal, seldom-used parlor in his home. He placed the clock on the mantel in that parlor. A few days later he told someone that he was puzzled about the newly acquired clock—every time he went in for the nightly winding, he found that it was already wound and ticking away.

After a week or so, the strange winding ceased. Maybe the ghost of Granddad Reeves became tired of chasing the clock all over town!

The Ghost of Pocahontas Hale

Toward the end of the nineteenth century, Pocahontas Hale, long the notorious madam of the Black Shawl brothel, died. Because of her unsavory reputation, the trustees of East Hill Cemetery would not allow her to be buried there. So she was laid to rest in Flat Hollow Cemetery, which was then considered to be a lowly burying ground.

Soon after the burial, a hired hand of the Susong family, who had been courting in Bristol, was returning home about two o'clock one morning. His path lay directly by the Flat Hollow Cemetery. A bright moon was shining above, causing night to be almost as light as day.

Long before the hanty old cemetery was reached, the young man had determined not to look in that direction. He likely would not have done so, but he said he heard what sounded like a woman singing a strange lullaby, and the sound came directly from the cemetery.

Pocahontas Hale operated the Black Shawl, Bristol's largest brothel.

He well recognized the voice and the melody. As a previous visitor at the Black Shawl brothel, he remembered that as the girls visited in their rooms with their male guests, Pocahontas Hale would walk the halls, crooning the very song that he then heard coming from the lonely old cemetery. He recalled that when she thought a girl was spending too much time with a guest, she would stand at the door of the room and sing the lullaby in a much louder voice. It was the signal for the girl to switch visitors.

Greatly frightened, he saw a tall figure dressed in black, standing at the cemetery gate. He knew he again was seeing Pocahontas Hale, the recently deceased madam of his favorite brothel. As he looked, the lullaby became much louder.

Well, if that had been the old signal to switch visitors, he took it as the new signal to switch locations! That he did—and in a mighty hasty fashion. He was at the Susong place, over a mile away, before he knew he had started. He may have gone courting in Bristol after that, but you may be certain that he took a different route home.

Several times after she made her opening debut to the Susong hired hand, the ghost was seen by others who dared pass that "hanted graveyard" at night. Several reported hearing the same lullaby that the well-known madam used to croon in the dimly lighted halls of the Black Shawl.

Around 1900, the Flat Hollow Cemetery was moved to just beyond the end of Piedmont Avenue. We know it today as the Citizen's Cemetery. Did the troubled spirit of Pocahontas Hale make that move? Maybe, and maybe not.

On occasion, since Rice Terrace was built (1940) over top of the old cemetery, there have been reports of a tall black figure walking around and around the site, and at least one person reported hearing what he called a "peculiar tune" coming from the figure. The sightings were always made in the wee hours of the morning when there was a bright full moon overhead.

Ghost at the Flat Hollow Hanging Tree

The hanging tree stood near the gate of the Flat Hollow Cemetery. Early Bristolians said it was just right for hanging or swinging. This conclusion was reached because a long limb of the oak tree reached straight outward from the main body, and it was just the right distance from the ground to be used for either purpose. It doesn't seem to have ever been used for swinging, but sadly, it was once used for hanging.

In the late 1880s, a black man was thought to have attempted to rape a white woman. The suspicion was largely based on circumstantial evidence; certainly there was no definite proof that the man was guilty. As usual at such times, emotions ran rampant. Unfortunately, emotions often overrule reason and any sense of well-founded judgment. It was so in this case.

Several relatives and friends of the lady involved found the man and forcibly took him to the Flat Hollow Cemetery, where they hanged him from the tree and left his body hanging overnight. Sometime the next day, relatives of the man, without benefit of coffin or funeral, buried him in the Flat Hollow Cemetery.

Perhaps a year later, one of the men who had been a leader in the lynching had tarried late in town, and on his way home he had to pass the hanging tree and cemetery. Heavy clouds hung overhead, causing the night to be "black dark." As the man came almost even with the hanging tree, which stood about fifty feet from the roadway, he saw what he described as short streaks of lightning begin to flash among the branches of the tree. Some of them circled around and around the limb that had been used for the tragic hanging. All the while, he heard a steady and loud hissing.

The terrified man froze in his tracks. That is, he froze until suddenly those short streaks of lightning seemed to all come together to form one big round ball of fire, which sailed straight at him, and the hissing became a loud roar. That "unfroze" him! Like a chased jackrabbit, he raced up Flat Hollow, with the ball of fire sailing right behind him.

Reaching home, he fell onto his front porch and passed out. When he finally revived, it was daylight. The ball of fire had disappeared.

Shortly afterward the man suffered a nervous breakdown. For days he could neither eat nor sleep. Finally, in his weakened condition, he developed pneumonia and died. Perhaps the ghost of the lynched man had evened the score.

The Ghost in King College Woods

It was a lonely and secluded place, back there in the closing decades of the 1800s. Where King College campus is now was then a great forest of giant trees that had effectively smothered out the underbrush. (Remnants of the forest yet remain today.) It was an easy and pleasant place to stroll if one's mind was at ease and the outlook promising.

James "Jim" King Anderson, who daily and nightly strolled there, had no peace of mind, and the future for him was only a black cloud portending worse to come. When he sauntered forth among the mammoth trees behind the tenant house on his father's Whittaker Branch Farm, he was likely seeking peace of mind rather than enjoying it. Perhaps he did find a small measure of such in the first appearance of colorful spring flowers or the myriad hues of autumn. In high summer, perhaps the singing of birds was a bit of solace to him. Or maybe the sighing winds of bleak winter were music to him in whose tortured soul there were no bright notes of harmony.

Jim had been placed on the farm to keep him from the temptations of the numerous saloons that were then flourishing in downtown Bristol. Some called it banishment by his stern, prohibitionist father, Joseph R. Anderson. Actually it was an act of great kindness, for Jim had nearly been killed by alcohol, and his mind and physical health had been irreversibly damaged by it. One drink could plunge him into months of torturous suffering. For him to go down the East Hill to Bristol was to go down the road to destruction.

So for well over twenty years, he was only twice in the town his father had founded. On those occasions, his mother, who was greatly concerned about his spiritual condition, had sent a servant with the family carriage to bring her erring son to church (First Presbyterian). Jim could not sit through the full service. He complained of feelings that suddenly swept over him, causing him to want to cry out and run from the sanctuary. Indeed, each time he came, he had to make a hasty exit before the service ended. Today, the behavior would be diagnosed as a panic attack. Alas, the medical world at the time seldom recognized the malady, and there were no effective drugs for treatment.

A black servant, a former Anderson slave, stayed with Jim for most of those years spent on the Whittaker Branch Farm. His report was that Jim

The ghost of James King Anderson is said to still walk in King College woods.

spent most of his waking hours in constant motion, either walking in the great forest, over the fields, or up and down Whittaker Branch. Sometimes he briefly sat down by the Whittaker Spring but was soon up and going again. Like a caged animal looking for a way of escape, his troubled spirit sought a deliverance that could never be found. His constantly moving body tried in vain to warm his frozen emotions.

Sometimes his wanderings took him farther than the farm. On the night following the burial of his father, it is told that Jim roamed through the darkness to the East Hill Cemetery and sat by the grave until daylight. He had not attended the funeral, likely because of the severe panic attacks.

To passersby he became a familiar sight. Even if it was midnight, perhaps under a bright, full moon, no one was surprised to see the tall dark figure moving slowly across the open fields or through the shadowy woods. One morning about daylight, he was seen walking homeward near Jacob Carmack's place on what is now King College Road. No one knew how far he had been.

But no matter how far he ever went, the servant always knew Jim would be back for a short nap—he never slept a night through—or for a bit of food.

In the spring of 1902, Jacob's son, Robert P. Carmack, made an extended visit with relatives who lived in Green County, Missouri. Arriving back in Bristol on the night of April 23, he walked from the depot to his home some two miles distant. His route lay by the great forest on Anderson's Whittaker Branch Farm.

At home his mother set a late supper for her son. During the meal he casually said to her, "You know, I saw Jim Anderson on his rounds in the woods at Whittaker Branch tonight. For some reason he didn't seem so feeble anymore. He was walking like a young man and was whistling a merry tune."

His mother gasped, turned pale, and with shaking voice replied, "Why, son, Jim was buried yesterday. Your father and I attended the funeral and burial."

Robert then gasped and turned pale. It is said that he would never again pass the woods at night, not even after he was an old man and King College had long occupied the site.

Soon there were other sightings of the ghost. About a year later, Robert's brother-in-law David J. Hart, who had recently moved to his new home on the Carmack place, was returning home from a trip into town. He had tarried a little longer than he had meant to, so it was late twilight when he reached Whittaker Branch. Across a small field and near the woods, he saw the figure of a man ambling along, dressed in jet black and carrying a walking stick.

The man looked just like Jim, who had used a cane in his final months of life. David had known him well, but he also knew that the man was dead and buried, so it couldn't be Jim. When the ghostly figure just seemed to sink down into the ground and disappear, David had second thoughts and quickly hurried on home. Evidently he was not in a hurry to tell the fearful story. It wasn't until he was on his deathbed, fifty-three years later, that David told his family about encountering the ghost.

By 1910, the Anderson farm had been long untended and Whittaker Branch Farm had become a notorious gathering point for gamblers, drunks, and a few prostitutes—so much so that a lot of folks living out that way were hesitant to pass the place even in broad daylight. Often there were fights, and it appears that a murder was once committed on the property.

One bright moonlit night, a few men and two prostitutes gathered there to have a wild party around the spring. In the midst of their revelry, one of the women cried out that a man was stalking them. Sure enough, a tall man dressed in black was slowly circling the group, coming closer with each round. One of the men drew a pistol and called out a command for identification. There was no response from the intruder. The man, a bit perplexed and angered, then called out, "Who are you and what do you want?"

Again there was no response, but it was plain to see that the silent figure was drawing closer, so the angered and fearful reveler opened fire. He emptied his pistol toward the strange, circling form, but without effect. Then the shaken revelers watched in horror as the figure seemed to rise up to about head height and continue his circular walk "as if on air." He seemed to be getting higher with each circle. No one knows how far the ghost ascended, for in moments not a witness was left!

There lived in Bristol a man who had known Jim Anderson for many years. He heard tales of the strange occurrences at Whittaker Branch Farm and vowed that he would not be afraid to spend the night there. "Jim's well buried," he said. "I helped to lower him down, and he sure is not going to pop up on Whittaker Branch or in those woods or anywhere else."

Some friends dared him to do it. One mellow, mid-spring night soon after the dare was issued, he took a bed roll and, loudly boasting to friends that there were not enough hants in Sullivan County to keep him from enjoying a night in the woods, left town, calling back that he would see his friends in the morning.

It is not known when he saw his friends again, but it is known that he was back in town by nine o'clock that night and that he was in an agitated, exhausted, and breathless condition, as if he had been running a long way. He would never explain why his outing was cut short; indeed, he would never talk of the experience. Perhaps he discovered that Jim Anderson was not so safely lowered into the ground after all.

A few years later, Jim's brother, Isaac Anderson, who had inherited the farm, gave much of it to King College for a new campus. About the time the first building was being erected on the new campus, the ghost appeared again. A man who had known Jim many years before was driving his buggy past the woods about an hour after nightfall. Suddenly, Jim stepped from the woods, took hold of the bridle, and led the horse for some distance up the road. He then turned and disappeared into the gloom of the dark forest.

Does the ghost of Jim Anderson still roam King College woods? There are some who think so. Perhaps if you are brave enough to walk there at night, you may see for yourself!

Mini Ghost Stories

Over the years this writer has heard many ghost stories which will be presented here in a mini version or a brief sketch; space will not permit their complete presentation. Perhaps the reader may determine from these and the other longer stories just how great is the extent of Bristol ghost lore.

GHOST ORGANIST: For several years there was an organ-playing ghost in the old Central Presbyterian Church, which long stood on the northeast corner of Cumberland and Moore streets. Folks passing there at night sometimes heard the sound of beautiful organ music; some said the music was indescribable, beautiful, unearthly. Two or three persons, including the town constable, bravely went in to investigate. They found no one, but the music continued. They even saw the keys being pressed down by invisible fingers. At least one of these brave souls who saw the work of those invisible hands decided it was time to close the investigation, and he quickly departed. It was generally believed that the organ was being played by the ghost of a former church organist, who had suddenly died during a Sunday morning service while playing the organ.

THE MYSTERIOUS WOMAN IN BLACK: There have long been reports of a mysterious woman in black who roams in and near the Jewish Cemetery on Bradley Street. She is usually seen on bright moonlit nights but has been seen wandering about in heavy rain or driving snowstorms. At least on one occasion she was seen in broad daylight sitting on a tombstone near the cemetery gate. (That gate is always locked.) No one seems to have an explanation as to who she is (or was) and why she sticks to the Jewish Cemetery area.

GHOST UNDER MARY STREET BRIDGE: For years there have been sightings of a woman in white, holding a baby in her arms, who appears in the railroad yards, directly under the Mary Street bridge. She might be taken for a real person if she did not suddenly sink into the ground. Railroad engineers have seen her, as have many of the yard crews.

It is known that just before the first overpass bridge was built, a woman and her baby were killed by a passenger train as they were attempting to cross the tracks at this point. Indeed, the bridge was built because of that tragedy.

She has been seen at night, but her appearances are usually in broad daylight. Once, a man attempted to commit suicide by jumping from the Mary Street bridge. Though he was badly injured, he long survived. Later he told that when he landed below, the first thing he saw was the woman in white. That caused him to think for a few moments that he had arrived in the great beyond. Alas, he was mistaken!

ROSETTA'S RETURN: Rosetta Bachelor was long an eccentric, legendary figure in early Bristol. Her husband, Lewis Bachelor (formerly spelled *Baecheler*), died in 1876 and was buried near the old gate of East Hill Cemetery. In her later days, Rosetta became infirm and was taken to the home of a niece in Catonsville, Maryland, and she died there in July 1903.

Her request had always been that when she died she was to be returned to Bristol and buried at the side of her late husband. Indeed, she renewed the request as a final plea in her dying moments. "I want to go home to Lewis," she had feebly begged.

Sadly, there were no funds to make her request possible, so she was buried in Catonsville. The night following her death, a purplish light was seen slowly moving around her late husband's grave in East Hill Cemetery. A late traveler first saw it. He ran back to the town with the frightful story. Two or three others hastened up Cemetery Hill, and they too saw the strange light. They said they got close enough to hear what sounded like an old lady muttering something which they could not understand.

Had the disappointed spirit of Rosetta Bachelor returned to where she wanted her body to be? Many Bristolians thought so.

This is the only such instance this writer has ever heard of purple ghost lights, which are usually white or red. That was the eccentric Rosetta, she would be different!

GHOST STOPS BURIAL: The bodies of three Confederate soldiers were once left unburied overnight in East Hill Cemetery because of a ghost. Early in the Civil War, coffins (actually plain pine boxes) were stacked there for the burial of soldiers who died in the local Confederate hospital. Very late one day the three bodies were taken up there for burial. As the graves were being dug, a loud knocking suddenly began in one of the empty coffins. The gravediggers dropped their tools and quickly fled. The bodies were left lying on the cold ground. Not until the next morning did the men venture back up to the graveyard to finish their task.

THE GHOST OF LITTLE WOODROW STALLINGS: A much-loved and adored little boy named Woodrow Stallings once lived with his parents on the south side of Second Taylor Street. At the age of five, he contracted scarlet fever, but he lingered long. After he died, he was buried in East Hill Cemetery on the hill behind the Stallings home.

One snowy night in the winter following his death in October, the mother was awakened by a low knock on the kitchen door. She arose, but before reaching the door, she heard the unmistakable voice of little Woodrow call out, "Let me in Momma, I'm cold, so cold." She threw open the door, but no one was there. She did see what appeared to be a ball of fire float back up through the woods, toward the cemetery.

SOMETHING AT THE BRIDGE: In the early days of Bristol a narrow wooden bridge spanned Baker's Creek (now usually called Little Beaver Creek) on what is now West State Street, near Builders First Source. Often, at night that bridge could not be crossed. "Something" (said by some to be indescribable) about three feet tall would appear, bouncing around in the middle of that bridge. Horses became so frightened that they could not be made to go forward. Indeed, they tried to run backward. Needless to say, footmen also ran backward until they had time to turn around. Some people reported seeing that "something" standing in the middle of the stream, just below the bridge. One braver man threw rocks at it, but those rocks went only a few feet, then sailed back to knock him flat. He threw no more rocks! The story was that a man had been murdered at that creek crossing long before Bristol was founded. For some reason this ghost ceased its bridge blocking when West Main (State) Street was macadamized. Perhaps it could not stand modern improvements.

GHOST AT LOWER KING'S SPRING: The bold lower King's Spring forms a lovely little lake in DeFriece Park near the intersection of Fifth and Stine streets. If one should go there on an icy winter night he or she may hear a girl's faint screams seemingly coming from the depths of the little lake. A moonlight skating party was held there in the very cold winter of 1876. Sixteen-year-old Viola Kennett broke through the ice that night and drowned in the frigid waters. A night or two later members of the John G. King family, living on the hill above the spring, heard screams coming from the lake. They investigated but found that no one was there. Later others heard the same thing. Other skating parties were attempted there, but they were all soon broken up by the ghostly screams coming from the water. Some say that, even now, on icy moonlit nights the weird screams can still be heard.

THE HAUNTED PARLOR: Many of the better early Bristol homes had double parlors (often called front and back). These parlors usually

had sliding (pocket) doors between them. Sometimes heavy curtains were hung over these doors. This setup existed in an early Windsor Avenue home. Once, the owners of this house were entertaining guests in the front parlor when the sliding of the dividing doors was heard. Then the curtains were slowly parted, revealing a daughter of the entertaining couple. For a few moments she peered intently at those seated in the front parlor, then slowly eased back into the darkened parlor behind her.

This couple's daughter appeared in their parlor long after she was dead.

The mother screamed and swooned away. The father loudly gasped and leaped from his chair. Why all this ado over a daughter simply looking in on her parents and their guests? Well, this daughter had been dead and buried for almost two years!

THE STINKING GHOST ON FOURTH STREET: In the earliest days of Bristol, a slaughterhouse operated between Fourth Street and the railroad where the southern edge of the Salvation Army property is now located (across from the east end of Shelby Street). The offal from that slaughterhouse was simply dumped on the ground around the place. This created such an awful stink that many homes and businesses in Bristol had to keep windows and doors closed even during the hottest part of summer. The smell was heavy, overpowering, and nauseating.

This slaughterhouse ceased its operations near the beginning of the Civil War. The buildings and pens were dismantled. The town breathed a sigh of relief as the horrible stench gradually faded away.

In 1895, more than thirty years after the slaughterhouse closed and after a thousand rains and numerous melting snows had thoroughly cleansed the ground, the horrid smell of that dread place again drifted over a surprised and perplexed town. There was no mistaking it. There yet lived many persons in Bristol who had lived through the period when the smell was real. They could never forget it. To them, it was as if the clock had suddenly turned back to those pre-Civil War years. There were those who claimed that the ground turned red at the old site, just as it had been red with blood when hundreds of animals were slaughtered there. Bristolians "allowed" that this was the ghost of those slaughtered animals.

In about three or four days the stench ceased just as suddenly as it had come. Now more than a century has passed, and there has not been a reoccurrence of the stinking ghost on Fourth Street.

THE GHOST IN THE MIRROR: The locally famous Nickel Plate Saloon was located on Front Street directly across from the west entrance of the Bristol depot. It was set up and long operated by Isaac Nickels. His wife was a sister of Capt. J. H. Wood, who built Pleasant Hill, home of this writer. The most outstanding furnishing in the Nickel Plate Saloon was a huge mirror which hung on a wall behind the bar.

Isaac Nickels died in 1891. He was buried near the highest point in East Hill Cemetery. The Saloon was reopened day or two after his funeral. That night, the patrons in the crowded bar were horrified when the image of the deceased Isaac Nickels suddenly appeared in the big mirror behind the bar. No one knows how long the ghostly image remained in the mirror, for in moments all the patrons had fled. The new operator long complained that they did not take time to pay their bills. The fact is, he did not remain long enough to receive them!

THE SHRINKING HORSE GHOST: Far back, a man was driving his wagon and team out the old Paperville Road (East State Street). As he reached a point near the eastern boundary of what is now the East Hill Cemetery, he was startled to see a large white horse racing along the road, toward him. It appeared to him that the racing horse would crash head-on with his team and wagon. When the horse was within a few feet of what seemed to be an inevitable collision, it suddenly shrunk down to about the size of a dog and ran right under the team and wagon. After it cleared the wagon and raced on down the road, it continued to shrink, first to the size of a large cat, then a squirrel; and then the horse was gone. It was told that a man had been thrown from a large white horse and killed there long before Bristol was founded.

THE PROPHETIC GHOST: In 1855, Jesse Aydlotte, pioneer Bristol carpenter, moved into a little cottage that stood on the southeast corner of

Moore and Scott streets. Slightly northwest of the intersection of these streets is a gently sloping hill, at the edge of what was then Rev. James King's pastureland.

One bright spring morning, Mr. Aydlotte was out preparing his garden for early planting. He became aware of the faint sound of women and children weeping and wailing. This strange sound seemed to be coming from near the top of the gently sloping hill in King's Pasture, and as he listened the sound grew louder. He looked but could see no one. Cattle grazing contentedly near that area did not seem to be aware of that which Mr. Aydlotte was clearly hearing. Finally the sound slowly faded away. A little later that morning, he heard the sound of hymn singing and preaching coming from the same area where the weeping and wailing seemed to have been. Still no one was there. Finally all was quiet again. He thought much on this strange experience and could never forget what he had heard.

A little over six years later, he heard all those sounds again, on numerous occasions, but these times the sounds were real. In that exact location the families of men who were going away to serve in the Civil War gathered to bid those men farewell. There was much weeping, hymn singing, and preaching. It sounded just like what Jesse Aydlotte had heard six years before. That area became well-known as Weeping Hill and was so called for several years. Mr. Aydlotte was not one to tell of unearthly happenings, so it is likely that few Bristolians ever knew that ghosts were the first to weep there.

GHOSTS IN THE FLOOD: The great Beaver Creek flood of 1917 is one of the worst on record. As the turbid waters were flooding downtown Bristol, some local youths went up to the second story of the Lockett Wholesale Building (southeast corner of Scott and Moore streets) to get a better view. As they were peering out the back windows of that building, they clearly heard what sounded like the screams of three or four children, which seemed to come from the swirling waters directly below the windows where they stood. Though they looked intently they could see no one. Thinking that children were drowning in the raging flood, they soon alerted the town. Many were alarmed until a very old man explained the mystery.

He told that the screams were of ghost children and that no one was really drowning in the current flood. He went on to tell that in the early 1800s, some children were playing near the creek bank when, without warning, a mighty flash flood swept down Beaver Creek and drowned them all. He stated that the ghostly screams had been heard many times before, coming from the waters of Beaver Creek practically every time it had flooded since that sad tragedy long before. The screams were always heard at the location where the children drowned. When the area had been a part of the vast James King Plantation, members of his family and his slaves had heard them. After the founding of Bristol, many town residents heard the piteous cries of the ghost children.

Does anyone want to go over and listen when there is another flood on Beaver Creek?

MODERN GHOSTS

Up to this point the author has written of ghosts of pioneer Bristol (pre-1900). Now there will be presented stories of several modern and, in some cases, current ghosts of the city. As one old-timer expressed it recently, "They's still plenty of hants around here." Well, according to what has been told to this writer, it would seem he was right. This section does not include all reports of recent or current ghosts, but here is given a sampling of some of the unearthly visitations that are still occurring in Bristol.

The Humming Ghost on Alabama Street

Soon after a young bachelor moved into an old (erected 1895) Alabama Street house, he began to hear strange sounds. Sometimes locked doors would be heard to open and close or windows to slide up and down. Occasionally there would be loud knockings on the door, though no one was there. These knockings might occur in the wee hours of the morning. (Shall we say that this was a rude and inconsiderate ghost!) The weirdest hant of all was a woman who walked about while humming the familiar hymn "What a Friend We Have in Jesus." If the resident was downstairs, the ghost would walk and hum upstairs. If he was on the second floor, the ghostly sound would come from the first.

The first time he heard the humming ghost was soon after he turned the downstairs of his home into an office. His help had gone to lunch. He was upstairs when he heard the sound, coming from below. He thought his receptionist had returned from lunch a bit early. When he called to her there was no reply, but the humming continued. When he went down to investigate, he found the doors still locked and the office vacant. The humming then began upstairs.

Sometimes he heard the sound outside—like the time he was behind the house, trimming a shrub. The strange humming began right behind him. He whirled around but no one could be seen. The humming continued for a few seconds but seemed to be growing fainter and slowly sinking into the ground. Once when he was sitting in the porch swing, he heard the sound coming from the porch roof. An even more frightening visitation occurred one night when he had just driven his car into his dark garage. He heard the humming suddenly begin in the backseat. That time he did not wait to see how long the sound continued!

The hauntings created a tense state of affairs. Once, the humming began in the little pantry just off his kitchen as he sat at his supper table. Another time it happened just outside his bathroom door as he was bathing. One other time he was awakened by the humming at 2:00 A.M., and it seemed to be on both floors at once.

Soon after that early morning occurrence, the young bachelor was visiting with an elderly neighbor who lived directly across the street. The neighbor had lived there for most of her life. In the course of their conversation she mentioned that a widow named White had once lived in the house then occupied by the young bachelor. She went on to say that the widow was a bit strange, and that she was very religious and went about every day, whether inside or outside the house, continually humming the same old hymn. The neighbor went on to say that the Widow White had been dead for fifteen or twenty years. The young bachelor immediately asked his neighbor what hymn the widow had continually hummed. He paled a bit when he was told that it was "What a Friend We Have in Jesus."

Strangely, after that shocking revelation, he never heard the humming ghost again.

Cousin Sinnie Still Calls Her Boarders

For many years, three sisters originally from Letcher County, Kentucky, operated a boardinghouse on Alabama Street in Bristol, Tennessee. They were cousins of this writer. Before he owned a home in this city he spent much time as a roomer in their fine, old, Queen Anne-style house. (It has fifteen rooms and he has slept in eleven of them.) He became well acquainted with the practice and customs of his cousins as they carried on their business operation.

One practice was to awaken boarders sleeping upstairs by knocking on steam pipes leading up to the radiators in their rooms. This early morning chore was usually performed by Cousin Sinnie, the youngest of the three sisters. Her room, the former back parlor, was entered from behind the grand front staircase, and it was in that room that she usually made her morning "attack" on the steam pipes.

On Mother's Day morning, 1969, those pipes remained silent. After an illness of only a few hours, Cousin Sinnie died in her room. Her death occurred at about the time she usually gave the wake-up call.

The two remaining sisters soon ceased operation of their boarding-house. However, they continued to live there until October 1983, when they moved back to Kentucky. At that time they sold the house to a nearby neighbor. For the first time in many years, the Alabama Street landmark stood vacant, the windows darkened and the furnace cold.

The new owner soon began to make plans for a large-scale renovation of the house. Perhaps the intense planning for the renovation project caused him to awaken early on a Sunday morning about two weeks after the ladies had left the place. He arose and went through the predawn darkness to his newly purchased property, intending to walk through the rooms, planning for their renovation. He went upstairs to the room directly over the one where Cousin Sinnie had died fourteen years before.

As he looked about, he was startled by a loud banging sound coming from the room's steam radiator, seemingly caused by someone beating on the pipes in the room below. (He knew nothing of Cousin Sinnie's former practice nor that she died in that downstairs room.) He well knew that radiators often make popping sounds when warming up, but he also knew that there was no fire in the furnace, nor had there been for weeks past. He remembered that he had locked the front door behind him. Thinking that someone might have already been in the house when he came in, he cautiously eased back down the stairs and switched on the light in Cousin Sinnie's former bedroom.

The knocking on the pipes continued but no one could be seen. He checked the other rooms and the basement but found that he was alone in the house. It was then that he decided to leave the house, and his exit may have been a bit on the hasty side. His exit was not so hasty, however, that he did not notice that as he left, the knocking became more insistent, as if to convey the message, "come back, come back." Needless to say, he had no desire to go back!

A few days later he told this writer of his strange experience. It was then that he learned of Cousin Sinnie, her room, her morning practice, and her death. When told all of this he became white as a sheet and was momentarily speechless. According to what he later said, he never went into that house alone again. Even in daylight he always took someone with him.

After the house was completely renovated, he sold it to a young family from Ohio. When the next Mother's Day morning came around, the family was awakened before dawn by a loud and unexplainable knocking on the steam pipes in Cousin Sinnie's former room. Months passed without any similar occurrences, but in the fall of that year they heard the knocking again. Before that family sold the house, the ghostly wake-up call was heard two or three more times.

Next, the house became the headquarters for a commercial firm. Since then there have been no reports of steam-pipe banging by unseen hands. Perhaps this is because there is no one there in the predawn darkness. Who knows, if conditions again become favorable, Cousin Sinnie might yet give the unique morning call to her boarders.

A Real Long-Distance Call

Back in the mid-1930s the noted Carter family of the Bristol area popularized a sentimental song called "No Telephone in Heaven." In this song it was told that there was no telephone connection between earth and far-off Paradise. In the light of a recent experience had by a West Bristol family, it would appear that the theme of that song may have been wrong. For this family tells of receiving a telephone call from the Great Beyond.

In this family was once a fine teenage son who was greatly adored by his parents and siblings. He was handsome, intelligent, industrious, and ambitious. His future appeared to be bright and promising.

He had a close friend who was not as civil as he was and who often had difficulties with his associates. Late one day this friend called and asked the much loved son of the family to come quickly. It seems the friend was being threatened and thus felt he might need help. The summons was quickly answered. With a wave of the hand to his mother and a promise that he would be back soon, the teenage son jumped into his car and drove away to what would become a rendezvous with death. In the violent confrontation that soon occurred with his friend's adversary, he was stabbed to death. His untimely and tragic demise cast a dark cloud of grief and oppressive sorrow over the family home.

Two weeks later, at about the time the son had left home for his date with a tragic destiny, the telephone rang. It was answered by one of his surviving sisters. Later, she told that even before lifting the receiver, she had experienced the weirdest and most foreboding feeling. At first there was no voice, only a sound very much like the roar of the ocean breaking upon a distant shore. In that faint roar there was a mystical sound of ethereal music, a music that was more felt than heard. The sound became a bit subdued, and then there came the somewhat quavering but unmistakable voice of her recently murdered brother, sounding and echoing as if he were in an empty hall or cavern. The girl was frightened but could not release the telephone. Her mother, who was standing nearby, said the girl blanched and swayed as if she would fall.

"I'm very happy over here," the voice said, then was drowned out by the breaking-waves sound. That sound subsided and the unearthly voice continued. "I love you all and miss you very much, but I do not want to return there." Again the voice came through. "Though I am far away, my presence is still with you. I am in all those places where I used to be. Farewell for now, but I will see you all here someday." Then, as if the circuit had been suddenly broken, there was complete silence. For about an hour afterward the telephone would not work, but later the service resumed as usual.

This was truly an unnerving experience, but it did much to lessen the profound sorrow of the grieving family. Perhaps great benefit can come from some ghostly happenings.

NOTE: This writer is well acquainted with another person who had a similar experience. This happened at Valley Springs in Boone County, Arkansas, in mid-July 1968. In that case a bereaved son received an unearthly telephone call from his recently deceased mother. Perhaps that story will be told someday.

The Dental-Office Ghost

Do ghosts need dental services? It would appear so. At least one ghost recently came into a Bristol, Tennessee, dental office during regular business hours. The apparition disappeared before the receptionist was able to extend greetings or offer services.

In this case the receptionist was a man. On this particular day in late 1995, his waiting room was almost full. He was busy at his desk with paperwork when he heard the front door open. He glanced up to see a woman coming in carrying a beautiful baby in her arms. Later, he remembered that the woman was dressed in old-fashioned clothes, possibly around 1920s vintage.

He went back to finishing the paperwork at hand, intending to greet the woman as soon as he was finished. By that time the woman had walked past the desk and had entered the rest room. This was not too unusual; mothers often took their babies to the rest room for a quick diaper change before taking a seat in the waiting area. He waited for about twenty-five minutes before becoming concerned about her, so he had someone check the rest room. The lady was not in the bathroom or anywhere else in the offices. (This building has no back door.)

Somewhat puzzled and perhaps a bit shaken, the receptionist returned to the waiting room and inquired if anyone had seen the lady come in. There were at least a dozen patients waiting in the room, but only one had seen the strange woman and her baby. That patient stated that she was expectantly waiting for the lady to return so she could "get a look at the most beautiful baby I have ever seen."

If the ghostly lady needed dental services, she must have chickened out, for she had disappeared without a trace. Perhaps there is no connection, but the receptionist soon gave up his job.

A lady who long had lived in the area remembered a tragedy that had happened in the old house before it had been turned into the dental office. That tragedy may have been the seed of this ghostly occurrence. Far back—my informant thought it was during the Great Depression—a young woman living there with her parents had become infatuated by a young man from the wrong side of the tracks. Against the will of her parents, she married this man. Soon after she left her home, her mother died. Her father soon remarried.

After a year or two, the daughter's husband, having never been kind to her, had become outright cruel and abusive. He had an alcohol problem and lost his job. Thus the young family was destitute. By then a beautiful baby had been born to them.

At last the situation became unbearable. Suffering from hunger and cold and the mental and physical cruelty of her husband, the young woman, carrying her baby, fled through deep snow to her father's house. She did not find the safe refuge she had hoped for. The father, said to have been acting under pressure from his new wife, told his daughter that she could not stay and that she must immediately return to her husband.

In panic and sheer desperation, the young woman rushed by her father into the bathroom. There, using her father's straight razor, she killed the baby and then slashed her own throat. The lady who told this story remembered that the baby was the most beautiful she had ever seen. The bathroom where the double tragedy occurred was later made into a rest room for the dental office. The murder-suicide had happened just before Christmas. The ghost woman and baby appeared in the dental office just before Christmas 1995.

This writer's great-aunt Margaret Allen, supposedly well versed in "hantology," used to say that wherever there had been a murder a hant was likely, and where there had been a suicide she would guarantee that a genuine hant would show up sooner or later. Maybe she was right!

The Depot Ghost

As long as there was passenger service in Bristol, incoming trains from the south were occasionally met by a ghost. If one was not observant of period dress, the ghost might easily have been perceived as just another man in the crowd. Indeed, one might not have been aware that she or he was standing shoulder to shoulder with a real ghost, as it often happened. Even some people had brief conversations with this strange phantom, without knowing that the earthly was communicating with the unearthly.

The story goes way, way back. Old Rev. James King had a son named Cyrus. The only son of Cyrus was Joseph Chalmers King. The Chalmers part of his name came from the stepfather of the wife of Rev. James King, Colonel James Chalmers of Halifax County, Virginia.

After the death of his parents, Chalmers King went to live in his grandfather's home. The rather wealthy Rev. King saw that his grandson received a good education. In time, Chalmers became a skilled surveyor and his future appeared to be promising. After the death of his grandfather (1867), he never really had a home. He lived part of the time with his sisters, Mrs. A. M. Carter and Mrs. Joseph W. Owen, and the rest of the time he lived in local hotels.

Chalmers was over thirty years old before he showed any interest in seeking a wife. He then began a courtship with Susannah Seabright. She was the daughter in a formerly affluent family from Eastern Virginia. The family had suffered great losses during the Civil War and had moved to Bristol, hoping to rebuild their fortunes.

The courtship was rapidly blossoming, when the Seabright family decided to move to Kansas. Chalmers King quickly proposed marriage to Susannah and she readily accepted. Being underage, she had to move west with her non-consenting parents. However, she promised that when she was of age she would return and proceed with the marriage.

The couple carried a heavy correspondence as they waited for the much anticipated time to come. Finally, she wrote that her twenty-first birthday was past and that she would be arriving in Bristol on the evening train from Knoxville on a certain date. On that evening, Chalmers was at the depot long before the train was due. Alas, his bride-to-be did not arrive on that train or the next. For several evenings Chalmers waited patiently at the depot, but Susannah did not appear. He wrote to her but there was no answer. He wrote to her again but still there was no reply.

Greatly disappointed and much alarmed, Chalmers finally took the train to Kansas. There, he found that the family had moved on to somewhere in California. He returned to Bristol in a depressed state of mind. Soon he turned to alcohol. As his drinking bordered on alcoholism, it became apparent that his emotions were becoming unstable. Often after a drinking bout in local saloons, he would then wander up to the depot, stating that Susannah would surely be on the evening train. Nervously (some said he had suffered a nervous breakdown), he would pace up and down the long platform, saying to anyone he met, "Susannah will be on the evening train." She never came. His disappointment more acute, Chalmers would wander back downtown to drink through the night.

His kind sisters still provided food and shelter when he would avail himself of their hospitality. He finally was reduced to begging on the streets for whiskey money. Yes, for the first time, a King was begging on the streets of Bristol, much to the dismay of his affluent relatives.

Regardless of what condition he was in, he always went up to the depot when a train from the southwest was due. Sometimes he was heard to mutter, "She'll surely be on this train." Alas, she never was.

Early on the morning of October 20, 1880, due to acute alcoholism, stroke, or whatever it was, Chalmers King was found dead in bed at the home of his sister Mrs. Joseph W. Owen. He is buried in the East Hill Cemetery but his grave is unmarked.

About a week after his death and burial, the lamplighter at the Bristol depot went out to "work the lamps" in preparation for the arrival of the night train from the southwest. In the dim light, he was shocked to see the form of Chalmers King coming along the platform. He was still watching and waiting for the coming of his beloved Susannah. (It is not certain that the lamplighter finished his job that night!)

So it was for years—former friends, railroad employees, and others occasionally saw the ghost of Chalmers King strolling along or standing on the platform, awaiting trains from the southwest. He might suddenly appear at the side of a waiting passenger, who might think he is real, and lowly mutter, "She'll surely be on this train."

It was later learned by James King English, a first cousin to Chalmers, that while the ghost of Chalmers King was grieving on the platform at the Bristol depot, Susannah Seabright was enjoying a new marriage in a prim little bungalow in Los Angeles, California. In a strange course of events, Mr. English bought a house next door to her.

When the new depot at Bristol was built in 1902, it was thought (and perhaps hoped) that the station ghost would disappear, but it was not to be. Hardly was the new facility opened, when King's ghost appeared again. The ghost of Chalmers King made many appearances. Notable ones occurred in 1918, 1929, and 1942. They continued on through the following years. What really made the ghost stand out was that he was always dressed as Chalmers had been during his real-life waits: black suit, snow-white shirt, bow tie, and derby hat. Otherwise, he could easily have been mistaken for just another person waiting on the platform.

The weather on December 24, 1955, was unusually mild. A local man who loved to watch the comings and goings of passenger trains strolled over to the depot on that Christmas Eve night in anticipation of the arrival of Number Forty-Two, the eastbound train from the southwest. He had not been there long when the platform lights came on and the baggage, mail, and express carts were rolled out to trackside. All this activity indicated that Number Forty-Two was rapidly approaching.

At the first faint low moan of the whistle sounding from far down the line, the man looked down the platform toward State Street. Coming hastily along the platform was a low, heavyset man. This was nothing unusual at train time, except that the man looked like he had stepped out of the past century. He was dressed in a black suit, white shirt, bow tie, and derby hat.

As the new arrival came close to the somewhat puzzled man, it was noted that the stranger's face was deathly white. "She will surely be on this train," he said and then quickly passed. In moments he was nowhere to be seen. Though Chalmers King had been dead some seventy-five years, it seemed that he was still hoping his bride-to-be would be on the approaching train.

The last sighting of this depot ghost was in 1969, on the day the last passenger train passed through Bristol. It appears that the disappointed lover watched in vain for his bride-to-be to the very end.

Little Boy Blue

How often it is that acts of love and kindness become causes of grief and bitterness, perhaps casting a dark cloud of regret and sadness over the remainder of one's years.

Regrettably, this is true of Mrs. King James, long a beloved and respected matron of the Solar Hill section of Bristol, Virginia. After the death of her husband, Mrs. James moved from her former home at the southeast corner of James and Cumberland streets to a large two-story house in the 200 block of Johnson Street. There she spent the remainder of her days. For her, what should have been a time of peace and contentment through her golden years was rather a dark period of sorrow and deep regret.

Though the Jameses were not blessed with children of their own, Mrs. James lavished a great deal of love and kindness upon the children of others. Her favorite of all was little Timothy Shreve, her great-nephew, son of her niece who lived in a little cottage on Broad Street. He was a beautiful five-year-old with a round, smiling face, extra-large blue eyes, and thick, curly blond hair.

Mrs. James often walked over to the home of her niece to bring little Timothy back to her house to spend a night or two. He delighted in this, knowing that his aged aunt would let him eat his fill of her homemade cookies and other delicacies that she often made just for him. Often on the trip back to her home, a stop would be made in town for ice cream and perhaps a bag of candy.

On the anniversary of her late husband's death, Mrs. James became rather depressed. She decided to walk over to get her "little bundle of joy," as she called Timothy Shreve. Usually the child was delighted to come home with her, but on that day he was a bit reluctant, saying he wanted to stay home with Mommy. Mrs. James would think much on his strange reluctance in the months ahead.

By the usual promise of ice cream and candy, plus a yo-yo thrown in, the doting aunt soon had Timothy willing to go. So, dressed in a blue sailor suit that his skilled mother had made for him, he took his aunt's hand, and the two started across town. After the promised treats, a stop was made at the Kress store for the yo-yo. He chose one in brilliant red.

Though Timothy had been chattering gaily when they stepped back into the street, he suddenly got serious and looked back toward his home on Broad Street. Then, looking up with big, pleading eyes, he begged his aunt to take him back to Mommy. With a little gentle persuasion and a promise to take him back to his mother the next day, he again took Auntie's hand and trotted by her side along Piedmont and up the hill to her home.

After supper, he played almost continuously with his new yo-yo until bedtime. Before the two ascended the stairs, he again renewed his plea to be taken home. Mrs. James told him it was dark and rainy outside but that the next day he would surely be taken to his mother and home.

Do children have premonitions of danger? In this case it seems to be so. Though Timothy usually delighted in spending the night with his aunt, on this occasion he seemed to feel he should not be there. Even after he was tucked into his favorite bed, said his prayers, and received his usual good-night kiss from his beloved aunt, he again asked to be taken to his mother.

Being assured by his auntie that morning would soon come, then soothed by her singing of a sweet lullaby, he dropped into deep slumber. Mrs. James retired to her adjoining room and went to bed, but she long lay awake pondering as to why little Timothy wanted so much to return home.

Sometime during the middle of that dark, rainy night, a fire broke out in a downstairs room. Dense, choking smoke billowed up the stairway and into the room where little Timothy lay sound asleep. Mrs. James, sleeping fitfully, awoke and recognized the imminent danger. She rushed into Timothy's room, grabbed him from the bed, and escaped through a window onto the front-porch roof. Her cries alerted neighbors, who called for help. Firemen came and rescued the two from the roof before extinguishing the flames inside the house. For Timothy all was too late; he lay dead in his aunt's arms. He had suffocated in the dense smoke before she had reached him.

Mrs. James lived on for another two or three years. For her the sun never shone again. Those final years were spent in deep sorrow and bitter regret. Often she would lament to friends, "Oh, why didn't I take him home that night?" After her death, the house was sold and strangers moved in. Through the following years, most of those who had then lived on Solar Hill died or moved away. The tragic story was all but forgotten.

Then, on a dark, rainy afternoon in the fall of 1999, a carpenter was working alone in the upstairs hall of the house, near the doorway of the room where little Timothy had perished long ago. A young couple had recently purchased the house, and the carpenter was doing renovation work for them. Neither they nor the carpenter had ever heard of the tragedy which had happened there. The couple was at work, the doors were locked; only the little family dog was in the house with the carpenter.

Suddenly, the carpenter felt a tug on his pant leg. At first he thought it was the playful dog, but then he heard the sweet voice of a child say, "Mister, oh, mister." Startled, the carpenter looked around and down into the face of the most beautiful little boy he had ever seen. The boy appeared to be about five years old and had unusually big blue eyes. His head was topped by a tangle of blond curls, he wore a blue sailor suit, and in his hand was a bright red yo-yo.

The beautiful child looked up with big pleading eyes and, in a somewhat quavery and far-off-sounding voice, begged, "Please, mister, take me home to my mommy." Having said that, he turned and fled up the narrow stairway leading to the attic. The shaken carpenter searched the attic, but the child could not be found.

A little later, when the owners of the house came home, they and the carpenter made a thorough search of the entire house, but to no avail. It seems that the beautiful little boy had simply vanished. Later that evening, as the owners sat at their kitchen table for supper, the sound of a child's feet pattering in the room overhead was distinctly heard. Another search was made but again to no avail.

A few minutes after they went to bed that night, they again heard the sound of a child running in the hall just outside their bedroom door. That time they did not search, as they were convinced that the effort would be futile.

To this day Little Boy Blue has not appeared again.

NOTE: The ghostly appearance of Little Boy Blue may have been rather costly for the carpenter. He would never work there alone after his encounter with the child ghost. The next day he brought an assistant whom he had hired sometime during the night. It was generally felt that he really did not need an assistant except for ghost protection!

The Clean Ghost on Windsor Avenue

Driving by, one would never suspect that a modest cottage on Windsor Avenue is home to a strange ghost, one who apparently has a bathing mania.

Years ago, a daughter of the family who then lived there was to graduate from Tennessee High School. On the night of her senior prom, she hurried home from her part-time job at a local drugstore, quickly took a bath, dressed, and then hurried off to the much anticipated social event.

After the prom, some of the students, including this girl, decided to cruise around a bit. The cruise finally led down the Bluff City Highway, and, as might be expected, the driver of the group became a bit reckless. Driving at a high rate of speed, he lost control of the car, which left the road and crashed into a concrete wall. The girl from Windsor Avenue and two or three others in the car were killed in the tragic wreck.

The night following their daughter's funeral, the parents, along with others of the family, were sitting in the living room of their modest home. Suddenly, the opening of the daughter's bedroom door was distinctly heard by the silent mourners. Then, a white-robed figure passed down the narrow hall leading to the bathroom. Some described the figure as floating rather than walking.

In moments, the clicking of the bathroom light switch was heard. The door was closed, and then came the sound of water running in the bathtub. Two or three of the group went to investigate. Indeed, the light was on and water was running in the tub, but no one was there.

Two or three more times throughout that long evening, the sequence was repeated. After the perplexed and somewhat shaken family retired for the night, the ghostly bather again turned on the lights and water in the bathroom. That time there was quite a debate as to who would arise to turn the lights and water off, hopefully for the rest of the night!

Through the remaining year that this family lived there, the ghost continued to take two or three nightly baths. Perhaps that is why the family sold the house and moved away.

Apparently the clean ghost didn't move. It soon visited the new family. The bedroom from whence the ghost emerged was made into a storage area. The bathroom was moved to another part of the house, but that didn't stop the ghost with the bathing mania.

Instead, the problem worsened. It seems that the troubled spirit of the deceased daughter soon found the new bathroom. The passage to reach the new location had to be made right through the living room, and because of that situation, the family got a closer look at the strange apparition.

It was a look they did not want. What appeared to be blood covered her neck and hands, and her eyes were like burning embers. (Perhaps this troubled spirit was trying to wash the blood away.)

The new family occupied the home only three more days after the ghost began to use the new route to the bathroom. None of that time was spent in the living room. The bathroom too became off-limits. How could one have a comfortable stay in the bathroom while expecting a bloody, fiery-eyed ghost to come breaking in at any moment?

This writer still has occasion to drive by the house now and then. Though it is known that through the intervening years several families have moved in and out, he does not know the people who live there now. Whoever does may yet have the company of a ghost with a bathing mania.

The Last Call for Help

It is not at all uncommon for an invalid or seriously ill person to keep a bedside handbell to summon aid when needed. Such was the case in a modest home near the Bristol Mall. The aging grandmother of the family occupying the house was brought there to spend her final days.

In time, she became bedfast. It was then that the handbell was placed within her reach. As her condition worsened, the ringing of that bell became a familiar sound throughout the household. Even the family dog sprang to attention whenever the grandmother's distress call was heard.

At last this grandmother had to be taken to the local hospital. Within a few days her condition became critical. Her devoted son stayed close to her bedside most of the time.

At twilight on the third day of this woman's hospitalization, the daughter-in-law and granddaughter were at home, anxiously awaiting the sad news they felt was soon to come.

Suddenly, the family dog sprang up and stiffened, giving a low growl as he looked toward the grandmother's bedroom door. (Dogs seem to have a way of sensing ghosts before people do.) At that instant the call bell sounded throughout the house.

The daughter-in-law, accustomed to quickly responding to the summons, jumped up and was almost to the bedroom door before it dawned on her that Grandmother was not there. She proceeded on to the room and switched on the light. The bell was in place and motionless, yet its familiar call was loudly sounding throughout the room, and it did not cease for another minute or so.

Shortly, a call came from the hospital—the grandmother had died at the exact time that her distress call had sounded from her vacant room.

A Soldier's Return

Though the fine old family home on Bristol's Solar Hill has been bought and sold several times in recent years, a soldier son of the original owners doesn't seem to know it. Recently, he has been returning to wander through the familiar halls and rooms of his youth. The big problem is that he was killed in World War I, and just before his ghostly appearances, his bereaved mother, dead since 1940, usually can be heard bitterly weeping in her upstairs bedroom.

When James Carlock Brewer left the house in 1917 to serve his country on foreign soil, he was a handsome, healthy, and bright young man, adored by his family and loved by his numerous friends. Alas, his promising life ended on June 11, 1918, during the Battle of Belleau Wood in France. Five years or so later, his body was brought home to rest in the family

Does James Carlock Brewer still haunt his old home in Bristol, Virginia?

plot in Bristol's historic East Hill Cemetery. However, it seems that he cannot rest; he keeps coming home.

The soldier's father lived on in the house until he died, in 1954. A sister remained there until about 1972. The house was then sold and has been resold several times since. Virtually all of the later occupants have commented about the distinct ghostly feeling that seems to pervade the place. A few went so far as to say that things could be seen and heard there. One person, a painter working outside in broad daylight, developed such a feeling of something "strange around" that he quit his work and hastily departed. This writer, working there alone as an interior decorator in 1976, sensed a creepy feeling—a feeling of not really being alone. He did finish the job!

It was not until the present owners moved in that the ghost of the soldier began to appear. Well, actually, it started before they moved in. On the day they decided to buy the house, the young husband saw a uniformed soldier appear at the side of the real estate agent. Then, as suddenly as he had appeared, the soldier vanished. The husband did not mention this to his wife, but he thought much about it.

A few months after the couple moved in, the wife awoke at two o'clock one morning to find the phantom soldier standing by her bedside. The ghostly figure was surrounded by a grayish light. In a few moments he disappeared. It was later learned that she was in the room he had occupied as a youth.

More months passed. Then, one night as they were in the kitchen, preparing the evening meal, they heard distinct footsteps in the little hall leading from the dining room into the kitchen. Looking up, they saw the phantom soldier standing in the doorway. This time he smiled at them before fading into nothingness. Nearly a year passed before he appeared again. One night, they were having a candlelight meal in the formal dining room. The smartly uniformed soldier was seen seated across the table from them. "He disappeared before we could ask him to partake of the food," the young husband once said.

Sometimes the locked front door opens, then the sound of footsteps enters the front hall and proceeds up the stairway. The den, formerly the back parlor of the fine old home, is directly under the dead soldier's former bedroom. Sometimes as the couple sits in this den, they hear footsteps that seem to come from the bedroom above. Apparently, the ghost decides to go to bed, for the sound of shoes dropping on the floor can also be heard.

The most recent appearance of the homesick soldier occurred on a bright, moonlit night late in the summer of 1999. On that balmy evening the owners of the house were sitting on the south-side porch, enjoying a quiet, peaceful evening at home. Maybe the restless soldier was enjoying the evening also. He was clearly seen coming up the driveway, whistling a merry tune. As he passed by the porch, he stopped a moment and waved to the young couple, then quickly passed on into the darkness of the heavily shaded backyard.

Where and when will he appear again? This couple, now used to his unexpected and sudden appearances, is not the least bit afraid of him. Indeed, they seem to now look forward to his ghostly visits.

Minor-House Ghosts

The old Minor home still stands tall and proud on Lee Street. It is well preserved and has been carefully restored. Perhaps Dr. Minor is well pleased, for he likes to come back from the grave for a visit now and then. A member of his family, long deceased, still enjoys practicing music in an upstairs bedroom in the wee hours of the morning.

Several years ago, the house was occupied by a young couple who knew nothing about its former owners and occupants. One night after supper, they retired to the living room, where they expected to spend a pleasant, quiet evening. About eight o'clock, they heard the front door, known to have been locked, swing open. Looking up, they were startled to see a short, portly man walk in. He was dressed in jet black, wore a derby hat, and carried what appeared to be a doctor's bag. He looked neither to the right nor left, but walked straight ahead and up the stairway. The couple finally gained enough courage to make a search for the intruding stranger. No one could be found. All was quiet upstairs. Seemingly, the man in black had simply disappeared.

A few days later they told a neighbor, who had lived in the area all of his life, about the strange occurrence.

"Why," the old man replied, "you have described old Dr. Minor to a T. He always came home about eight o'clock and always went right upstairs to change before supper." That revelation was a bit unnerving to the young couple but they were determined to stay on in the house they loved so well.

Soon after this incident, the husband's younger brother came to spend the night with the couple. They put him in the north upstairs bedroom. The next morning he was found sleeping on the living room couch. His explanation was that he couldn't stay in that room because "something" was in there. The youth later explained that he saw nothing, but that there were sounds of footsteps around his bed and drawers being pulled open; a chair was moved from one corner of the room to the other, and even a shade was raised and lowered, seemingly by unseen hands. It was later learned that the brother was trying to sleep in Dr. Minor's former bedroom.

About a week later, the couple awoke around 2:00 A.M. to the sound of a flute being played in that room. It was faint but distinct. The husband, forcing himself to be brave, arose, went across the hall, and snapped on the light in the room. The playing instantly stopped. No one was there.

Perhaps there is no connection, but the couple soon sold the Minor home and moved elsewhere. The following owners had some weird experiences there also.

Though there have been no reported sightings of the restless Dr. Minor, lately the flute player has performed again on several occasions, and always in the wee hours of the morning. We are awaiting further developments!

Pseudo Ghosts

Along with the numerous purported real ghosts that have terrorized Bristolians since the city's beginning, there have been a few pseudo ghosts (fake or manufactured, if you please). Some were created just for fun or pure devilment. Others served to make better situations or to alleviate bad ones, while some just happened to be. For whatever reason they were created—or just happened—they were real, at least for a time, to those who saw or heard them.

Ghost Meets Ghost

The original Susong home stood on the site now occupied by the Dollar Store in the Little Creek Shopping Center on Euclid Avenue. After the last of the older Susongs left there, the house was let out to tenants. Around 1895, a family living there had a number of grown and nearly grown sons and daughters. The children were fun-lovers, so they often had parties, dances, and so on, usually called *frolics* by the old-timers of this area.

At one of these frolics, talk turned to local ghosts. One of the sons of the family then living in the old Susong house told of seeing a white-robed figure strolling through the Susong family cemetery when he had been out hunting late one night. His story was pure fabrication.

The old cemetery is high on the hill back of where the old Susong house then stood. As he told the story, he noted how nervous his visitors seemed to be and he got an idea. He knew that many at the party would be passing that cemetery on their way home.

Just before the party broke up, the boy slipped from the crowd, picked up a sheet in a back bedroom, and quickly went up to a brush thicket adjoining the south side of the supposedly haunted graveyard.

Unknown to him, another party visitor had gotten the same idea. He, too, had slipped out, raced home, gotten a sheet, and returned to a thicket on the north side of the cemetery and there impatiently waited for the fun to begin.

In a little while, the boy in the south-side thicket heard the partiers coming up the hill. He then wrapped himself in the sheet and strolled forth to near the center of the moon-bathed cemetery. Shortly, the other "ghost" heard the approach of the crowd, and he too strolled forth from his thicket. Neither saw the other until only about twenty feet or so separated them. The startled yell of the first one, who realized he was not alone, caught the attention of the other. Then both of them, each thinking that the other was a real ghost, gave a bloodcurdling yell, and the wild race was on!

The youth from the Susong house took the trail toward home, while the other boy went northwestward blindly, not knowing where he was headed, just so long as it was away from what he then believed to be a truly haunted cemetery.

The crowd coming up the hill got a shocking surprise when a white-sheeted figure suddenly came into view just a short way up the trail. That ghost was running right at them, yelling as he came. You may be sure they hastily cleared the trail for him. They scattered into the brush, running wildly in all directions and raising horrendous screeches, screams, and yells as they fled.

The ghost-playing youth paid no attention to them. He sped on down the trail until it made a turn that he couldn't. Rather, he ran straight ahead right into a dense thicket of saw briars. There he lost his sheet, part of his clothes, and a considerable amount of his hide. He finally reached home, completely exhausted and bleeding from his numerous saw-briar slashes.

The youth fleeing northwestward fared no better. His flight took him through the backyard of a nearby farmhouse. In that yard was a big, bad, white English bulldog. Now, that dog apparently resented having his sleep disturbed by a running, yelling hant, pseudo though it was. He sprang up, snipping and growling, and charged right after the white-robed figure. In no time he had the sheet, bits of the youth's clothes, and a chunk or two of his flesh. Luckily, the then doubly frightened youth found the low limb of a tree, swung up on it, and then climbed higher, thus avoiding further damage. He stayed treed for a good while before the dog's owners came to his rescue.

The reader may be sure that neither of those youths ever played ghost again!

Polite Ghost

Oliver Caswell King grew up at Poor Hill, his paternal home in Holston Valley near Bristol, Tennessee. (Poor Hill is somewhat of a misnomer—neither the land nor the family was poor.) The Civil War began just as

Oliver Caswell King

Oliver reached manhood. He soon volunteered for service in the Confederate Army and was sent to Northern Virginia. There he was severely injured in a fierce battle. His injury was such that he could not stand or sit without suffering unbearable pain. His only comfort—and that in a but small degree—was when he was completely reclined.

He spent some time recuperating in a farmhouse near the battlefield where he had been injured. Finally, he decided to try to return to his family home in Holston Valley. To make this trip he had a coffin-like box made in which he could lie down during the long train ride to Bristol. He and his box were placed in a baggage car along with several other real coffins containing the bodies of dead soldiers, all bound for Bristol.

At the Bristol depot several men had gathered for the sad duty of unloading the coffins. The door of the baggage car was high, thus the men had to slide each coffin onto their shoulders before lowering it to the platform.

Finally, thinking it was another coffin, they started to remove the box containing the injured Mr. King. As they pulled it onto their shoulders, one of the men sadly queried, "Wonder whose box is this?" (All the coffins were simple and boxlike.)

Well, young Mr. King had been properly reared. He had been taught to speak when spoken to and to promptly answer all questions. He quickly raised his head, peered over the top of his box, just above the face of the man who had asked, and kindly replied, "Why, this is my box, Oliver Caswell King."

A supposedly dead man introducing himself was considered to be mighty ghostly and a bit disconcerting, to say the least. The men instantly released the box and fled in all directions. The box had already been pulled far enough out so that it tilted and slid downward, dumping its hapless occupant onto the depot platform. As was usual at train time, a large crowd was milling about the platform. Seeing a supposedly dead man dumped near their feet caused a stampede to ensue.

Somehow Oliver Caswell King managed to get to his family home, near Bristol. The severely crippled veteran spent a few years as a "lying-down" schoolteacher. Finally, he regained the ability to stand, sit, and walk about, though he walked in a pronounced halting manner. He eventually settled in Morristown, Tennessee, where he became a successful businessman and noted politician. He always delighted to tell of his never-to-be-forgotten arrival in Bristol when he came home from the war.

The Healing Ghost

An antebellum house stood on Washington Street until a few years ago. Within its plain but sturdy walls there occurred what old Bristolians referred to as a case of "hant healing."

During the Civil War, a tragedy occurred in this house. At that time, Bristol was often the target of roving bands of heartless bushwhackers. Upon the approach to this place by such a band, the man of the house hid in the loft over the living room. He was found and shot. As he lay dying, his blood ran through cracks in between the floorboards and formed a pool on the living room floor below. The large stain could be seen there as long as the house stood.

A few years after the close of the war, the widow sold the house to another family. A little later, members of that family began to tell of what they called "hanty happenings" that occurred in the place. Sometimes a gunshot or two could be heard in the loft over the living room. At other times, groans and hard breathing could be heard there. There were other reports of strange knockings and sounds of walking in that loft. Once or twice there was a dull thud, as of a body falling, followed by what appeared to be blood dripping through cracks in the loft flooring.

In time, the father of this family became very ill. It appeared that his death was imminent. As was the practice in those days, kind neighbors came in to aid as they could. Many of them sat up with him through the night. Often the living room, where the sickbed was located, was almost full of concerned friends and neighbors. Most of them had heard that the place was haunted, so some of them seemed to be a bit "juberous" (nervous) most of the time.

In this family there was a half-nitwit son. One day he got to thinking of creating a ghost for the benefit of the neighbors who were helping care for his sick father. Because no real ghost had chosen to perform for the nightly assembly, he decided to make one. One morning, when the house was just about clear of all visitors, he slipped up into the loft, carrying a jar of pokeberry juice and something (the informant had forgotten what it was) to simulate the sound of a falling body. He then rigged strings and dropped a pull cord through a hole in the floor to a dark corner of the room below, where he would take his seat that night.

About twilight of that never-to-be-forgotten day, neighbors again gathered in the sickroom. About an hour or two after dark, the nitwit son got the conversation going on ghostly happenings which had occurred within recent months. In a short time most of the people were sitting on the edge of their chair, as if ready to jump up and run at a moment's notice. Some of them began to nervously look left and right, as if they expected the soon and sudden appearance of a big bad hant.

The time was right and the nitwit son knew it. He jerked the cord. There was a heavy thud in the loft, which muffled the sound of the breaking jar. In an instant a flood of "blood" came pouring through the cracks in the ceiling.

Those people sprang up, gasping, screaming, and yelling, all bent on sailing out the windows or the door, whichever was closer. Guess who was the first one through the front door?

The mortally ill man sprang up from his bed and, with sheets and covers still tangled around him, made it to the door in no more than two leaps, and was gone. When he finally returned later that night (to an empty house, needless to say), he seemingly was well and strong. Indeed, he remained in good physical condition until he contracted a fatal sickness some fifteen years later.

However, it is fair to inform the reader that he died far across town from the haunted house on Washington Street. He sold that house within a few days after he was visited by the healing ghost.

NOTE: The writer knows of at least three instant cures like the one described here. One happened during extreme fright, another in extreme anger, and the third resulted from an urgent need for action.

This writer well knew the last resident of the old house mentioned in this story. The occupant was a widow, then around ninety years old. She was deaf in her left ear. He once asked her if she thought the house was still haunted.

"Oh, yes," she quickly replied. "They's thangs to be seed and heared here. Hants groan and knock around here at night. But I don't feel like foolin' with them, so I jist go to bed and put my good ear in the pillow, and I don't hear 'em anymore!"

"The Devil's Rat Ahind Me"

Young Willie Sturgill's mother had often warned her son that if he didn't stop "night trottin'," then the pure old devil was going to get him. Evidently Willie loved his night trottin', whatever that may imply, more than he feared the devil, for he kept right on trottin'.

The Sturgills lived on the far outer reaches of Third Street, directly in front of the old Mud Flat Civil War prison grounds (present Rotary Field). One night Willie had tarried especially late in a little settlement of squatters in the present Spruce Street area. On the way home he reached the top of what is now Ash Street Hill, and that is where his race began. There

Willie Sturgill

was a little brush thicket to the right of the trail there. As he hastened by, a commotion began in that thicket, which included the sound of a rattling chain.

That is all it took. Young Willie just knew that his encounter with the pure old devil had begun. He shot down the hill at record speed, a speed that greatly increased when he heard a distinct *thump, thump* and heavy breathing right behind him, along with the wild rattling of a chain.

By the time he reached the old prison grounds, he was traveling in high jumps. He was across the field in nothing flat and crashed through the back door of his home. He landed on the kitchen floor, completely exhausted but still blurting out that the pure old devil was "rat ahind" him.

Sure enough, just moments after he collapsed upon the kitchen floor, there was a heavy thud as something landed on the back porch, followed by the wild rattling of a chain. Now, Mrs. Sturgill froze in horror as she became convinced that her Willie had really stirred up the devil.

She had but a moment to wonder, for through the open door sprang the family dog. Evidently, he had broken loose from where he was chained in the backyard and, taking a portion of the chain with him, had tried to follow Willie. Perhaps he became tired and just lay down in the thicket on Ash Street Hill to await his master's return. This revelation meant nothing to Willie. At the sound of the "devil" landing on the back porch, he had completely passed out and was not revived for an hour or more.

Devil or dog, the race did something for Willie. It is said that he never went night trottin' again.

A Voice from the Grave

Many years ago, an old man lived just across from the east end of East Hill Cemetery, on Williams Street. As he grew older he slept less and less. Thus, on summer nights he often spent long hours sitting on his front porch, looking up through the silent city of the dead that spread before him. Usually he saw or heard nothing out of the ordinary, but one morning about 2:00 A.M. there was a little excitement.

The family living next door had a teenage son who had become a bit wild. The teenager was spending more and more late hours along vice-ridden Front Street in downtown Bristol. It was not at all uncommon for the elderly man to see his wayward neighbor boy come strolling homeward through the cemetery late at night. (The boy used the cemetery route as a shortcut to his home.)

On this particular occasion, the boy was heard before he was seen. His yelps broke the stillness of the night as he came, not running but leaping, down the north driveway through the cemetery. At that time the old burying ground was fenced, and the lad, barely missing the gate, cleared the fence in one jump. He then sprang across Williams Street, and in another leap or two, he landed against his door, which he practically broke down in his maddened frenzy to get into the house.

The next day, the old man, talking to the sexton of the cemetery, was able to piece together what had happened.

On the day before, the sexton had dug a grave in the dark shade of the large trees that stood immediately north of the Confederate lot. Near midnight, a drunken man, taking a shortcut through the cemetery, had fallen into the open grave. In his somewhat tipsy condition, he could not climb out, though he made every desperate effort to do so. He had just about given up when he heard the lad whistling as he passed near the open grave. So the drunken man loudly called out, "Come here, boy, and help me get out of this deep dark grave."

The boy instantly stopped his whistling, stiffened for a moment, yelled out "Oh, Lord!" and shot down through the cemetery in frenzied, record-breaking leaps as he desperately sought the refuge of home. To say that he was not long in reaching that refuge is putting it mildly.

As far as is known, the wayward lad never knew what the real situation was. It is known that he never again used the cemetery as a shortcut on his late-night returns from downtown Bristol.

Ghost with a Purpose

In 1876, Isaac C. Fowler, fearless editor of *The Bristol News,* wrote that a few prostitutes of the town, too low down to work in the regular houses of prostitution, had set up shop in the City Cemetery (now known as East Hill Cemetery) to carry on their lascivious trade. His summary was that "women and men of the basest form of morality, the scum of the town and off casts of the town's society were resorting there almost nightly for the most debauched of purposes, desecrating in the most damnable manner in the most sacred place here." He went on to call for help from the town constable in stopping "this loathsome practice." Alas, the cemetery was then outside the city limits. In that none seemed to know the exact location of the state line, there was little that county officers could do. (The state line runs through the cemetery.)

Joseph R. Anderson, founder of the town and prominent local merchant, then decided to take the matter into his own hands. His first strategy was to create a ghost with a purpose. He well knew that most of the town prostitutes, and likely a great portion of their clients, were a superstitious lot, dreadfully afraid of what they usually called "hants."

At that time Daddy Thomas, who later supplied this writer with reams of local history, was a lad of nineteen and spent much of his time doing odd jobs for Mr. Anderson. One day Mr. Anderson offered him a dollar to play the role of a ghost in the cemetery. Young Mr. Thomas quickly agreed to the offer. He was given his dollar in advance and enough white cloth from the store to fashion a shroud.

Soon after dark that night, young Thomas slipped up to the cemetery and donned his white shroud. Let us have the rest of the story as he told it in late 1953:

They wuz heavy brush and lots of high weeds all over the place at that time. I wrapped up in the white cloth and got behind a tree near a real weedy place. I hadn't been there very long when I heared one uv 'em comin' through the lower gate with her man. I recognized her high, screechin' voice, knowed who she wuz without doubt. They called her Red Penny, and she wuz one of the worst uns in town. That night she were leadin' Tim Dare, whose daddy run a drinkin' place [saloon] down on Front Street. Reckon Tim wuz jist a late teenager at that time, but she had roped him somehow.

Well they come close to my tree and got down in the weeds. I let them open court afore I jumped out from ahind that tree, a-wailin' powerful strong. Land! Your ort to uv seed 'em. They jumped up a-yellin' till you could uv heared 'em plumb down in town. Red Penny took back toward town jist a-flyin'. Tim Dare tuck down over the north hill, a-tearin' rat through brush and briar thickets.

I thought I had shore created a hant scare that night. But I didn't know that a town drunk was a-layin' in the weeds not fer from me. Now he heared me down a-rollin' and laughin' and talkin' to myself about what I had done. Now, he told it on me, and I had to dodge Tim Dare fer weeks after that, fer he were tore up powerful bad and vowed he wuz gonna tear me up worse. But, he never did. I reckon that wuz the only time I ever played hant. I think Uncle Joe [Joseph Anderson] begrudged that dollar after he learned the hant scare didn't last long.

Ghost Solves Mother-in-Law Problem

Even today many people comment on how close the last two houses on Second Taylor Street are to the East Hill Cemetery. Indeed, they are all but in it! Certainly the outhouse for the one on the north side of the street is in the very edge of it. So much so that a monument marking a grave is within a few inches of the back side of that little necessary building, almost against it.

Far back, the house on the north side of the street was rented to a couple who had moved to Bristol from Abingdon, Virginia. The man of the house was employed by the nearby Bristol Door and Lumber Company. Perhaps life would have been pleasant for him there had it not been for one major problem. His mother-in-law, whom he actually detested, came often, for what became longer and longer visits. The longer those visits became, the more frustrated and miserable the young son-in-law got. He dearly loved his wife, and for her sake he tried to adjust to the unpleasant situation but that became harder and harder to do.

The mother-in-law, a rather obese and lazy woman, was querulous and nitpicking, daily giving an abundance of unsolicited, and certainly unappreciated, advice. Though she came often and stayed long, she didn't like the location of the house and was constantly pestering the son-in-law to find another place to live.

Her chief complaint was that the house was too close to what she called "that scary old graveyard." Her bedroom was on the cemetery side of the house, so she constantly grumbled about the fact that on moonlit nights she had to lie with her face away from the window to "keep from seeing those white tombstones and no telling what else."

That "what else" is what really bothered her. She was terrified of what she called "hants," and she supposed that East Hill Cemetery was "working alive" with them. At that time it was a "boogery-looking" place, being a virtual jungle of brush and high weeds with only a well-kept family plot here and there.

Nine o'clock in the evening was a time dreaded by the old lady. That was her bedtime, and just before retiring she usually felt compelled to take a trip to the outhouse. She knew that a grave was directly behind it, and that grave was all sunken in and rather scary looking. At such times she always went there singing an old ballad, continuing while there and most of the way back. Apparently, she hoped to drown out any ghostly sounds that might come from the cemetery. The way she staggered along on these nightly trips caused the son-in-law to think that she was traveling with her eyes shut.

When the widower of the woman who was buried behind the outhouse died, he was buried at her side. This caused the mother-in-law to become nervous, especially when she thought of having to go to the outhouse in the dark. As the mother-in-law trembled in dreadful anticipation, the son-in-law coolly conceived a plan to take advantage of the situation.

Two or three houses down Haddon Street, there lived a big strip of a boy who would do just about anything as long as he was paid enough. Shortly before nightfall, the lad had a visitor from the house at the edge of the cemetery, and the husband made a deal with the boy. He was to be behind the outhouse at 9:00 P.M., and when the old lady made her nightly trip, he was to really do his thing.

Well, nine o'clock came and the old mother-in-law was mighty reluctant and nervous about her nightly trip. However, necessity finally overcame fear. She sang extra loud

This woman was tricked into leaving her daughter's house.

that night as she staggered out to the outhouse and took her seat.

Hardly was she settled in, when, over her singing, she heard a loud moan that turned into a wail. Her song suddenly stopped and she shrieked out, "Lordy, what wuz that?"

Immediately, there came a loud knocking on the back of the outhouse, and a quavering, ghostly voice called out, "I'm coming in there to get you."

In stark terror, the old lady shot up from her seat and, squalling to high heaven, lunged against the door, since there was no time to unlatch it. At the first lunge the hinges gave way and the door fell outward, forming a gangplank for her hasty exit.

To call that exit "hasty" is putting it mildly. She leaped over the fallen door like a frog in front of a pursuing snake, and she continued to leap wildly toward the house. You see, she had to leap. She had lowered a certain part of her clothing when she took her seat in the outhouse, and there had been no time to draw that part back up, since she supposed a real hant was just behind her. Running was impossible, so she made her maddened flight in long, frog-like leaps. She did miss the trail a bit and leaped right into the middle of a thorny, spreading rosebush. She leaped right out, and in no time made it to the porch. One more leap took her through the front door, which she slammed shut and locked behind her.

Once she was safe in the house and had regained her breath, she began a long harangue against "fool people living in such a hanty place." She vowed she couldn't stay where there were hants so close. She went on to say that if she wasn't afraid to walk to the depot in the dark, she'd go home that very night.

Well, it seems that the long-suffering son-in-law suddenly became chivalrous. Kindly, he told his mother-in-law that if she felt she must go then he would escort her to the train station. He got her there in time to catch the 10:30 P.M. train to Abingdon. Before she left, she delivered the ultimatum that unless they moved from that awful place she would not be back. It was noticed that the relieved son-in-law made no effort to move for several years. In fact, he did not try to move until after the querulous old woman had died.

A Parting Word

The ghost tales recorded here, numerous as they are, barely scratch the surface of local ghost lore. More stories, both old and new, come to light nearly every day. From reports often received by this writer, it would seem that ghosts are still active here—and that in large numbers. Perhaps at some future time more will be written about Bristol boogers. Meanwhile, if you have such stories, please contact the author.

Hell on the Border

Murder and Violence in Early Bristol

It is apparent that the paradise Joseph Anderson had hoped to create on the Tennessee/Virginia border soon slipped fast in the other direction. For some reason, border towns seemed to have a way of fast becoming lawless. Bristol was also a railroad-terminal town, another situation that often led to wild and wooly actions. Further, the early settlers of the town made up a widely varied strata of humanity, ranging from the most holy of saints to the worst of the debased, violent, and immoral. Conflict was inevitable.

Something else must also be considered: Though Anderson had planned for his town to be bone dry, it actually became soaking wet. Whiskey flowed freely. The resulting drunkenness caused much violence and sometimes murder. Along with the saloons, gambling flourished, often creating disastrous confrontations.

Ladies of the street began to ply their trade soon after Bristol began. Their number swelled until there was "quite a swarm of them," as one old-timer once expressed it. In spite of the fact that there was "quite a swarm of them," the prostitutes were greatly outnumbered by potential male clients. Vying for the favors of these easy women often resulted in maiming fights and worse.

Of course, the fame of this center of vice soon spread far, and Bristol became a strong magnet, drawing many who delighted in such things. The rough, rowdy, and lawless soon outnumbered the civil and law-abiding citizens. This undesirable element was often joined by those of like interests who lived in the immediate area. While not residents of the new town, they often visited, intent upon having a rip-roaring time. So what had been planned as paradise soon became described as "hell on the border."

Two Killings in One Afternoon

How often in the early days of Bristol were peaceful scenes and pleasant gatherings suddenly and unexpectedly marred and interrupted by the vilest of crimes. The afternoon of July 30, 1872, was rather pleasant for mid-summer. Several men and women, guests of the Virginia House Hotel on Front Street, had gathered in the lobby of that prominent establishment for a pleasant time of socializing and game playing. Most of them were seated around a huge game table in the center of the lobby, when an obviously drunken man came through the front door. He likely had overimbibed in the Nickel Plate Saloon, which was next door to the Virginia House.

The drunken man came over to the gaming table and centered his unwanted attention upon two of the younger ladies seated there. Pretty soon he was making indecent and suggestive remarks to the disturbed and frightened women. Naturally, the men in the party began to bristle, and they firmly asked him to desist from his vile annoyance of their female friends. By then, as Editor Fowler reported in his *Bristol News,* the drunken man was acting scandalously. He was in the act of indecently exposing himself to the women.

A guest from New Orleans, one of the men in the party, could take no more. He jumped up, seized the offender, and attempted to forcibly eject him from the lobby. In the ensuing struggle, the drunk pulled out a long knife and stabbed the man in the heart, killing him almost instantly. He died in a pool of blood on the fine carpet of the hotel lobby.

Meanwhile, someone had alerted the town constable to the trouble brewing in the lobby of the Virginia House Hotel. He arrived just as the murderer, bloody knife in hand, staggered out the door and onto the hotel porch. Recognizing the officer of the law, he went for him with his knife drawn. The constable quickly drew his pistol and ordered him to stop. The drunken man instead continued to lunge forward, brandishing the deadly knife. Three shots reverberated along Front Street. As the New Orleans traveler lay dying in the lobby, the drunken murderer lay dying on the hotel porch.

It was a rather exciting afternoon for the town of Bristol, but it was not really all that unusual. Similar events happened often during the early years of the city.

Murdered Man Testifies Against Murderer

Is it possible for a murdered man to testify against his murderer? As unlikely and strange as it may seem, it once happened in Bristol. In 1863, young Robert Droke was employed as a clerk in the Famous Hotel. (Later called the Thomas House, this hotel stood on the lot now occupied by the Paramount Theatre.) A man called Colonel Prentice was then staying in the hotel. Someone told Colonel Prentice that young Mr. Droke had called him a drunken sot, not worthy of the respect or association of honest and upright men. This angered the colonel and he vowed a hasty settling of the matter.

On the morning of November 9, 1863, the two men met in the street in front of the hotel. Colonel Prentice confronted Mr. Droke with the alleged statement. Droke denied it. A violent argument ensued, during which one of Robert Droke's uncles walked up and tried to make peace between the two. All efforts at such were in vain. The end result was that Colonel Prentice pulled his pistol and shot Robert Droke.

Hardly had the gun smoke drifted away when friends of the mortally wounded Droke carried him into the lobby of the hotel. They sat him at a table and, as death crept upon him, he wrote his version of what happened. The original paper is yellow and crumbly, but the faint and trembly handwriting is still legible. It reads as follows:

> During the argument I asked Col. Prentice if he was armed. He replied that he always went armed. I then went to my room and got my pistol, and then returned to where Prentice and Mr. Droke [the uncle] were standing. I then remarked to him [Prentice] that he was mistaken about that he had been told I had said. He then said that if I denied it I was a damned liar. I then said that I did not want a difficulty with him, and that I would not shoot unless he shot first at me. Prentice then shot at me and I fell. He then shot again and gave me a fatal wound. I think I shot at him twice after he first shot me.

The paper was duly witnessed and did become a piece of damning evidence in the trial that soon followed. Though the court records of Sullivan County, Tennessee, for that period are not available, the writer was long ago told that Colonel Prentice was convicted and received a long prison term, largely on the strength of his victim's written testimony.

Election Day Murders 1872

Election Day was always a perilous time in early Bristol, largely because of the manner in which voting was done. In those days the voter (only men voted at the time) did not take a ballot, go into a booth, and there mark it in secret. Instead, he was required to go stand in the door of the mayor's office and publicly and loudly call out the name of his chosen candidate. Often this was done before a crowd of other voters who had proclaimed their choice and then stood around to hear what others would do. At the very best, it was a volatile situation. Oftentimes voters were heckled, argued with, and castigated for their choices. It was not uncommon for one who had called out his choices to be called a damned fool for having made a particular choice. Often such banter led to blows.

The town election of 1872 was especially bitter. Many a verbal fight, and a few with fists, had taken place in the streets of the town long before Election Day arrived.

Hiram Pickford and Lucian "Luke" Keeton were certainly on opposite sides of the political fence, and they had been steaming at each other for several weeks. Perhaps it was fortunate that they did not arrive at the voting place at the same time. (The mayor's office was then located near the intersection of Lee Street and the old route of Cumberland Street.) Hiram Pickford and his son, Guss, voted first. Then, as did many other voters, they went on to the noted Nickel Plate Saloon, located near the corner of Cumberland and Front streets. Next came Luke Keeton and his son, Timothy. They, too, voted and then went on to the Nickel Plate Saloon.

A violent clash was inevitable. The Pickfords were well boozed up by the time the Keetons arrived. The Keetons had hardly finished ordering their drinks when Hiram Pickford strode up and loudly stated that he supposed the Keetons had just played the fool by voting for the wrong man.

Witnesses later stated that Luke Keeton never said a word, but for a moment he "looked daggers" at his adversary and then reached for a weapon. No, he did not go for a pistol in his pocket. Strangely, he did not have one. Instead, he used what is likely the most unique weapon that ever figured in a Bristol murder.

Isaac Nickels, owner and operator of the Nickel Plate Saloon, had brought a fine Seth Thomas weight-driven clock from his old home in Nickelsville, Virginia. He had set it on a shelf on the wall over the end of his bar.

It was his pride and joy. He often boasted of its accuracy, usually pulling out his fine watch and showing that the two were keeping time together, to the minute. Mr. Nickels liked to bet, so he would often wager someone a dollar that if he set the two timepieces together they would still be minute-to-minute twenty-four hours later. He usually won his bet.

Result of a battle on First Street. Two limbs were so badly shattered by gunfire that they had to be amputated.

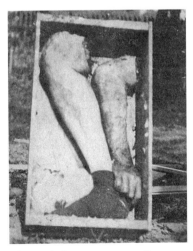

These leftovers came from a battle on Bristol's notorious First (later Front) Street.

Alas, Election Day 1872 was a sad day for Isaac Nickels and his prized clock.

Luke Keeton knew something of the inner workings of a weight-driven clock. He whirled around, pulled the clock door open, and seized a weight from inside. With a mighty jerk, he broke the weight's cord and came out with the three-pound piece of metal held tightly in his hand.

Keeton's action also toppled the clock from its shelf. It fell to the bar with a mighty crash, breaking the glass in both doors and badly damaging the handpainted and decorated dial. No one, except perhaps Isaac Nickels, noticed the fallen clock.

All eyes were fastened on the enraged Luke Keeton. With one mighty swoop he threw the weight at Pickford. It hit him in the face and broke his left jawbone.

In a maddened rage, Pickford grabbed the fallen weight from the floor and threw it wildly, hitting Keeton in the forehead and knocking him flat. Then he grabbed it again, straddled the fallen victim, and, with several hard blows, bashed in his skull.

Timothy Keeton, enraged by the murderous attack on his father, grabbed a whiskey bottle and broke it on the bar. Then, using the neck of the bottle and the jagged glass that remained as a weapon, he seized Pickford, pulled him backward, and inflicted several deep slashes across his throat.

Mortally wounded, Pickford fell to

the floor, blood spurting from his severed neck arteries.

Guss Pickford then attacked Timothy Keeton. Timothy, using the same broken bottle, inflicted mortal wounds on his attacker. Guss fell across the body of his dying father. Their blood mingled on the carpet of the saloon floor.

Isaac Nickels then drew a pistol from his pocket and shot Timothy through the hand, making him drop the deadly weapon. By then the constable had arrived. He, with the aid of two or three bystanders, subdued Timothy and took him to the local jail.

Timothy Keeton, likely by the aid of friends, escaped jail that night. (Considering the flimsy condition of the local jail at that time, such was not hard to do.) It was later told that he slipped by his home, viewed his father's body by flickering candlelight, bade the rest of the family farewell in the backyard, and then disappeared into the darkness, never to return.

Thirty-seven years later it was discovered by one of his nephews that Timothy, using an assumed name, was living in Oregon County, Missouri, and was operating a thriving country store.

There was another murder in Bristol before that long-to-be-remembered Election Day was over. That night, in Bosang's Saloon, located just a short distance from the Nickel Plate, several local men had gathered to celebrate the victory of their chosen candidate. Among them were two brothers, Hiram and Boone Whitson. A cousin of theirs, Marcus Whitson, was also present, playing lively tunes on his banjo. The Whitson brothers, both of them rather tipsy, got to dancing a jig.

In the course of this dancing, Boone bumped into Hiram, causing him to lose his balance and fall to the saloon floor. Angered, Hiram sprang up and attacked Boone, knocking him backward over a table. Boone went into a rage, drew a small pistol from his pocket, and shot Hiram right between the eyes. He died instantly.

Boone was arrested and put in the local jail. When he was taken there, it was discovered that Timothy Keeton had escaped. The town constable hired someone to guard the jail and its prisoner the rest of the night. The next day, Boone was moved to Abingdon, where the county jail was more secure than the little room which served as the jail in Bristol. Apparently overcome with guilt and remorse over killing his own brother, Boone Whitson soon became stark raving mad. He was then moved to the Western State Hospital in Staunton, Virginia. Within a few days after he was taken there, he somehow managed to commit suicide.

Well, a murder or two in a town with a reputation of being hell on the border was not unusual. Yet, three in one day, followed closely by a suicide, caused a bit of excitement. It was long told that Isaac Nickels grieved more over the damage done to his prized clock than he did over the men who died on his saloon floor.

Bloody Battle on Railroad Street

Free-for-all gang battles in early Bristol were not at all unheard of. One of the bloodiest battles of this type took place in the middle of Railroad Street (now Randall Street Expressway) on May 26, 1883, between one and two o'clock in the morning.

Lemuel "Lem" Hardy, a railroad switchman, lived in a little cottage on the west side of Railroad Street, a short distance north of the present First Christian Church. He and his wife had several children. Alice, the oldest, was a few weeks short of her fourteenth birthday.

There lived in the neighborhood a twenty-seven-year-old widower named Steve Richardson. He was a good friend of the Hardys and often visited in their home. He and Alice began courting, and when her parents saw that the casual friendship had turned into a full-fledged courtship, they strictly forbade the young widower from coming on the place again. By then, Steve thought he was madly in love with Alice and she in turn was extremely infatuated with her handsome suitor.

Though they were strictly forbidden to see one another, they managed to carry on their courtship by sending love notes to each other by the aid of mutual and sympathetic friends. Finally the two made plans for marriage, but they would have to elope to carry them out.

They formulated a plan. Alice was to slip from the cottage at 1:00 A.M. and come across the street to a grove of saplings that spread between the street and the railroad yards. There, Steve would be waiting with a horse, upon which they would make a hasty escape.

The best-laid plans of men often go astray. In this case a common saw briar not only caused an upset in plans but also led to one of the bloodiest gang battles that ever occurred in Bristol.

Young Alice Hardy was still a student in a local school. She received the elopement note through the aid of a schoolmate. After gleefully noting the contents, she placed it in the pocket of her dress. On the way home that afternoon, she veered from the usual path a bit and, while passing through a weed patch, caught and ripped her dress on a saw briar. Upon her arrival home, Alice removed the damaged dress and handed it to her mother for repairs.

Alas, she forgot to remove the elopement note, and it was discovered by Mrs. Hardy. Though seething with anger, she remained silent but quickly began to make plans to thwart the elopement.

At one o'clock on the morning of May 26th, Steve and his horse were waiting in the grove of saplings across from the Hardy cottage. A pale moon up above, frequently obscured by fast-moving clouds, gave a little light to the scene. Just in case there might be trouble, Steve had brought along three other men and his rather tomboyish sister, who was known to be good in a fight. He had assured the party that things would likely go smoothly, that they would likely not be needed, but at least they would get to see a first-class elopement.

Unknown to the party in the grove, there were battle forces waiting in the Hardy cottage! Alice's parents had sent for Mrs. Hardy's two brothers and a man who worked in the railroad yards with Lem. The three allies pretended, for the benefit of young Alice, to have come for an overnight visit. Their plan was to pounce upon Steve Richardson and give him the beating of his life. Of course, they were unaware that Steve was also well prepared for battle. They all went to bed but lay awake awaiting the fateful hour.

In her little room just off the kitchen, Alice happily anticipated the time when she would ride swiftly away with her sweetheart. While she would indeed ride swiftly away, it would not be quite in the way she had planned. When the kitchen clock struck one o'clock, Alice quietly arose and tiptoed from the house.

Steve Richardson was lovingly lifting his bride-to-be into the saddle when the front door of the Hardy cottage burst open and the attackers raced out, loudly shouting curses as they sprang across Railroad Street. Steve's allies-in-waiting realized what was happening and rushed to launch a counterattack. Everyone met in the middle of the street, and a battle royal was on! All were armed to the teeth. (They were not necessarily armed for this particular encounter; at the time, most Bristolians went well armed anyway.)

Lem Hardy seized Steve and threw him to the ground. In that instant Mrs. Hardy landed upon him. In the dim moonlight, Steve saw the glint of a knife in her hand. She, then realizing that it was no longer a matter of fisticuffs but that it was going to be a battle to death, began slashing at

Steve's throat. Somehow, he managed to grab the handle of the knife and then rip it through her hand, cutting it almost in half. In another vicious slash, he ripped open her left breast. He turned upon Lem Hardy, cutting his throat from ear to ear, and then he pulled a pistol and began shooting.

The first shot felled one of his friends, who, in the dim light, was mistaken for one of Hardy's men. About that time, one of Mrs. Hardy's brothers, blazing pistol in hand, shot Steve three times—once in the chest, once in the stomach, and once in the groin. By then Steve's sister, brick in hand, had attacked Mrs. Hardy's other brother. In moments, he lay in the street with a smashed skull. It was then that Lem's fellow worker from

Alice Hardy's torn dress led to a bloody battle on Railroad Street.

the railroad yard opened fire on Steve's remaining ally. Steve's friend fled down the hill and into the railroad yards. Shot twice, the man ran for about a half of a block down Railroad Street, then fell onto the porch of Hiram Bickley's undertaking establishment and there died in a pool of blood.

Meanwhile, the horse, greatly frightened by the melee, raced madly away, with the bride-to-have-been hanging on for dear life. The frightful race ended four or five miles away. Alice did not make it back home until well after daylight. By the time the fighting ended, the entire neighborhood had been roused by the sounds of the horrible street battle. Law officers and doctors were summoned and soon were on the scene.

Mrs. Hardy survived, but barely. She almost bled to death, and it was months before she recovered. Lem Hardy quickly bled to death, lying in the street where he fell. Steve Richardson was carried to his nearby home, where he suffered indescribable agony until death mercifully came a little over twenty-four hours later.

Two of Steve's friends died in the battle; one he accidentally shot, and the other was felled by Lem Hardy's friend and coworker.

The brother of Mrs. Hardy who shot Steve Richardson survived the battle. He was jailed but was soon free on bond. Soon after being released, he was passing the W. W. James mercantile, at the corner of Front and Main (State) streets, when Steve Richardson's father, standing in the doorway of that store, pulled a pistol and pumped four bullets into the body of his son's slayer. The mortally wounded man ran across Front Street, blood spurting from his wounds. He made it across the depot lot and fell on the railroad tracks, where he died.

Steve's sister survived the battle without a scratch. She later became the first woman to operate a saloon in Bristol.

Lem Hardy's friend also survived the battle, but, under threat of retribution by his victim's brothers, he slipped away from town, leaving his wife and several children behind. He was never heard from again.

Mrs. Hardy, blaming Alice for the tragic battle, was never good to her after that. Less than two years later, Alice managed to successfully elope with a younger brother of the slain Steve Richardson. It is said that they fled to Newton County, Arkansas, and permanently settled there.

"Brush" Jim Buford, who lived on Railroad Street when the battle occurred and who told the writer all that happened those years ago, ended his tale by commenting, "Ain't it a sight what one little saw briar can cause!"

Deafness Leads to Death

Lewis Eanes, a deaf man, was well-known to about everyone in Bristol, but unfortunately, he was not known to the new town constable. Eanes made his living by doing light, short-distance hauling around town.

One day in 1881, Eanes backed his wagon onto the sidewalk at W. W. James's warehouse on Front Street. He then started walking down the alley, intending to enter the warehouse from the back and open the front door so that a small amount of goods could be loaded for delivery.

At that point, the new constable came walking along Front Street. Perhaps a bit tipsy on his newly vested authority, he may have, shall we say, overreacted when he saw a minor infraction of the law.

At that time, Goodson, Virginia (always popularly known as Bristol), had an ordinance against parking a vehicle in a way that blocked a sidewalk. The practice of all previous constables had been to disregard this ordinance when it came to the work of local draymen.

Lewis Eanes

The new constable did not act as had his predecessors. Instead, he quickened his step to the head of the alley and ordered Lewis Eanes to come to him. Of course, Eanes, not hearing the command, walked on as if ignoring the order. This angered the constable, and thinking that his command was being ignored, he curtly ordered Eanes to halt. Again, the unsuspecting man walked on.

Much angered at what he thought was a blatant disregard of his authority, the constable drew his pistol and again called for a halt. Being, as wrongly supposed, ignored again, he fired. Later he claimed that he meant to shoot the man in the arm to show him that he "meant business."

Whatever the constable had meant to do, deaf Lewis Eanes was shot through the heart from the back. He died instantly, not knowing why or who had shot him.

The town was outraged. There were serious threats of lynching, and as the furor increased the constable "resigned." Resigned, that is, by suddenly disappearing from town. He was never heard from again.

Unexpected Confession

How often does a decision made by someone seal his or her fate, whether for good or bad? It was so with Jonas Page, a widower in his mid-sixties, who came to Bristol from Pittsylvania County, Virginia. He set up a store on the Virginia side of Main (State) Street and soon began to prosper.

Among his early customers was the Prangle family from the mountain country beyond Holston Valley. In this family was a daughter, Ada Hicks, who was about thirty-five years old. Widowed by the Civil War, she was again living in her parental home.

She always went with her parents on their shopping trips to Bristol. She was rather coarse, unlearned, and a bit on the rough side, but somehow she was appealing to Jonas Page and was often in his thoughts. One day, as he worked about his store, he made the decision that come Sunday he would ride his horse out to the Prangle place and talk a little "business" with her.

His talk must have been successful, for when he returned to town, Ada Prangle Hicks was in the saddle behind him. They were married as soon as arrangements could be made. Jonas, who had been living in a little room over the back room of his store, rented a house on Virginia Street, and the two settled down to marital bliss.

Jonas Page

Not long after the wedding, Jonas made another decision that would contribute to the sealing of his fate. His business was prospering so much that he badly needed help. A friend told him of a man, then living in Abingdon, who had some experience as a store clerk and was looking for work.

Orbey "Orb" Cook had come to Abingdon from Eastern Kentucky. He was a Civil War veteran in his mid-thirties and had recently been left a widower. His five or six children were in the care of his parents. Jonas worked out a deal with him, and Orb moved to Bristol. Jonas not only gave him employment but also gave him room and board in the Page home as part of his compensation.

All went well for a while and continued to do so as far as Jonas Page knew. Orb made an extra-good hand in the store. However, unbeknownst to Jonas, Orb was also making an extra-good boyfriend for Ada Prangle Hicks Page. While Jonas pored over his books at the store until far into the night, Orb was home enjoying "merry fellowship" with Ada. That merry fellowship reached a point where the two wanted to enjoy it for the rest of their lives, as man and wife.

It was then that they fell upon a plan to put Jonas out of the way and gain possession of what had become a very profitable store. Ada went to Bunting's drugstore and, on some pretext, was able to buy a quantity of a deadly poison. The next morning a dose of that poison was in her husband's coffee. He became very ill but was still alive at suppertime, whereupon Ada urged him to drink more coffee, as it might help him "rest better."

That cup contained a double dose of the poison. Indeed, it did help him rest better, as he was in the everlasting sleep before nightfall.

From that very day, there was much suspicion as to the cause of his death. In a very short time, Jonas's son by his first marriage had enough evidence to convince a Washington County, Virginia, grand jury to indict Orbey Cook and Ada Prangle Hicks Page for murder. The case soon came before the circuit court.

One of the chief witnesses at the trial was Jeremiah Bunting, who had sold the poison to Mrs. Page. On the stand he gave much damning testimony concerning the matter. The more he told, the more Mrs. Page became frightened and agitated. Finally she turned toward Orb, anger flashing in her eyes, and screeched out, "Dog take it, Orb, I told you that we ought to have bought that pizen somewhere besides Bristol!"

That unexpected confession clinched the case. Where Ada and Orb spent the rest of their lives, they could neither enjoy the store nor their "merry fellowship."

Blacks Lynch Black

It is tragic and sad, but true, that Bristol has been the scene of at least three lynchings of blacks by whites. Most unusual as it is, Bristol once had a lynching of a black man by other blacks.

Hibert Lough (pronounced *low*) came here from New York City. It was told that he had never been in the open countryside until he started his journey to Bristol. He secured work in the town with a group of stonemasons who were erecting stone walls, chimneys, and house foundations. He was a fast learner and, while beginning as simply a laborer, soon was considered to be as good a mason as his employers. In time, he went out on his own and apparently was doing well.

It soon became obvious that Hibert was rather hedonistic. He drank heavily, attended frolics (parties) in the black section of town, and frequented the brothel known as the Black Shawl. (The Black Shawl kept a few black women, supposedly for the benefit of men of the same race. However, there were rumors that white men wanted them as well.) He also womanized a great deal among the black population, which almost got him killed several times.

A year or two after Hibert arrived in Bristol, he married Miss Lilly King, a former slave of Rev. James King who had been but a mere child when freed. All seemed to go well for a while. Then Lilly inexplicably disappeared. Many suspected foul play but were never able to prove it.

About a year later, Hibert married Jane Rader, a widow with several children. Fortunately, the children remained with their grandparents, for the Lough home soon became a virtual battleground. Hibert and Jane were not at all compatible. Severe conflicts erupted almost every day.

Once, after an especially severe conflict, Hibert stormed out of the house and went downtown to his favorite saloon, the Nickel Plate on Front Street. After getting tanked up, he hastened back home, apparently determined to permanently end his marital conflicts.

On the back porch Hibert picked up a sharp-edged piece of stove wood. Jane was bending over a tub of dirty laundry when he entered through the kitchen door. She did not look around when she heard him coming, and in a moment she was knocked to the floor. Her angry and drunken husband then continued to brutally batter her head, neck, and shoulders. Before she lost consciousness, she heard him growl that he'd kill her just like he did Lilly. This would have been very damning evidence had he been brought to trial. As it was in his case, swift justice bypassed the law.

When he thought Jane was dead, he dragged her into a dense thicket behind their home and threw her into a ditch. He then shoveled dirt over the body. Having, as he thought, settled his troubles, he went back to the saloon and resumed his drinking.

But Jane was not dead. When she regained consciousness a little later, she found herself buried alive. However, two things were in her favor: Hibert had not covered her well and the dirt was cloddy (lumpy), which evidently allowed some air to reach her. In stark terror, she heaved and clawed her way out of the shallow grave. She then ran to a neighbor's house, blurting out the fearful story. Like wildfire, the news spread through the neighborhood. In a short time, two or three men went running for the constable.

The constable, acquainted with the habits of Hibert Lough, knew just where to find him. He also knew that Hibert was a dangerous character. So, with his most trusted deputy, he quietly entered the Nickel Plate. Before Hibert knew it, the constable and the deputy were in the room and had cocked pistols at the back of his head. He was told that if he moved he would be a dead man. Then, with pistols in hand, they marched Hibert to the town jail, which was then a flimsy little building far up Washington Street. They intended to move him to the more secure Washington County jail in Abingdon on the following day. The constable hired Lemuel Strait, best known as the town's woodcutter, to stand guard that night.

The black community had always feared Hibert Lough. After his heinous crime, the fear became mixed with extreme anger. Now, anger and fear combined is always a potentially volatile mixture. Hardly had the crime become known among the black population, when talk of swift retribution began.

It has long been thought that it was Adam Flint, an influential leader in the black community, who decided what that retribution would be and how to bring it about. By nightfall, a lynching party was organized and was waiting for the chosen time.

At 1:00 A.M., Lemuel Strait was having a hard time. Hibert would not sleep. He was pacing about in the little jail, kicking the walls and vehemently swearing. Occasionally, he would turn his wrath upon Lemuel, shouting out threats of what he would do to him and his family if ever he became free.

He would not rant and rave for much longer. Suddenly, the jail was surrounded by thirty or more men and women. Adam Flint ordered the somewhat startled guard to throw down his gun and surrender the prisoner. Of course, Lemuel knew that most of that crowd carried arms and that they would not hesitate to use them. Resistance, if he had been of a mind to offer any, would have been useless. Perhaps he had had enough of Hibert's wild ravings, and he may have been fearful of his threats. In any case, he quickly obeyed Flint's command.

The jail door was broken down, and by sheer force the resisting prisoner was subdued. A rope was put around his neck and he was jerked down and dragged into the street. Several of the strong men swooped him up and carried him to the nearby Mary Street overpass bridge. (At that time the bridge was a wooden structure and not as high above the tracks as is the present one.) From that bridge Hibert was hanged, directly over the mainline track. This was done purposely, as it was well-known that a passenger train would be arriving from Lynchburg at about 1:20 A.M.

That night the train was on time. At the right moment, the rope was cut, allowing the body to fall upon the track, directly in front of the approaching train.

The next morning, the mutilated remains of Hibert Lough were taken up and buried outside the fence at Flat Hollow Cemetery. Around 1900, the bodies in that cemetery were moved to what became known as the Citizen's Cemetery, at the end of Piedmont Avenue. Hibert Lough, being in an unmarked grave outside the fence, was not moved. His bones moulder somewhere near the intersection of Oakview and Buckner streets in Bristol, Virginia.

First-Class Murder

Not all Bristol murders took place on the wrong side of the tracks, nor did all those who committed murder come from what was considered to be the lowly element of the town.

The family of Maj. Z. L. Burson was among the most elite in Bristol. By the 1880s, Major Burson had apparently become the wealthiest of local citizens. His real estate holdings were extensive, and he always seemed to have plenty of ready cash. The Burson home, known as "The Oak," at 342 Moore Street, was one of the finest in town. (The stump of the great oak that gave the place its name can still be seen in the backyard at the above address, where the house has been replaced by a larger brick structure.)

Major Burson was twice married. He fathered about fifteen children, only a few of whom survived to adulthood. Those who were yet living in the 1880s were considered to be prominent and upstanding citizens. It was a great shock to the town when, on August 27, 1889, one of Major Burson's sons, himself a prominent and well-known businessman, shot and killed Stephen Bonham, another prominent Bristolian.

At noon on that long-ago day, Major Burson and his son were walking up Moore Street on their way home for lunch. Near the Beaver Creek bridge (northwest corner of the present Cumberland Square Park) they met Stephen Bonham, who was on his way downtown. Without a word, Burson's son drew a pistol and shot Bonham through the heart. Bonham died in a pool of blood at the south end of the bridge.

Immediately after the murder, young Mr. Burson went into hiding until he could consult with his lawyer brother, "Hell" John Burson. John was then out of town but was due back the next day. It was later learned that the murderous Burson used the steeple of his father's church (Burson Baptist), on the 800 block of Main (State) Street, as his hiding place. After Hell John arrived the next day, he went there and advised his brother that it would be best if he surrendered. The murderous son then went to the Goodson City Hall and surrendered himself to Charles Worley, the town constable.

At 5:00 P.M. on August 28, 1889, Burson's son was given a preliminary hearing before W. L. Cunningham, a local justice of the peace. After this hearing he was turned over to R. R. Hughes, the sheriff of Washington County, Virginia. Sheriff Hughes immediately took Burson to the county jail in Abingdon.

One can imagine how this son of one of Bristol's most elite families must have felt. He did not dine sumptuously that night as he had before, but ate—if he ate at all—the coarse and meager fare of a county prisoner. He, who had long been used to sleeping on a fine, carved-walnut bed, had to sleep on a wretchedly uncomfortable and filthy cot.

Perhaps he was made to reflect upon his crime and to fear an uncertain future wherein his own life would be in jeopardy.

The next day he was taken before the county court, with Judge George W. Ward presiding. However, Judge Ward disqualified himself. Judge George W. Richardson of Smyth County then took the bench. Burson demanded to be tried by the circuit court and asked to be released on his own recognizance. His case was turned over to the circuit court, but his request to be released was denied. He was returned to the county jail. His trial was set for the fourth Monday in September 1889.

From the hour of the murder, there was much and varied speculation as to what had been the motive. Rumors were rampant. Burson's first and persistent plea was that it had been done in self-defense. Indeed, a gun had been found in a pocket of Bonham's coat. That is hardly unusual for that day and time; most of the men (and a few of the women) of the town went armed.

Burson claimed that Bonham had vowed to shoot him on sight because of a bitter dispute between the two. Why the dispute? There were rumors that a woman was involved, perhaps the wife of one or the other. The most plausible claim, one that was used by Burson in the ensuing trial, was that a property line was the source of the trouble. Whatever the cause, it had ended in a shocking murder, one that Bristolians remembered and talked of for years afterward.

Burson was able to hire the best legal counsel to serve in his defense along with his brother Hell John Burson. The matter was not settled during the September 1889 term of court. By various legal maneuvers it was pro-longed until the May term of 1890. Apparently, Burson's plea of self-defense was successful. During that term of court, the jury, acting under foreman J. W. Wyrick, found him not guilty.

Though free, Burson's life was far from pleasant. Members of the Bonham family and a close friend or two of the murdered man had threatened to even the score. Daily Burson went about the town, fearing for his life. He would not sit on his porch on summer evenings, nor would he allow a light in his house until all window blinds were closed. Of course, he went armed at all times, expecting at any moment to be drawn into a shoot-out. Finally, he took his family and moved to Seffner, in Hillsborough County, Florida. Later, several others of the Burson family, including his mother, also moved there.

Though he had escaped imprisonment, the Burson son could not escape the tortured mind that is the lot of many who commit murder. Moving far away from his enemies may have made him feel more secure, but it did not lessen his guilty conscience and troubled mind. He soon sickened and died. He now sleeps under the Florida sand.

Murder-Suicide at the Bristol Depot

The Bristol depot which was erected in 1881 and served until 1902 was the setting for many an exciting event, some pleasant and good, others sad. One of the most tragic events happened on the morning of May 5, 1887. It was near time for the arrival of the eastbound passenger train. As usual at such times, a crowd of people had gathered on the station platform. Many of them were travelers, some were awaiting the arrival of friends or family members, and a goodly number just liked to see the trains and the people who arrived or departed.

In the crowd that bright spring morning was a young, obviously unhappy couple, Emma and Will Tompkins. The wife held a satchel in her hand, apparently waiting to depart on the expected train. The distraught husband was becoming more agitated by the moment as

Emma and Will Tompkins perished in a murder-suicide at the Bristol Depot.

he alternately verbally abused and pled with his wife not to leave him. His haggard appearance and bloodshot eyes, as well as her fatigued countenance, strongly indicated that their marital distress had extended through the previous night. A look of sheer panic seized the young man as the approaching train swung into the big bend just south of the state line. The shriek of the whistle drowned out the last words he shouted to her.

When the engine was only a few feet away, he seized his wife and, half dragging, half carrying her, jumped onto the tracks, directly in front of the swiftly rolling train. The scream of the poor doomed wife was joined by the screams of many of the women in the crowd who saw the frightful spectacle unfold before their eyes. Men stiffened and gasped. In seconds the couple was horridly crushed as the heavy engine and wheels passed over them. A lad who was standing on the other side of the tracks often told of how the woman's neck was directly across the right rail. Her head was completely severed and went bouncing toward him, and, of course, he went "bouncing" in the other direction! Folks on the platform watched in horror as the man's body was cut asunder at the waist.

Thus was the tragic ending of a bitter marital dispute.

Wedding Night Surprise

When Bristol was truly hell on the border, violence sometimes took a strange twist. Perhaps almost unique in the period was an event that occurred in the Virginia House Hotel on Front Street on June 16, 1886. On that day a young couple married in Marion, Virginia, and then came to Bristol on the train. They planned to begin their honeymoon in Bristol and then travel on to visit points of interest in and around Chattanooga, Tennessee.

They registered at the Virginia House and, as was usually done with newlyweds, were assigned to what many locals called the "Presidential Suite." This was the most lavishly decorated and best-furnished room in the hotel, and was so called because President U. S. Grant had once spent a night there.

Another train, arriving in Bristol about nine o'clock that night, brought three more Marion residents to Bristol—an angry-looking young man and his two male companions. It seems that this young man had also been a suitor of the new bride. As it turned out, near the end of the supposed double courtship, the young lady had more or less promised to marry the one who got to her first with the proper license. It seems that the other fellow was more fleet of foot or a better horseman. For when potential bride-groom number two arrived at the Smyth County courthouse, he found that his competitor had bought a license about an hour before. This threw him into a jealous rage. He stormed from the courthouse, enlisted the aid of two allies, and made plans for an exciting evening.

The Virginia House was the nearest hotel to the Bristol depot, so the trio went there first. Of course, the clerk, desiring to protect the privacy of his guests, refused to divulge any information about them. The clerk was knocked out cold by one of the ruffians, and the register was then scanned and the room number found. The men then rushed up the stairs and, using a hall bench as a ramrod, knocked the room door from its hinges with the first lunge against it.

The happy couple within was preparing to retire for the night when the door to their room came crashing inward. One can imagine their conster-nation as the three uninvited guests rushed in over the fallen door.

They had not long to fear or wonder what was happening. The bride-groom was knocked out cold and thrown behind the bridal bed. The jilted suitor then swooped up the half-undressed bride and threw her over his shoulder. Closely followed by his two allies, he then rushed down the stairs and out the front door. The party raced up Front Street and disappeared into the darkness. Somehow the kidnapped bride managed to escape. Just after daylight she, in somewhat of a dazed condition, wandered into Abingdon.

It is told that as soon as her new husband regained consciousness, he immediately left Bristol and was never heard from again. Suitor number two, apparently fearing the law, also fled and was never back in the area. The bride went home to her folks and remained a bitter woman for the rest of her long life.

Battle in East Hill Cemetery

Violence in early Bristol was not always confined to the rougher sec-tions of the downtown area. As surprising as it may be, a violent and bloody fight once took place at the side of an open grave in East Hill Cemetery. It all came about because of the marriage of a beautiful young Bristol woman to the boy who was her neighbor. Even though he lived next door, there was a world of difference between them.

There were seven daughters in the Leander Parks family. The youngest, Alvira, married her neighbor Ike Brewton. He was a ne'er-do-well who spent more time in the vice dens along notorious Front Street than he did at

— 160 —

Leander Parks engaged his son-in-law in a battle in East Hill Cemetery.

home. Working to provide for his young wife was certainly not his top priority. Indeed, when he did do an odd job now and then, his meager earnings were fast squandered on strong drink and local prostitutes. Occasionally, dire necessity forced the deprived wife to do menial tasks for more fortunate Bristolians.

In February 1887, this state of dire necessity reached the point where there was no fuel for fires or a morsel of food in the Brewton home. (Home was a drafty shack in Burson's Grove, a notorious slum west of Moore Street and between Scott and Mary streets.) In desperation, Alvira walked to the A. H. Bickley home, which was just north of the present First Christian Church, and asked for work. (The Bickleys had used her to do washings on several past occasions.) Mrs. Bickley did have laundry to be done, but she insisted that it was too cold outside to do any washing on that particular day. Alvira begged to go ahead in spite of the freezing temperature. Finally, Mrs. Bickley gave her consent.

All through that frigid day, Alvira washed and hung out clothes that froze stiff by the time they were pinned to the lines. Near dark she finished the job and received her pay. She was too tired and cold to walk the short distance to the D. A. Wheeler store to buy food. Instead, she went straight home. Chilled to the bone, she went to bed in a vain effort to get warm. There was no heat in the shack, and the bedcovers were inadequate.

When her drunken husband came home at about 2:00 A.M., he found Alvira to be very ill. She was in the rigors of a hard chill that was soon followed by a high fever. She begged Ike to go for Dr. Minor, who then lived on Lee Street. Ike, in a drunken stupor, paid no heed to her plea. Instead, he fell into bed and was soon fast asleep. It was near noon the next day before he sobered up.

By then, a neighbor who had learned of the problem had gone for Dr.

Minor. The doctor came as soon as he heard about the situation, but it was too late. Alvira had developed double pneumonia, a condition almost certain to be fatal in those days. Poor Alvira, weakened by toil and malnutrition, survived only to the third day after she became ill. (Pneumonia victims usually survived about seven days.)

"Oh, if only I had been called a few hours earlier," the sympathetic doctor lamented to Alvira's father. Leander Parks became enraged at that statement. It caused him to consider that his neglectful son-in-law was, in effect, guilty of murdering Alvira, and he vowed certain revenge.

Ike Brewton was downtown in a saloon when his wife died. Leander sent him word not to come back home while Alvira "lay a corpse" and not to show up at the funeral. "I'll take care of you if you do," he was told. Ike didn't return home.

But the funeral? Well, that's a different story.

The weather had gotten warmer by the time of Alvira's funeral, in East Hill Cemetery. A large crowd had gathered for the last rites, which were to be conducted by Maj. Z. L. Burson, who owned the shack where the poor woman had died.

About halfway through the sad service, Mrs. Parks nudged her husband and excitedly whispered, "Here comes the old scamp." Indeed, Ike Brewton was fast approaching up the path from the cemetery gate.

A stack of short boards lay near the grave, intended for use in covering Alvira's coffin. Leander lunged forward, seized a board, whirled around, and charged toward the despised son-in-law. Ike immediately stooped down and swooped up a loose brick that had fallen from a curb surrounding a family plot. The battle was on!

Before Ike could straighten up, Leander walloped him over the head with the board. The board slipped and nearly tore off Ike's left ear. Enraged and with blood flowing from his wounded head, Ike hurled the brick at Leander. It missed, but in jumping backward Leander lost his balance and fell flat on his back. In an instant, Ike, with pocketknife in hand, landed upon him.

Major Burson, realizing the imminent peril of his good friend (Leander), quickly dropped his open Bible, jerked off a boot (he always wore heavy half-shank boots), and, using the boot as a club, waded in on Ike. In moments Major Burson had knocked Ike senseless.

But the battle wasn't over. Leander jumped up and began stomping his fallen son-in-law. Ike's brother was in the crowd, and he immediately

The Parks-Brewton battle occurred near the location of this funeral in Bristol's historic East Hill Cemetery.

attacked Leander, knocked him out cold, and then turned upon Major Burson. The major was shoved backward in the frantic struggle that ensued, and he tumbled into the open grave. He was not alone. He still had hold of his attacker, and pulled him into the grave as he fell.

Now, Ike's brother had a horrible fear of graves. Realizing where he was, he lost all desire to fight, and with a mighty leap he landed back up among what few of the crowd remained (most of the people had fled). His troubles were not over. A sister of Alvira, an Amazon of a woman, collared him the instant he cleared the grave, and, using her fists, she soon had him prostrate and moaning on the ground.

It took considerable effort on the part of what few people were left to pull the rather corpulent Major Burson from the deep grave. Someone ran for Dr. H. T. Berry and Dr. M. M. Butler. (The latter was a veteran of the Civil War and was used to caring for battlefield casualties!) All participants survived the battle, but none of them ever forgot it, including the doctors who patched up the casualties. Both of the respected medical men often talked of it as long as they lived. Poor Alvira was buried that day— but much later than planned. The town constable had to summon several men to finish the task.

Leander Parks boldly threatened to settle with Ike Brewton at the first chance he got. Ike, though drunk most of the time, had enough sober mind to know that it would be a permanent settlement. Thus, knowing that he was in mortal danger, he fled Bristol, using freight trains as a means of travel.

Some twenty years later, a Bristolian who had known Ike well was visiting relatives in Springfield, Green County, Missouri. While there he was sure he saw Ike working as a laborer for the city street department. Though the man he thought was Ike was using a different name, it was noticed that he had a badly damaged left ear.

Today, Alvira Parks Brewton sleeps in an unmarked grave in Bristol's historic East Hill Cemetery. Thankfully, she is forever unaware that her death was the cause of a brutal fight in the sacred burying ground.

Bristol's Only Legal Hanging

In the days when Bristol was truly hell on the border, there were at least three lynchings, or illegal, mob-conducted hangings. It appears that there has been only one legal hanging in the city's history. Had not extra security precautions been exercised, a lynching might have circumvented the due process of law in that case.

According to Old Daddy Thomas, Annie Fogarty, then barely past her twelfth birthday, lived with her family in a little house by the railroad yards. The father of this girl hired a black man, Kit Leftwich, or Left-ridge—he seems to have been known by both names—to pick beans in the family garden. Mr. Fogarty and his wife then walked to Bristol to buy canning jars in which to preserve the bountiful bean crop. Annie, the young daughter, was in school and was not expected home until well after the return of her parents. However, for some reason, school was dismissed early that day, and Annie arrived home well ahead of her parents.

Kit had worked for her father several times before, so Annie thought nothing of finding him laboring in the garden that day. Seeing her home alone must have caused Kit to quickly concoct his devious plan. He called to her, saying that he was thirsty, and asked if she would please bring him a drink of

Annie Fogarty was the cause of Bristol's only legal hanging.

fresh water. The kind girl drew a bucket of cool water from the well and, along with a tin cup, took it to him.

Kit took a long drink, and as Annie turned to go back to the house, he grabbed her and dragged the screaming girl into a thicket at the backside of the garden. There, waving a knife in her face, he threatened to kill her if she did not cease her screaming and submit to him. Then he attempted to rape her.

Kit might have accomplished his purpose if one of Annie's playmates, who had promised to come back as soon as she went home and put up her books, had not returned and heard the struggle in the thicket. She ran to a nearby house, where only an old woman was at home. The aged lady grabbed a pistol from somewhere near her bed (many people kept pistols under their pillows in those days) and hastened as fast as she could toward the commotion, firing as she went. Whether she fired as a means of frightening the man or out of pure fright on her part is not known, though her gun was empty by the time she reached the garden, and the shots caused Kit to release his victim and flee across the road, down into the freight yard.

The sheriff was sent for, as was Dr. W. B. St. John. Before either arrived, Capt. Joseph W. Owen, one of Mosby's Rangers during the Civil War, came riding along the road, returning from his upper farm. Captain Owen was always loaded for bear, carrying two or three pistols and usually a suitable knife or two. That day his personal arsenal came in handy.

Once informed of the situation, Captain Owen quickly dismounted and, with pistol in hand, proceeded to search the freight yard for the criminal. He finally found Kit crouching in a dark corner of an empty freight car. Captain Owen immediately put Kit under citizen's arrest. There was not another man in the area to help bring the culprit in, so Captain Owen gave one of his pistols to Maggie Babcock, the girl who had come to visit Annie Fogarty. With her aid he marched the arrested man to the local jail.

Before he gave her the gun, Captain Owen tried to give Maggie a crash course in its use, but the girl quickly informed him that she already knew all about them. To prove her claim, she raised the pistol and shot an apple from a nearby tree. Her prowess with a pistol impressed Captain Owen and likely helped to keep Kit in line. Maggie Babcock never forgot, nor allowed anyone else to forget, that she had served as a deputy sheriff when she was only twelve years old.

Word quickly spread of the detestable crime, and, as expected, a mob began to form, intent upon administering swift frontier justice. However, Judge William F. Rhea managed to quell the enraged citizens by promising them that he would see that Kit Leftwich would "stand on the gallows" in less than three months. Nevertheless, heavy guard was placed at the jail that night. The security was needed, for around midnight there was an attempt to storm the jail, but the attackers were repelled by the guards.

Several prominent Bristolians sat on the grand jury that was soon assembled. These included William H. Trammell, one of the earliest pioneer settlers of the town; H. M. Millard, long a city official; and Charles F. Gauthier, who would later become the first postmaster of Bristol, Virginia. Among the witnesses were Annie Fogarty, the victim; Dr. W. B. St. John, the medical examiner; and J. V. Gast. The grand jury rendered an indictment in which it was stated that "Kit Leftwich did violently and feloniously ravish and carnally, and against her will, and by force did know the said Annie Fogarty."

The wheels of justice turned rapidly, so that on the morning of September 9, 1895, the summoning of a jury began. Due to much local prejudice, it was decided that an impartial jury could not be assembled from Bristol residents. Consequently, a jury was summoned from the county. A review of the names indicates that most of this jury came from the upper-Holston Valley area.

The court assigned Col. Abram Fulkerson and John S. Ashworth counsel for the defendant. Certainly, it could never be said that Kit Leftwich did not have competent legal defense. Both lawyers were local legal giants. Indeed, Colonel Fulkerson had served in the U.S. Congress.

Most of the actual trial was held on September 10, 1895. That night the prisoner was returned to the well-guarded jail and the jury was put in custody of the town constable.

The trial was concluded soon after nine o'clock on the following morning. A little later a hushed courtroom heard the jury foreman, J. Stanton King, read the verdict: "We, the jury, find the defendant not guilty as charged [he had been charged with actual rape], but do find him guilty of an attempt to commit the offense as charged, and fix his punishment as death by hanging."

The prisoner was given a chance to speak but said nothing. Judge Rhea ordered the prisoner to stand before the bench, for sentencing. The original handwritten sentence still survives. It reads as follows:

Therefore, the judgement of this court is that you be safely kept and confined by the officers of this court until the 11th day of October 1895 and further judgement of this court is that you be hanged by the neck until you are dead and that execution of this judgement upon you be made and done by the Sergeant of this City on Friday the 11th day of October next between the hours of ten o'clock in the forenoon and two o'clock in the afternoon of the same day, as provided by the law of this state, at the legal place of execution, and may God have mercy on your soul.

Judge Rhea then ordered Sgt. John H. Gose (the town constable) to transport the prisoner, with the aid of one guard, to Lynchburg, Virginia, for safekeeping, and to deliver him back to Bristol in suitable time for the hanging. Sergeant Gose, who had been instructed on the art of execution in Lynchburg and Norfolk began the search for a suitable rope, immediately after his return to Bristol.

A news note in the *Bristol Courier* dated September 29, 1895, tells that the rope had arrived in town from a firm in Cincinnati, Ohio. The article further states that "it was made for the job, free from knots and lumps that might cause it to hang, and has been coated with a slippery substance to cause the noose to draw without friction." Instructions for its use were enclosed in the box in which the rope had been shipped, and the noose was already formed.

The prisoner was brought back to Bristol on the night train from Lynchburg, arriving there a little before daylight on the day of execution. In spite of the predawn arrival, a large crowd had gathered at the depot to witness the return of the condemned man.

The morning dawned a bit on the cool side but it was very bright, as only early October days can be. The scaffold had been erected near the gate of the burying ground located near the intersection of present Oakview and Buckner streets. It was made of rough oak lumber from a sawmill that then operated just south of the present railroad overpass on Piedmont Street. It was built by Will Graham, a local carpenter. The grave had been dug on the afternoon of October 10.

Annie Fogarty's father was allowed to drive the wagon that transported the prisoner from downtown Bristol to the place of execution. Schools were closed "so that the pupils might view the awful end of sin and crime." Most businesses closed for the event. An endless procession of people moved from the town up to the "place." By 10:00 A.M., Flat Hollow (Rice Terrace section) was a "vast sea of humanity," so described by *The Bristol News*. Somewhere in the crowd stood Annie Fogarty and her playmate who had gone for help on the day of the attempted rape.

When the wagon bearing the prisoner arrived, a deep hush fell over what had been a rather noisy crowd. That hush continued as Kit Leftwich, with steady steps, was led up the crude stairs leading to the high gallows. Standing on the trapdoor through which he would plunge to his death, he still maintained the surprising calmness that had marked him since the time of sentencing. The open grave and coffin nearby were well within his sight but he never looked toward them. He declined the offer of a final statement. The hood and noose were then applied. At about 10:30 A.M., Sergeant Gose applied the ax to the rope holding the trapdoor. Kit Leftwich plunged to his death.

Old Daddy Thomas, who said he was "standing as close as I could get," told that when Leftwich's neck broke there was a sound "like the crack of a rifle." At that sound, "a heap of the women and children fainted like flies and some took off running back towardge town." Long before noon, the executed man was buried, but there was "not a flower on his grave."

On October 15, 1895, John H. Gose, the town constable, filed his final report of Bristol's only legal hanging. It states, "I hereby certify that the foregoing sentence upon Kit Leftwich was executed by me in the manner and at the time therein directed."

The remains of Kit Leftwich were moved soon after 1900 to the Citizen's Cemetery at the end of Piedmont Street. They remain there today, in an unknown and unmarked grave.

Though the hanging took place over a hundred years ago, a grim reminder of it still remains. The noose, which was long kept in the Bristol, Virginia, courthouse, was recently given to the Bristol Historical Association. It is now kept with the many relics belonging to that association.

The Murder of Fred Rust

One of the most sensational murders ever to be recorded in Bristol occurred shortly after midnight on January 21, 1897. This murder caused one of the most unusual situations ever known in Bristol—the jailing of a baby.

Fred Rust was not liked much by anyone who knew him. In fact, he was strongly disliked by most Bristolians, largely because his extreme cruelty to his family was well-known. Too, his hostile and overbearing nature caused him to be in frequent difficulties with acquaintances and neighbors.

Fred's cruelty to his wife and children was so severe that they dreaded to see him come home. Seldom was there an easy moment when he was with them. More to escape than anything, the oldest daughter, then barely fifteen years old, eloped and married a man twice her age. Knowing how unreasonable Fred could be, especially when he had been drinking, the family doubly feared his homecoming on the day of the elopement. They knew he would likely heap his fury upon the person who told him what had happened.

Late that day, after drinking for a while at a local saloon, Fred Rust finally arrived at the humble rented house on Second Taylor Street where he and his family lived. It was not long before he missed Isabel (the girl who had eloped) and demanded to know where she was. The family, cringing in fear, remained silent. Finally, he singled out Charles, the ten-year-old son, whom he always seemed to dislike. He grabbed the quaking boy by his long hair, backed him against a wall, and began banging the boy's head mercilessly, threatening to kill him if he did not reveal Isabel's whereabouts.

Dumb with terror, Charles remained silent. Enraged and insane with fury, Fred then threw him to the floor and began to brutally kick and stomp him, breaking two or three of the helpless boy's ribs. It was then that the mother, fearing that Fred would actually kill their son, rushed in and screamed out to her husband that Isabel had eloped. Fred then turned his fury upon his wife, finally knocking her unconscious.

When she slowly came to an hour or so later, Fred, overcome by the liquor he had consumed before he came home, had fallen into bed and was sound asleep. The children remained huddled around Charles, who screamed in agony every time he moved.

Hours later, after the children had been fed and put to bed, including the wounded Charles, the light was finally extinguished. But there was no sleep for Mrs. Rust. She began a slow walk through the darkened rooms, wrestling with a decision she knew she had to make. Occasionally, Charles, moving in his troubled sleep, cried out in pain. That helped her to reach her final conclusion.

She could not go on in such a situation. She feared for her life and more so for the lives and well-being of her children. For years, life had been a living hell, and she felt that she could bear no more. She concluded that there was no relief other than in what she felt she must do.

Time and again she had appealed to local law officers. Fred had been jailed several times, but he was always released within a few days. He would come home meaner than ever, sparing none of the family from his angry vengeance. Mrs. Rust fully believed that if any relief were to be had it, would have to come by her own hand.

Near midnight, a full moon rose over Cemetery Hill, back of her home, filling the little cottage with an eerie light. About that time her firm decision was made. Quietly she stepped onto the back porch, picked up an ax, and returned to the room where her husband was soundly sleeping. He lay flat on his back, snoring away. She raised the ax high, and with one firm, sure lick, she split his head asunder. Fred Rust would never again torment his family or anyone else.

Mrs. Rust quietly closed and locked the door of his room and, being so relieved of danger, immediately cast her weary body into bed with one of the children, sleeping soundly until daylight. Upon awaking, she called out to the children and told them to go to the home of their grandmother, some two or three blocks away. The oldest son (Isabel's twin) was told to first go for Dr. W. B. St. John to attend to the wounded son, Charles.

Then, carrying her nursing baby, Stephen, who was about one year old, she went to the local police and gave a full confession to the crime. She feared that her oldest son, who had publicly stated that he would kill his father if the abuse continued, would be suspected and arrested once the crime was known. Taking her word for it, the police chief arrested her and placed her in the city jail. There was nothing to do but to put the baby with her. On old jail records may be found the following notation: "Sarah Rust placed in jail to be indicted for murder. Baby Stephen placed in jail, uncharged."

Well, if Sarah Rust was ever indicted or tried for murder, there is no record of it either in Bristol or Abingdon, Virginia. The town knew the situation, as did the local officers of the law. Perhaps the sympathy of all concerned caused poor Sarah to be set free without official formalities. My informant of long ago did not seem to know what had happened.

A fragment of a newspaper article published two days after the murder mentions that Mrs. Rust's grandfather had killed William King Hesikell, High Sheriff of Washington County, Virginia, several years before she murdered her husband.

It is known that she and the children later moved to Indiana and then to Hardin County, Ohio. Stephen, the baby who was jailed with his mother, later settled in or near Camdenton, Missouri. He died there a few years ago at the age of ninety-two. As far as can be determined, he was the only baby ever jailed in Bristol.

Man/Woman Fight on Front Street

A man-to-man fight on Bristol's notorious Front Street was almost a daily occurrence. So common were such altercations that they commanded little attention and did not cause much excited comment. A man-to-woman fight was a bit uncommon, even in a town where the uncommon was very common! When such a fight did occur, it caused quite a stir among local citizens and was talked of for years.

Edward Stanley had come to Bristol from Lynchburg, Virginia, as an engineer on the Virginia and Tennessee Railroad. After settling here, he engaged in various business pursuits, including tobacco processing, hotel keeping, and the operation of a Front Street pool hall (called ten-pin alleys in those days). His nature was such that he often had difficulties with those he associated with. Often these difficulties ended in actual battles. It was nothing unusual for him to come to blows with some local man over the slightest offense or disagreement. Though a veteran of many a hostile engagement with men of the town, he is best known and remembered for his one fight with a woman.

One day in the early spring of 1887, Stanley and two or three of his friends were engaged in a lively card game inside his establishment, when a commotion in the street caught their attention. It was found that three young boys were chasing Stanley's milk cow along the street, just for fun. (Cows ran loose in the town at that time.)

This enraged Stanley. He left the card game and chased the boys. The two older ones outran the angry man, but little Tommy Wells was caught. Using a riding crop that he had grabbed when he left the game,

Edward Stanley whipped a woman on Bristol's notorious Front Street.

Stanley inflicted a severe beating upon the frightened little boy. When finally released, Tommy ran straight home and told his mother.

Stanley, thinking the matter had ended, went back to his game. His peace was of short duration.

In no time, Elsie Wells, the boy's mother, came running down Front Street "like an old flogging hen," as one bystander expressed it. She carried a brick in each hand, and it was clear that she was ready to use them.

At her call, one of Stanley's friends appeared at the door of the pool hall. Glaring at him, she yelled out, "Tell that damned old blackhearted son-of-a-bitch to come out here and take it like a man."

Hearing what she had said, Stanley became enraged again. He shoved his friend aside and stood defiantly in the doorway.

Elsie Wells lost not a moment in hurling one brick at him, quickly followed by the other. Brick number one missed him but broke a side light of the doorway. Stanley dodged brick number two, which sailed past him and broke a hanging lamp that happened to be in line with the door.

Seeing that the woman had exhausted her ammunition, Stanley sprang toward her, and she toward him. They crashed together, fell in the street, and went into what a bystander called "a rolling wildcat fight."

Womanlike, Elsie Wells grabbed for his hair. Alas, he had none—he was slick bald. She then tried to bite off an ear, hammering him in the eyes all the while.

Stanley jumped up and, holding her by the hair of her head, swung her around and around while beating her with his riding crop. (Somehow he had managed to hold on to it all through the violent fight.) She later testified that he raised whelps on her back, hips, and neck. As he was whipping her, she was wildly kicking him on the shins.

Reinforcements were coming! Little Tommy Wells, who had followed his mother back to Stanley's place, saw what was going on, ran back home, and awakened his father. Lige Wells was a night worker in the railroad yards and thus was a day sleeper. In no time, someone in the crowd of onlookers yelled out, "Lige Wells is a-comin' and all hell is gonna break loose!" Indeed, Lige Wells was charging down Front Street like an enraged bull, swinging a big club in the air as he came.

Lige was a giant of a man, all muscle and strong as an ox. As Old Daddy Thomas used to say of him, "He warn't afeared of the Devil, and would have fit [fought] him even if he'd had to a done it in the middle of tarment [torment—hell]."

Seeing Lige coming, Stanley quickly released Elsie and rushed forth to meet the greater foe. They clashed head-on near the south bend of Beaver Creek. One mighty blow from that big club put Stanley out cold on the ground. Lige dragged him a few feet and threw him into Beaver Creek. The battle over, he then went to see about his wounded wife, who, as he later told it, "was wandering around sort of addled, not knowing where she was or what was going on."

Perhaps the cold waters of Beaver Creek revived Edward Stanley. Later that day he sneaked back to his place of business, and he, too, was "sort of addled" for several hours.

Not only were there three trials for assault, but the Wellses had local attorney A. H. Blanchard file suit against Edward Stanley, seeking three thousand dollars in damages. A jury found for the plaintiffs but reduced the claim to seventy-five dollars.

Such was life on Front Street when Bristol was truly hell on the border.

Baby Victims of Violence

In the early days, crowds always gathered at the Bristol depots (there were two then) to watch the arrival and departure of the trains. To see the steam-powered trains come huffing and puffing to a grinding halt and then see them depart with equal flourish was exciting to many of the town's citizens. There was one memorable occasion at the Virginia depot when there was more than the usual excitement, and the train was still more than fifteen minutes away.

On that balmy day in late April 1887, a larger-than-usual crowd had gathered to see the arrival of the southbound train. Before the distant and faint wail of the train's whistle was heard, a mongrel dog came trotting down the station platform.

Women began to scream, two or three fainted, and strong men gasped in horror. No, the dog was not that much feared; wandering dogs were commonly seen in downtown Bristol, and few people feared them. What brought on the mass consternation was that the dog was carrying the upper part of a baby's body in its mouth.

The other half of the mangled body was soon found near the end of the railroad yard. Apparently someone had placed the unclothed newborn across a rail.

It is likely that the freight train which preceded the passenger cars by about an hour had severed the body. Engineers had but little view of the rails in those days and could have easily passed over the body without knowing what had happened.

Though the mystery was never solved, locals strongly believed that the baby had been born in one of the several brothels that then flourished in Bristol.

When the foundation trench for a new building for King College was being dug about 1872 (present site of King Pharmaceuticals), the body of a baby was found in a shallow grave. It had been buried only a few days. It appeared that the baby's skull had been fractured by a blunt instrument, likely a hammer.

As late as July 1902, a dead baby was found in a coal car parked in the Knoxville, Tennessee, freight yard. The car had been sitting there only a few minutes when the ghastly discovery was made, and no strangers had been seen in the yard. The car had been attached in Bristol and there had been no opportunity for the baby to be placed on the coal car between the two cities. It was strongly suspected that this was another Bristol brothel baby. If the baby was tossed alive atop the coal—and there was every indication that it had been—it likely died from exposure to the blazing summer sun.

Courthouse Battle

Even the local halls of justice were not free from the violence which was part of daily life in pre-1900 Bristol. In those days there were no sophisticated metal detectors set up at courtroom doors to protect contenders in trials from anyone who might be intent upon administering their own form of speedy justice. In Bristol, it was generally conceded that likely half of those in attendance at court sessions were armed—and that included the judge, jury, and participating lawyers.

In 1898, a bitter and hard-fought campaign was waged in Virginia's Ninth Congressional District. The contenders were Gen. James A. Walker, Republican, of Wytheville and Judge William F. Rhea, Democrat, of Bristol. General Walker, somewhat of a Civil War hero and former lieutenant governor of Virginia, had been elected to Congress in 1894 and 1896. The present campaign had been marked with violence, most often between followers of the two, but in Gate City Walker and Rhea had come to blows on the speaker's platform. When the speaking was held at Lebanon in Russell County, the county sheriff had to sit with them on the platform to preserve peace.

Judge Rhea won the election by 744 votes. General Walker immediately filed a lawsuit contesting the result and charging that there had been widespread election fraud. Evidence later came to light that there indeed had been much deliberate, coldly calculated, deceptive, and criminal fraud practiced throughout the Ninth District.

Just before General Walker left Wytheville for Bristol to take and give depositions in the case, he received two letters, one signed by a prominent Bristol resident and the other unsigned. Both warned him that a plot was under way to murder him while he was in Bristol. One named the man who was set to do the shooting. The plan was to get him angry, which they knew would not be hard to do, then instigate a general scrimmage, during which the general was to be shot, supposedly in self-defense. Upon receiving these warnings, General Walker better armed himself and went on to Bristol.

The taking of depositions commenced in the jury room of the old Bristol, Virginia, courthouse on March 11, 1899. The room was packed to capacity long before the depositions began. The crowd included many strong supporters of both men. W. S. Hamilton, a local lawyer, represented Rhea, while General Walker served for himself. Soon after the depositions began, Walker became highly irritated by Hamilton's browbeating of witnesses. Finally, he told Judge Rhea that he would refuse to proceed unless Rhea replaced that "damned drunken bully Hamilton."

Hamilton went into a rage; he swore loudly, then pulled out a knife and started to rise from his chair, all the while vowing to "cut Walker's damned throat." Instantly, General Walker whipped out a small derringer from his hip pocket and shot Hamilton in the stomach. The wounded man fell back into his chair. Thinking he was mortally wounded, he begged a friend who had sprung to his side to "take care of my widow and orphans." (Actually he was not mortally wounded and lived many years after the battle.)

Even as Hamilton thought he was dying, the battle raged on. General Walker threw the smoking derringer to the floor and quickly reached under his coat. George E. Davis, Judge Rhea's law clerk, saw the action on Walker's part, drew a pistol, and shot the general twice. One shot injured Walker's right shoulder so that his arm dropped, useless, to his side. Walker later stated that he had been reaching for a fully loaded .44-caliber pistol, and that if he could have gotten it he would have "cleaned out the whole shebang!"

One of Walker's close friends then jerked out a pistol and aimed for

Davis's head, but for some reason he could never explain, he did not fire a shot. He later confided to a friend that he had meant to get Davis and that Judge Rhea would have been next.

The wounded and bleeding General Walker was carried by several friends to the nearby Palace Hotel (later known as the St. Lawrence), and Dr. W. K. Vance was quickly summoned.

The next day Walker's daughter arrived from Wytheville, and she kindly cared for him throughout the many anxious days which followed. As the general lay critically wounded, many of his friends took up guard in the hotel lobby. One of them later stated that all of them were loaded for bear and fully intended to make sure that no one could slip through and finish the job. Even the daughter made sure that she had two loaded pistols within easy reach.

After several days, General Walker showed considerable improvement and finally was able to be moved to his home in Wytheville. He was carried to the train by several of his friends, and they were surrounded by others of the well-armed group. Four of these men rode in the baggage car with Walker to make sure that he safely reached his home.

Three trials resulted from this courthouse battle: the trial of General Walker for shooting W. S. Hamilton, the trial of George E. Davis for shooting Walker, and a civil suit filed by Hamilton, seeking damages for his injury.

Strangely, some of the leading legal giants of the area, though strong Democrats, took up the defense of General Walker, among them Capt. J. H. Wood and David F. Bailey of Bristol, as well as the noted Daniel Trigg of Abingdon. Knowing that a fair jury could not be found among local citizens, these lawyers succeeded in having the jury made up of men from Montgomery County. Walker's trial dragged on for several days. At its conclusion the jury rendered a verdict of not guilty.

General Walker was never well after the courtroom battle, though he had recovered sufficiently to challenge Judge Rhea in the 1900 election. Again he was defeated. He died in 1901, as he was making preparations to go to Washington for a consultation with Theodore Roosevelt.

After serving in Congress, Judge Rhea served in a state position at Richmond, Virginia, where he died on March 23, 1931.

Murder with Long-Lasting Effect

It is a clear and demonstrable fact that murders often have long-lasting effects, perhaps enduring through several generations of the victim's descendants. Bristol certainly long had a visible reminder of a brutal murder that occurred here in 1866. This living reminder became a legend in his own time.

Somewhere in a long-lost and unmarked grave in Bristol's historic East Hill Cemetery sleeps William "Pat" Ryan, Sr. He rests far from his native homeland. He was born in Limerick County, Ireland, about 1833, a son of Timothy and Mary Ryan. Shortly before he was twenty years old, he left the beautiful Emerald Isle and sailed to America, landing in the port of Philadelphia. For several years he worked as a laborer in that thriving city.

On December 8, 1853, he applied for U.S. citizenship, which was granted May 18, 1856. Soon thereafter he left Philadelphia and came to Estillville (now Gate City), Scott County, Virginia.

How did a stranger in a strange land find his way to such a remote location as Estillville then was? In those days merchants from Western Virginia and East Tennessee hauled much of their merchandise from New York, Philadelphia, and Baltimore. It has been told that Pat Ryan hired on as a wagon hand for a Scott County merchant, likely Mr. H. S. Kane. Evidently the beautiful hills and valleys of Scott County and the kind and friendly people who inhabited them appealed to the young Irish immigrant, for after his first haul here he never returned to Philadelphia. It appears that a young lady of the area, Matilda "Tildey" Coley, especially fascinated him. She was born in 1839 in Guilford County, North Carolina, a daughter of William and Abby Coley. Pat married her on June 3, 1858.

Soon after their wedding, Pat Ryan and his wife, Matilda Coley Ryan, having heard of the many opportunities which awaited the young and energetic in the new town of Bristol, Tennessee/Virginia, decided to move to that "promised land" on the border. For Pat it was a fatal decision—it would cost him his life.

The Civil War soon ravaged the land. Pat and Tildey suffered much war-wrought hardships along with their fellow Bristolians. The years immediately following the close of that lamentable conflict brought even greater suffering. By then the Ryans had children to provide for. In desperation, Pat took whatever work he could find in order to put bread on the family table.

In spite of the severe economic conditions of the time, brothels were flourishing in the wild and wooly town of Bristol. Many of the clients wanted whiskey along with the usual offerings of such places. Pat Ryan became the delivery person for Bosang's Saloon, which was then located on notorious Front Street and was the chief caterer to the town's brothels.

One small brothel was then operating in a home on upper Washington Street. It was called a three-stall operation by the locals because only three women were working there. Pat was called upon to make a delivery to the three-stall house almost every night of the week. His route to this place was well-known. He picked up the whiskey at Bosang's Saloon, then crossed the depot lot to Washington Street and proceeded along the "elite" section of that street (Main Street to the Beaver Creek crossing), then passed on to the little cottage that served as a brothel.

According to Old Daddy Thomas, Henry Liston had come to Bristol from Knoxville, working as a railroad laborer. He lost his job and soon afterward became a drunken street bum. He always needed money. He well knew that Pat Ryan collected pay from three or four brothels before returning to Bosang's saloon. So Liston conceived a plan which he thought would yield him enough money for several days of feasting and drinking.

Liston broke into E. H. Seneker's store on the northwest corner of what is now State and Lee streets and stole one of that merchant's pistols. He knew that Seneker kept several pistols around the store to be handily reached in case of an attempted robbery. Thus armed, Liston hastened up to Washington Street. There was a narrow footbridge over Beaver Creek at the Washington Street crossing. (Vehicles had to ford the stream.) At the south end of that bridge was a huge sycamore tree. Liston concealed himself behind that tree and waited.

He did not have to wait long. Pat Ryan, his rounds made and money collected, soon came across the bridge, merrily whistling as he headed toward home and bed. Reaching the big sycamore, he was suddenly confronted by the gun-wielding Henry Liston, who demanded his money. Almost automatically, Pat swung out with his big fist, knocking Liston to the ground. At the same time, Pat called Liston by name.

The would-be robber, realizing he was recognized, and expecting more severe resistance from his intended victim, opened fire with the stolen pistol. Pat, shot through the head, crumpled to the ground and died almost instantly.

A resident of the area heard the shots and ran to the scene. He saw Liston, pistol still in hand, running toward the railroad yard. He immediately notified the town constable, who captured Liston a little later, as the murderer was climbing into a boxcar of a departing freight train. Before dawn

Liston gave a full confession to the crime, stating the details.

About noon the next day, the town constable and a deputy, fearing a lynching, started on foot with the prisoner to the more secure jail in Abingdon, Virginia. Somewhere on the Mulberry Grove Plantation (present industrial-park area near Wallace), Liston managed to break free—he was being led by a rope tied around his waist—and flee into a nearby wooded area. He was never recaptured.

The constable and deputy fired several shots at the fleeing prisoner and felt sure that he was hit one or more times. Several years later, the skeleton of a man was found in a heavily wooded section of nearby Walker's Mountain. It was strongly believed that the remains were those of Henry Liston.

Little Pat Ryan and How He Grew

The murder of Pat Ryan left his widow and family destitute. She had no means of providing for her orphans. (All fatherless children were called orphans in those days.)

Those were the days when there were no social services to look after those in need. Consequently, the bereaved family suffered much hardship. Continual hunger was their lot for many years.

Among the suffering children was Pat, the namesake of his father. He later told that as a small child he often wandered around the town, searching for garbage cans where he might find scraps of discarded food. Even so, he was always hungry.

When Little Pat was fourteen, he married a twelve-year-old neighbor girl, Anna Augusta Atkins, a native of Tennessee. In time they became the parents of twelve children. (Only eight were still living by the time of the 1910 census.)

For several years after his wedding, Pat was able to make a fairly good living. Even during those good years with sufficient food on the table, he still imagined himself to be starving and could never get enough. True, this supposed hunger was mental, a craving left over from a deprived childhood, but it sought a real physical satisfaction.

Naturally, this constant gorging on food caused Little Pat to grow larger and larger, so large that he finally had to have his clothes special made. He reached four hundred pounds, then four hundred and fifty, and finally five hundred. Still he continued to expand. An old-timer once told of seeing Pat use two regular chairs upon which to sit. His bed had to be reinforced (large blocks of wood were placed midway under the rails), and still it sagged under his tremendous weight.

Strangely, even after he became corpulent to a marked degree, locals still continued to call him "Little" Pat Ryan, much to the amusement of acquaintances and strangers alike. In time he became a measure of size for the town. That is, folks would say something is as large or as heavy as Pat Ryan. There are people living in Bristol today who remember hearing such expressions.

Of course, he could not work at regular jobs. Making a living soon became a problem for him. Once, he tried operating a restaurant on Bristol's notorious Front Street, but he literally ate up all the profits, causing the venture to fail. In later years he turned to trading watches in order to make a living.

He often went to the nearest restaurant and ordered food by the multiple plates full. Some local restaurant operators dreaded to see him coming, for more than once chairs had given way under him. There were instances when tables had broken as he leaned upon them.

Pat was long a familiar sight in Bristol. He would waddle along the streets, usually with a watch in hand, trying to sell or trade it to whoever he might meet. His large pockets held more. Folks said he was a walking jewelry store. He tried his hand at watch repair but did not succeed because his hands were too large for such tedious work.

After a day on the streets about town, Little Pat would waddle up to his home on Haddon Street. Worn out, he would fall into bed as soon as supper was finished. Family members later told that he usually slept the night through in the position he had assumed when slumping into bed, since it was too much effort to turn over.

When walking became a problem for him, Little Pat ceased his strolling about on the streets. Instead, he sat on a low wall above the train depot at the junction of State and Washington streets. There he would spend the day, hoping that buyers and traders would come to him, and many did.

While Pat traded watches, trying to make a meager living, his wife tried to help out by taking in boarders and doing washing and ironing for others.

Finally, he became so fat and short of breath that he could not walk down to his trading place; indeed, he was all but bedfast. Through the efforts of Father Myer of St. Ann's Catholic Church, Little Pat was admitted to a Catholic institution in Richmond, Virginia.

The late Ernest Emmert remembered seeing him placed on the train

Pat Ryan became a legend in his own time. This trick photo was likely made by Philip Painter.

for the trip to Richmond. Of course, Little Pat was too large to sit in a regular passenger seat. Instead he was placed on a wooden bench that had served in front of a local store as a seat for loafers. Mr. Emmert told that it took as many men as could get around it to lift the bench, with Little Pat on it, onto a freight wagon. The wagon was then rolled along the station platform, and Little Pat, with much difficulty, raised a large but weak hand to wave to the crowd which had gathered to see him depart. He would never see Bristol again.

After a year or two in Richmond, Little Pat's health had improved to the point where he could be cared for in a private home. It was then that he was taken to the home of a daughter who lived in Damascus, Virginia. He died there in 1927.

In death he was still a problem—a casket could not be found big enough for his body. Finally, a local merchant came forth with a piano box that had been kept in the attic of his store. Little Pat Ryan was buried in this box in the Mock Cemetery at Damascus.

This big, big man was long a constant reminder of the lasting effect of an early Bristol murder. Indeed, he was part of those events that truly made Bristol hell on the border.

The Brutal Lynching of Robert Clark

On the bright but rather cool morning of December 15, 1891, Andy Crusenberry loaded up his wagon with cookstove and wood and started into Bristol. He hoped to make a few sales so that he might have a little extra Christmas money. He was rearing three orphaned grandchildren and wanted to be able to buy them some trinkets to brighten up their holiday celebration. His route into town led down Moore Street.

As he was crossing Mary Street, he was startled by a clearly angry man, who ran alongside the wagon and stopped the team. Thinking the man was after him, Andy grabbed a stick of his wood, preparing for battle. The man quickly explained that he needed Andy's trace chains and promised to buy him another set in "just a little bit." Hearing a commotion some distance behind the wagon, the still-startled driver looked around to see four other men clutching a frightened but resisting black man.

Shortly, the trace chains were taken from the wagon and team. The man ran back to his group with them and soon had them around the neck of the intended victim. The brutal lynching of Robert Clark was under way. What followed was a display of horrible, blood-chilling brutality, seldom equaled even in those days when Bristol was indeed a bit of hell on the border.

What inspired this brutal lynching? It was not an aggressive action by Robert Clark but was simply a lewd suggestion.

Clark had the reputation of being one of the most capable handymen in the town. On that particular December day, he had been engaged by Charles Davis to apply a new lock on Davis's smokehouse door. Clark had often worked for Davis, usually doing yard and garden work at Davis's home, on Mary Street.

As Clark worked, Mrs. Davis was at home alone; her husband had gone across the street to play cards with a neighbor, Nick Dettor (or sometimes Detter). Flem Luttrell, Frank Nave, and Stephen Collin, friends and neighbors of the two, had also come to join in the game.

When Clark finished the lock job, he called Mrs. Davis to come out and see if the work pleased her. She came, and as he demonstrated how well the lock was working, he suddenly looked straight at her and suggested that they go into the smokehouse and "play" a while.

Horrified, Mrs. Davis fled across the street to the Dettor house, screaming out that Clark was trying to rape her. The men jumped up from their card table and, boiling with anger, ran over to the backyard of the Davis home.

Meanwhile, Robert Clark, sensing that he was in mortal danger, had concealed himself under the smokehouse. The family dog sniffed him out and was barking at the hole Clark had crawled through to get under the little building.

In moments, the angry men had dragged Clark from his hiding place and had started down Mary Street with him. It was then that they came upon Andy Crusenberry and took the trace chains from his team.

What followed may best be told from the wording of the indictment that was soon entered against Charles Davis and his friends.

The jurors of the grand jury, empaneled and sworn in and for the body of the City of Bristol, in the State of Virginia and upon their oath present that Charles Davis, Nick Dettor, Flem Luttrell, Frank Nave and Stephen Collin on the 15th day of December in the year of Christ, 1891, in the City of Bristol, did with force and arms in and upon the body of Robert Clark, feloniously, willfully, deliberately, premeditatedly and of their malice and aforethought, make an assault, and with certain trace chains, in their hands, did put and fasten around the neck of said Robert Clark, and then and there did hang him to a tree, of which said hanging by neck, he there instantly died, thus did they murder against the peace and dignity of the Commonwealth of Virginia.

And that afore said hanging they, the accused, did with their hands, feet, clubs, chains, and stones, did strike, beat, drag, stomp, and kick in and upon the head, breast, legs, back, belly, sides, neck, and other parts of the body of the said Robert Clark, and did then and there cast and throw him down with great force and violence, and doing unto him as afore stated, in such a manner as would have been fatal to him.

Robert Clark had been strung up from a low limb of an oak tree that stood on the northwest corner of Wood and Mary streets. Several witnesses to the crime later expressed the opinion that he was dead before being hanged, the victim of the cruel beatings as told in the indictment.

Members of Clark's family were afraid to venture out to bury the body. He was left hanging until almost dark, when the town constable and a few other men went up to the site, took the body down, and conveyed it to the Flat Hollow Cemetery (near the corner of Oakview and Buckner streets). The actual burial was done by lantern light.

Notwithstanding many witnesses who testified in the resultant trial for the brutal crime, all the guilty men, by some quirk of justice, were cleared of the first-degree murder charges lodged against them. Though free from the penalty of law, they were not free from an adverse public opinion. Most of them, under severe censure from their fellow citizens, soon left Bristol.

When the Flat Hollow Cemetery was moved to the end of Piedmont Street around 1900, Robert Clark's skeleton was found with the hanging chain still in place. It was left on when he was reburied.

Eye for an Eye

There were instances in the early days of Bristol when even innocent children were victims of brutal violence.

In late 1883, two women of the rather pronounced shady type rented a cottage in Burson's Grove. The house stood near the intersection of what is now Quarry and Piedmont streets. They placed a red light in the window—a well-known sign of a house of prostitution. Word got around, and soon they were in business.

One of them had a little boy of about three years of age. He was a hyperactive fellow and thus was hard to put to bed early. That somewhat interfered with the nightly activities of his mother and the other shady lady.

Late one night the ladies were "well drunked up," as Old Daddy Thomas expressed it, and they had a couple of male visitors in like condition. Midnight neared, and still the little boy showed no inclination of wanting to go to bed. Some person or persons in the group—no one ever found out who—drunken and enraged, soaked the child's clothes in kerosene, shoved him into the backyard, and set him afire. He was left there to die alone and in unspeakable agony. The child's screams awoke a neighbor, who arose and ran to him, but it was too late.

The town constable was alerted and soon arrived at the dreadful scene. As he looked upon the charred little body, a plan formed in his mind which he believed would bring on a more complete and swifter justice than could be obtained in a court of law. The wheels of justice might grind, and in this case, the constable felt that the grind would be far too slow.

He put the body in care of the neighbor who had been awakened by the child's dying screams, assuring him that full justice would be rendered before daylight. He then hastened to the home of Rosetta Bachelor on lower Main (State) Street. She was the town's resident moralist and was easily enraged at the mere mention of lewd women. The constable knew that this atrocious act would bring Rosetta to speedy action.

She sat on the edge of her bed, tying her shoes, as the constable told of the awful crime that had been committed. (Her feet were so large that she always had to wear men's shoes.) As expected, moralistic Rosetta became incensed. The constable told her to go to it; he would in no way interfere with whatever she decided to do. And to it she went.

For the next two hours or so she went about the town, gathering up her cohorts, ladies who had much reason to hate wild women and who, a few years before, had helped her attack and all but destroy a Bristol brothel.

It was nearing 3:00 A.M. when this "holy band" began the march toward Burson's Grove. Near where the spur railroad now crosses Piedmont Street, Rosetta called a halt at Luttrell's woodyard. There she had the women load up with much kindling wood, including several well-seasoned pine knots.

A elderly lady who died here in 1955 was in that band. She used to tell that as they gathered up the kindling, Rosetta began quoting Scriptures, two of which were "eye for eye, tooth for tooth" and "they that take the sword shall perish with the sword." Then, as she was prone to do whenever the occasion demanded, she added a "scripture" of her own making: "They that kill by fire shall by fire be killed." It was fast becoming clear to her cohorts what Rosetta planned to do.

The little shack in Burson's Grove was dark and quiet when Rosetta and her holy band arrived. Likely the women and their male visitors inside had, aided by alcohol, fallen into a deep sleep. At the orders of their commander (Rosetta), the women piled the kindling against the front and back doors. Then, still muttering her invented scripture, Rosetta strode forth and lighted the kindling. She then stepped back to the edge of the small yard and drew both of the pistols she always carried, vowing that she would shoot anyone who tried to escape.

Not a sound or movement was detected within. A little later Rosetta and her band of cohorts, having executed and witnessed their brand of frontier justice, silently marched back to their homes.

Those in charge of the town cemetery (East Hill) would not allow the bodies of the women and their visitors to be buried there. The little boy was buried there, at the foot of the grave of Lewis Bachelor, Rosetta's late husband.

Surprise in the Garbage Box

Then, as now, there were babies born in early Bristol who were not wanted. Apparently some of them were murdered outright, while others were cast away and left to die.

Soon after the Civil War (my informant of long ago thought it was in the late summer of 1867), young Pat Ryan awoke hungry. He knew there was no food in the house. His mother had been widowed the previous year ,and the family had become destitute. It was not yet daylight, but the boy arose and went downtown, hoping to find some fresh scraps of food in the garbage box behind the Virginia House Hotel.

It was still pitch dark behind the hotel, but he found the garbage box, opened the lid, and began to feel around. His eager hand took hold of something that was round, soft, and warm. It didn't feel just right and Pat couldn't figure out what he had found. He began to draw it out but suddenly released his hold when the "thing" began to move and cry. He ran into the hotel kitchen, yelling out that something was alive in the garbage box and it was making a sound like a crying baby.

Upon investigation, a newborn boy was found. Apparently he had been placed in the garbage box just minutes before Pat had arrived. Dr. Flavius Hartman was called. He found the baby to be normal, and took him to his own house. The baby was reared to manhood in the Hartman home. He was named Patrick Flavius Hartman, after the boy who found him and the doctor who took him in.

In early adulthood, he became a schoolteacher and taught in Bristol for a year or two. According to Old Daddy Thomas, Professor Hartman left about 1888 and began teaching in Arkansas, "somewhere on yan side of Little Rock and might nigh in Oklahoma."

In western Johnson County, Arkansas, there is a little town named Hartman. It is a good way "yan side of Little Rock and might nigh in Oklahoma." This writer wonders if this might possibly be the place where Professor Hartman settled and perhaps had a town named for him. Could be.

Train-Wheel Justice

Sam "Tiger" Goins, a giant of a man, lived up to his nickname. When provoked—and it didn't take much to provoke him—he easily flew into a violent rage. At such times he seemed to be devoid of conscience and any resemblance of human kindness or compassion. As a result of his barbaric nature, he had gone through a succession of wives; some said five, others claimed seven.

Most of them fled his home, greatly fearing for their lives, and likely their fears were well-founded. Thus, Tiger often found himself alone in the little rented shack on James Row. (The shack stood a short distance south of the present King Masonic Lodge building.)

Finally he took in, without the benefit of license or ceremony, a young widow and her one-year-old baby daughter. All seemed to go well for a while, though the young widow soon detected in Tiger a seething resentment against her child.

One night Tiger came home late from a local saloon. When he slipped into bed, he found that the baby had made a large wet spot up near his pillow. In a murderous rage Tiger jumped from the bed, grabbed the baby by the feet, then repeatedly slammed her head against the bedpost. Her brains were scattered all over the pillows and headboard, with some lodging in the mother's hair.

The woman sprang from the bed just as Tiger flung the lifeless and near headless body into a corner, calling out, "Now you won't wet my bed no more." He then grabbed for the mother, but she managed to evade his reach, jumping through an open window and fleeing through the dark to the home of W. W. James, which stood high on the hill behind the shack.

Tiger was sober enough to know that as soon as word spread he would be facing Bristol's version of frontier justice. That likely meant a rope around his neck and the low limb of a tree. He quickly fled across the darkened town to the Tennessee freight yards. As he reached the yards a freight train was pulling out, heading for Knoxville. This suited him fine; he would soon disappear from an angry town and be safe.

The train was already moving too fast for safe boarding. Tiger raced alongside it until a point was reached behind the present King Pharmaceutical Plant. There he made a desperate jump for an open boxcar door. He missed and was thrown under the train. He landed in such a position that his head was directly on the track. Fast came the crushing wheels. His brains were scattered for several feet along the crossties. He had been brought to swift justice beneath the wheels of a train, no more than thirty minutes after he committed the heinous crime.

A Parting Word

Before leaving this section on the violence of early Bristol, let it be said that the city we know today is rather peaceful, civil, law-abiding, pleasant, and safe when compared to that era when she was truly a bit of hell on the border. Time and many other contributing factors have made a great change here. We, who live here happily and in comparative safety today, are very thankful for that change. May it thus ever remain.

Hearts of Gold

Let it not be assumed that all the happenings in early Bristol were of a negative nature. No, indeed; from the very beginning there were many Bristolians who clearly demonstrated that they had hearts of gold. Their many notable acts of compassion and kindness are legion, and their fame spread to distant points. Whenever and wherever there was a need, local citizens were always there to help, often going far beyond the call of duty.

Perhaps this marked kindness was a natural outgrowth of the fact that Bristol was not a town that grew from a few closely knit families. Instead, it was a melting pot of people who came from many varied backgrounds and widely scattered places. They came and settled here as strangers in a strange town and thus felt a need to be of mutual help, one to the other. Having shared kindness with one another, they were quick to extend it to those who came after them. It was a case of gratitude becoming actions that would become a reason for gratitude on the part of others. Those who needed compassion were quick to extend it to others.

The author is happy to note that Bristol is still filled with citizens who have hearts of gold. The first impression he had of Bristol was the notable kindness and friendliness of her people. On August 20, 1953, he arrived in this city as a complete stranger, not knowing one person here. It soon became clear that the kind hospitality and helpfulness that was so marked in early Bristol had not ceased. The first people he met opened their hearts, hands, and homes to one who, at best, felt insecure in his new surroundings. It soon became clear to him that the city slogan proclaiming that Bristol is a good place to live is true, because of the goodness of her people.

Over the years, many stories have been told to this author of kind and noble deeds that were done by the early settlers here. So numerous are these stories that only a relatively small selection of them can be included in this work. Those which have been included show that kindness and goodness were not confined to a small segment of Bristol society. Such was practiced by a great cross section of her citizens.

It is true that there was much cruel crime, violence, vice, and outright meanness in the fast-growing town that spread across the peaceful fields and meadows of the old King plantation. Against that dark backdrop of the baser nature of man, there blossomed here and there bright flowers of compassionate deeds done, the memory of which may yet gladden the hearts of the present generation.

Cow From Heaven: How Angel George Nickels Got His Nickname

In the summer of 1877, lawyer Capt. J. H. Wood won an important case in the court of appeals at Wytheville, Virginia. For this victory the grateful client paid him handsomely, after which Captain Wood boarded a train for home. He arrived in Bristol shortly before dark. On the station platform he met an old friend and paused for a brief visit. While standing there conversing, he witnessed a tragic happening on the nearby tracks.

Miranda Carter, a poor black woman, had come down to Circus Bottom (area where the Bristol, Virginia, city jail now stands) to find her cow and drive it home for the evening milking. She had just started across the tracks, when a freight train struck and killed the unfortunate beast. The cow was mangled beneath the heavy wheels of the train.

Later, as Captain Wood walked toward his comfortable home on Johnson Street, he could not forget Miranda's pitiful cries. She had wailed out, "Lawdy, lawdy, they's 'nuff milk fer supper but won't be none fer breakfus. What will my little chillun do."

He knew she was a poor widow with five small children at home who depended on her domestic work to provide a meager living for the family. He also knew that milk from the prized cow was a large part of the children's diet. He thought ahead to home where there would be a sumptuous meal with plenty of milk for his own children.

In his pocket was the handsome fee ($100) that he had received at Wytheville. He remembered that a neighbor on Solar Street had a cow for sale; ten dollars would buy her. Usually rather thrifty—some said downright tight and grasping—he quickly calculated that if he bought the cow he would still have ninety dollars left, along with an easy conscience.

Once at home (Pleasant Hill—home of this author) he found that George M. Nickels, a younger man who lived nearby, was there and had been invited to remain for supper. That fit the captain's plans. He placed ten dollars in George's hand and told him to go buy the neighbor's cow.

Then George was to wait until well after dark before completing his mission of mercy. He was to lead the cow across town and stealthily put her in Miranda Carter's cow lot. Captain Wood knew his act of charity had to be kept a secret, or demands on his generosity would exceed the supply.

Now, George Nickels thought of the possibility that Miranda might hear him at the cow lot and perhaps might call out to him. He asked the Captain what he should do in such a case.

"Oh," Captain Wood replied, "if Miranda hears you and calls out to know who is there, just call back that 'the angel of the Lord has brought you a fine milk cow.'"

Angel George Nickels

About ten o'clock that night George quietly led the cow across the dark and sleeping town. Miranda lived in a little rented hut located near the present intersection of Buford and Lottie streets. The cow lot adjoined her fence immediately south of the hut.

Miranda was in bed but, worried about the loss of her cow, could not sleep. She heard the gate of the cow lot open and close, and the cow mooing a bit. The startled woman jumped from her bed and, peering into the darkness from her door, called out, "Lawdy, who's out there?"

In the most celestial tone he could manage, George called back, "It's the angel of the Lord and I've brought you a fine milk cow." As the "angel" quickly departed, he was thoughtful enough to call back through the darkness, "I don't think she's been milked tonight. You better get to her early in the morning. I think she needs it bad." Apparently, the heavenly milkmaids had not done their duty late that afternoon.

Well, for several years following, there was a supposedly "holy" cow from heaven at the Carter place. Perhaps appropriately, the cow was named "Angel."

The grave of Angel George Nickels in Bristol's historic East Hill Cemetery.

The cow was not alone with that strange name. Somehow, some of the close friends of George Nickels found out what he had done, and ever after he was called "Angel" George. In his case that name was a bit incongruous. It was well-known that he was far from being an angel. Actually, he was a bartender, a rather avid gambler, a noted womanizer (he once "stole" his brother's wife), rather profane in speech, and a general trader who would bear watching in any deal. He hated the nickname and would about fight over its use, but he could never shake it.

Under a huge and spreading maple tree in East Hill Cemetery, not far from Miranda Carter's former homesite, rests Capt. J. H. Wood (1842-1917), who long ago matched the gold in his heart with gold from his pocket. Some distance west of him sleeps Angel George Nickels (1849-1886), the "angel of the Lord" who delivered the "holy" cow to the poor widow Miranda Carter.

Permanent Relief

R. T. Lancaster, an early Bristol merchant, is easily classed among those with hearts of gold. He was a son of Thomas C. Lancaster, a hotel-keeper here. They came to Bristol in the late 1850s. R. T. set up a store on what soon became Front Street (old Fourth Street). At the beginning of the Civil War his new business was prospering. As the war wore on, more and more of the town's destitute, many of them war widows, sought credit at his store—credit which soon became charity.

A local man, who had enlisted in the service of the Confederacy and who fell mortally wounded on the first day of fighting at Gettysburg, left here a young widow and two little orphan boys. The widow soon became destitute and time and again was sustained by groceries bought on credit from R. T. Lancaster. Of course, he well knew that the woman would likely

R. T. Lancaster
His charity broke him.

not be able to pay him. The golden heart that throbbed within the breast of young Mr. Lancaster caused him to keep on giving to her and others. He could not bear to see the hungry suffer, especially children, so he was charitable as long as he could be.

Finally, he saw an opportunity to give permanent help to this particular young widow and her two little boys. Lancaster had a friend, a widower of some thirty-four summers, who lived near Paperville but often came into town to trade at Lancaster's store. He too had been left with young children. Once, while trading with his Bristol friend, the widower mentioned that he would like to have a wife to help rear his motherless children. Almost instantly Lancaster made a match in his mind.

The next time the young widow came to his store, he had a long talk with her. Yes, she would be glad to "enter into negotiations" with the widower. That night, after the store was closed, Lancaster saddled a horse and rode out to Paperville to talk to the man.

Yes, the lonely widower would gladly negotiate with the destitute woman in Bristol. Assuring his friend that an end to his loneliness might soon be at an end, the matchmaker rode back into town, happy that he could be of help to both of them.

Early the next day, the widower and the widow, who had never seen one another, sat down on a bench in front of their kind friend's store and indeed did earnestly enter into "negotiations." In less than half an hour the deal was made.

Two days later there was a wedding at the home of Rev. James King, on the corner of Moore and Main (State) streets. All of the children (his and hers) were present. Ann Bachelor, who later wrote down her memories of life in early Bristol, was on the street in front of the King home when the newlyweds came out. She wrote that she wept for joy when she watched the groom load his family into a surrey for the trip to his home, in Paperville. What really touched her was that his two children were clinging to the skirts of the new bride, glad to have a new mama. In time, five more children were added to this mixed family, and one of them was still living when this writer came to Bristol.

R. T. Lancaster walked back to his store from the wedding, glad and thankful that he had given the widow more than temporary relief. Matching her with a provident husband was far more helpful than the little bags of flour and small cuts of bacon that she had been receiving at his store.

R. T. Lancaster relieved this woman's destitute condition by finding her a husband.

A little later, Lancaster opened his store one morning and sent out word to the poor of the town to come and get it—free as long as his merchandise lasted. By night not an article was left in his store. He had given all to the suffering of his chosen town. He, whose heart of gold was long remembered by old-timers of Bristol, sleeps in the historic East Hill Cemetery, his grave marked by only a small stone.

She Hath Done What She Could

When Julian Droke came to Bristol as a brakeman on the railroad (about 1872), he was a widower with one child, a daughter. The daughter, Julia, was then about nine years old. Julian first rented a couple of rooms in the home of Austin M. Appling, a pioneer merchant of Bristol. Mrs. Appling looked after the little girl when Julian was away on his railroad runs.

Perhaps six months after he came here, Julian met and married a young Bristol woman. He then bought a small cottage on Railroad Street and moved his new wife and daughter there. Over the next five years or so four children were born in this home. Perhaps two or three weeks after the birth of the fourth child, Mr. Droke was killed in a tragic railroad accident.

Fortunately, Mrs. Droke was a fine seamstress, so she was able to eke out a living by sewing for the town. Her stepdaughter, Julia, not only served as a second mother for the children, but all the while, she assisted her stepmother and learned the art of fine sewing. The two also cultivated a little garden behind their cottage. Having a knowledge of gardening would prove to be valuable in years to come.

During the summer of 1879, Mrs. Droke became ill with a fever. Though she lingered for several weeks, she finally succumbed to the severe illness. Her death left Julia, then about seventeen years old, alone with her four half brothers and half sisters, the youngest then only about two. Ordinarily, under such circumstances the family would have been taken over by the county authorities and placed in various homes. The golden-hearted Julia Droke could not bear to see the family separated and scattered. She proposed to rear them herself. She had become a skilled seamstress and believed that she could "sew them out a living." The authorities agreed to let her give it a try.

The lamp in the little cottage burned far into the nights as Julia sewed hour after hour, in a noble effort to provide for those in her charge. In summers, she labored long in the little garden so that she might better provision her table. The entire town soon came to admire the girl who, at such a tender age, took on such a weighty responsibility. Many were the golden-hearted local citizens who frequently shared their bounty with her. Local merchants often gave her cloth so she could keep the children clothed (one of those merchants was E. H. Seneker). In December 1881, *The Bristol News* reported that the Presbyterian church had sent a basket of Christmas goodies to "Julia Droke and the orphans she is rearing."

Early in 1882, a man who had

Julia Droke

worked on the railroad with Julia's father became a widower and was left with five small children. Though he was at least a dozen years older than Julia, he soon began a courtship with her. Within a month, they were married and had moved to a larger house on Russell Street. Her four and his five made a family of nine children, but the kind Julia unflinchingly took his children into her care and loved them as her own.

Over the next several years Julia became the mother of nine more children. Her golden heart was big enough to love them all, and all received kind care from her as long as it was needed. Virtually her entire life was devoted to the rearing of this family of eighteen children, and certainly they all "rose up and called her blessed."

No more fitting epitaph could have been engraved upon the monument of this golden-hearted Bristol woman of long ago. It reads: "She hath done what she could."

How Merchandising Began in Bristol

In the early 1850s many residents of the Bristol area moved to Illinois, where much fertile land was available for settlement. Bristol's population had increased to the point that many of the younger generation were having difficulty in finding enough land upon which to establish a paying farm.

Out near what is now King College Road lived a successful farmer whose last name was Rutherford. He had a daughter who had married a young man of the neighborhood, and for a few years they had lived as tenants on her father's large farm. Hearing of homesteads available "way out west" in Illinois, the couple decided to move there. At the time of the move they had only one living child, a little five-year-old girl whose name was Rebecca but who was fondly called Becky.

A short time after the young couple and little Becky settled in Illinois, Philip Bushong, a prosperous farmer who lived near the Rutherford farm, decided to go see the area where the family had settled. He wanted to "view out the land," intending to settle there if "things looked just right." Indeed, he did procure some Illinois land, but he could never persuade his wife to make the move. So he "gave up the notion," as his yet-living great-granddaughter expressed it.

Mr. Bushong established contact with his former young neighbors soon after arriving in the area of Illinois where they lived. He was still staying near them when a virulent plague of some type swept through that locality, swiftly taking the lives of many settlers. The young Rutherford woman from Sullivan County, Tennessee, died early one day. And before darkness fell, her young husband was also dead. This left little Becky an orphan alone in a strange land.

Philip Bushong was determined to deliver the little girl back home to her Rutherford grandparents. Late fall had come and the weather was very cold. He bought a heavy wool blanket in which he snugly wrapped the child, and, placing her in the saddle behind him, the two started before daylight one frosty morning for Tennessee.

When an old woman, "Aunt" Becky still carried memories of that long, cold, and arduous journey. She remembered crossing the Ohio River on a ferry, along with other horsemen and a few wagons. She recalled the cold winds that swept down the river, chilling all aboard the slow ferry.

In Louisville, Kentucky, Mr. Bushong stopped to visit with relatives for perhaps two or three days. The extreme kindness of those kinsmen would never be forgotten. Becky recalled how they begged to keep her, and when Mr. Bushong would not agree to do so, they then tried to persuade him to leave her until spring, when some of the family would deliver her to Tennessee. Her kind and protective benefactor felt that Becky had to be taken to her grandparents as soon as possible.

While in Louisville, Mr. Bushong bought himself a "warm blanket" in the form of a flask of whiskey. That flask, embossed with an image of George Washington, still exists and is owned by this writer.

After leaving Louisville, Becky remembered traveling through heavy snow for some distance and then stopping at a wayside home to wait out a storm. Farther on, Mr. Bushong became ill and had to stop for several days with a family that Becky remembered as living in a crude log cabin, probably in the mountain country of Southeast Kentucky. It was later told that while there, the ill Mr. Bushong made arrangements for the orphan girl to be delivered to her grandparents in Tennessee, in case his illness was fatal. He survived, and was soon able to continue the trip.

Becky well remembered passing through Cumberland Gap. There a stop was made, and she was told to look long at that historic cleft, for she would likely never be there again. Though she lived to be over ninety years old, she indeed was never back at the Cumberland Gap.

Once settled near Bristol, she was never any farther from home than Abingdon, Virginia, and Bluff City, Tennessee. (Such a lack of travel was not uncommon among the residents of the area at that time.) Of course,

Becky could never forget the arrival at Grandfather Rutherford's home. The two travelers arrived in the misty dusk of a cold, rainy day; the grandfather saw them before they drew rein at his gate and came running to meet them.

Becky always had a special love and gratitude for Philip Bushong. When he died less than six years later (1859), she mourned as for a family member. She was always fond of and very kind to his widow and daughter, and she was grateful that she could nurse Mrs. Bushong in her final illness (1883). As long as she was able, Becky always took flowers to Mr. Bushong's Paperville Cemetery grave on Memorial Day. When she was no longer able to do so, she had others of her family carry on her custom of gratitude.

The reader may well be wondering by now how the events thus far described connect with the beginning of merchandising in Bristol. To find out, one must return to the little orphan girl who was placed in the loving care of her grandfather.

Within a short time after Philip Bushong brought her home, Becky had become a friend and playmate of a little neighbor girl whose name is unknown to this writer. This little neighbor girl had been given a red scarf as an early Christmas present.

Of course, Becky wanted one like it. Her doting grandfather vowed he would get her one before the fast-approaching holiday season had passed. He walked over to the store then operating at Paperville where the little girl's scarf had been purchased. He had to return home with the sad news that the stock had been sold out.

Becky was so disappointed that she cried herself to sleep that night, even though Grandfather Rutherford had promised that he would yet get her one even if he had to go "plumb to Blountville." However, he had heard that Joseph R. Anderson had bought a stock in goods and would open for business on Christmas Eve (1853), in the newly planned town of Bristol. So he determined to first try there.

When he arose on Christmas Eve morning, Rutherford found the ground covered with snow, and more was falling. Undaunted, he took a piece of bacon for bartering purposes and, facing the bitterly cold wind, waded the snow along the ridges and finally down what is now Cemetery Hill to what was then King's meadow. There, smoke curled upward from the chimneys of Joe Anderson's new brick home. (The site is now the southwest corner at the intersection of State and Edgemont streets.) Anderson, thinking that the heavy snow would preclude any business that day, had taken two of his male slaves and had gone to a wooded area on what is now Solar Hill to cut firewood.

Fortunately, once Mr. Rutherford had explained himself to the kind and understanding Melinda King Anderson, she sent another servant to bring her husband home.

Anderson was not sure that he had one of the coveted scarves, but he willingly proceeded to search through some previously unopened crates in the back of his store. At last he came up with a scarf that was prettier than the one owned by Becky's friend. The basic color was red but there were white splotches on it as well, each of which contained the image of a flower. The price was ten cents, which Mr. Rutherford paid with his piece of bacon.

Later that day there was a happy little girl far out on what is now King College Road. Indeed, Becky was so pleased that she spread the scarf on her pillow and slept with it beneath her head that night. She treasured it and kept it.

When a young woman, Becky came to trade at Anderson's store, then grown into a large mercantile firm. Anderson asked her if she still had the scarf. She replied that she did, and he then told her that it was the first article sold in his store and the town of Bristol. A few years later, Joe 's son John C. Anderson, who was by then in charge of the family store, tried to buy the scarf. He wanted to display it as what was even then considered to be a priceless Bristol artifact. He offered her a fine bedroom suite for it. She considered it to be a token of her grandfather's love and care for her and would not let it go. At her death it became the property of her only daughter.

When this writer came to Bristol in 1953, Becky's daughter was then an old woman living in one of the little shacks on Poverty Hill (Second High Street). This writer became acquainted with her through his first work here, and in time she became one of his closest friends. Though Becky's daughter was in rather humble circumstances, she was rich in local historical knowledge. Thus many trips were made to her home to hear her tell of Bristol's unique and interesting past. She died in "apple blossom time," 1956. On her deathbed she directed that the treasured scarf be given to this writer.

"He loves Bristol and its history, and will keep it," she said. This was her last act and nearly her last words. Though over forty years have passed, he still has the scarf. It is doubtful that any city in America can be sure of the first article sold within her boundaries, but Bristol can be, and all ought to be proud of this distinction.

In this story there are four persons who certainly may be counted among those early pioneers in paradise who well proved that they had hearts of gold— Philip Bushong, who brought little Becky to her grandfather's home; Grandfather Rutherford, who was so kind to the little orphan girl in his care; Melinda King Anderson, who understood the situation and acted accordingly; and

Becky Robinson Osborne, whose childhood Christmas gift started merchandising in Bristol.

Joseph Anderson, who left his work to search for the scarf so desired by the little girl. Perhaps we should include that unknown servant who waded through the snow to bring Mr. Anderson home. Though all of them have long been on the other side, their kind deeds are here noted and fondly remembered.

Campbell's Charity Cup

As late as 1954, a little tin cup remained in a humble home on Second Taylor Street, though its principal purpose had ended some eighty years earlier. That little cup, as insignificant as it may have then seemed, was proof that a heart of gold had long ago throbbed within the breast of a Bristol pioneer. For several years that cup hung from a nail over Charles C. Campbell's grain catch bin in his mill on Goodson Street. A little later we will learn why it was kept there.

Around 1870, C. C. Campbell set up a water-powered mill near the Goodson Street crossing of Beaver Creek. His mill operation was the largest and most modern in the town at that time. For some reason, Campbell was not well liked by his fellow Bristolians, seemingly due to some grudges carried over from the Civil War. Even so, because of the high quality of his mill products, he enjoyed the lion's share of the town's milling business.

In that neighborhood lived one of the town's best-known characters. Chad Barwick was not well liked by local citizens either. Some thought he was "soft in the head," as most Bristolians then called mental retardation. Retarded or not, his mind conceived some mighty far-out examples of what today would be called practical jokes. Many of his victims found the jokes to be highly impractical. (Perhaps this author might write of those jokes at a later time.)

Chad lived with his widowed mother and a much younger sister (his mother had been twice married) in a little cottage on Second Taylor Street. The little family was as poor as poor can be. C. C. Campbell knew this, and he started his own form of a relief program for them. His customers supported that program, though none of them were aware of it.

In those days millers were usually paid in toll, that is, they took a certain portion of the finished products of their grinding. It was so at the Campbell mill. Campbell used the aforementioned tin cup to take his toll of the meal that flowed forth from his whirling burrs. He always took his toll, then took one extra cupful, which he put into a separate wooden pail. By the end of a work week, he would have perhaps a peck of meal. Late on Saturdays, Chad Barwick would come to the mill and would be given the charity meal. For years the Barwicks had bread on the table because of the kindness of C. C. Campbell.

Then came the dark time when Campbell became so heavily in debt that the court finally ordered all of his property sold in order to satisfy his creditors. Of course, that included the mill and everything pertaining to it. Actually, that would have included the little tin cup, but it was no longer in the mill. The last time that Campbell was able to give Chad a pail of meal, he gave him the cup with it.

Doubtless there were many breadless meals for the Barwicks in the years that followed. The tin cup was always kept hanging in the kitchen as a reminder of a man who indeed did have a heart of gold. Chad's younger sister lived until 1954. She left no family and no one knows what became of Campbell's charity cup.

Careless Culler

It was common practice among early Bristol merchants to periodically cull their apple bins. Most merchants then kept their apples in shallow, square wooden bins. Of course, some of the apples would soon begin to decay. Thus the prudent storekeeper had to cull out the rotten fruit from time to time. Usually the culls were just thrown into the streets, where they would soon be crushed into the ground by passing wagons, horses, and mules if they were not picked up first.

In those days many of the poor of the town watched and waited for the culls to be thrown out. Often those culls still had a good bite or two left in them. Some of the women might even gather enough of them now and then to make a little applesauce.

When this writer came to Bristol, there lived an old woman in Crumley's Alley (a notorious slum that lay between Shelby and Broad streets and extended from Ninth Street to Tenth Street) who, as a girl of twelve summers or so, along with her nine-year-old brother, often used to go downtown to see if any good bites could be had from the culled apples. W. W. James then had a large store on the northwest corner of Main (State) and Front streets, and it was there that this sister and brother soon learned to go first.

It seems that if Mr. James was culling when they arrived, he would greet them kindly and tell them to stay close by, for they might find apples "with a lot of good eating left in them" if they would just look. It seems that Mr. James always got a bit careless when they were there. For, invariably, after a while there would be found two, maybe even four, perfectly good apples among the culls. How the two hungry children enjoyed them!

Much later they came to realize that the golden-hearted merchant, understanding their dire poverty, had been deliberately tossing out good apples for them.

"I never eat an apple now what I think of kind old Mr. James," the lady said as she told this story nearly fifty years ago.

Kindness to a Stranger

John Singleton Mosby (later Colonel Mosby, CSA) became the most famous stranger ever to come to Bristol. In November of 1858, Mosby started to Memphis, Tennessee, where he intended to set up a law practice. He stopped in the new town of Bristol to pay a brief visit to a cousin, Joseph W. Owen (later Captain Owen, CSA). Owen persuaded Mosby to stay in Bristol.

Actually, Mosby was not too hard to persuade. He had little money with which to establish himself in a new location and, perhaps, felt that he would be better off in Bristol, where he at least had relatives to help him. As it turns out, relatives were not the only ones who were kind to this stranger in a strange land.

Of course, the first things Mosby needed included an office and a place to live. As it was, he found both in one unit. Standing a bit east of the northeast corner of Lee and Main (now State) streets was the then-vacant office of the late Dr. B. F. Zimmerman. It was owned by Dr. Zimmerman's widow, who by then had married a man named John Keys. The golden-hearted Mrs. Keys came forth and offered to rent the building to the aspiring young lawyer, for the reasonable sum of seventy-five dollars per year. Without a dime down, she took a two-year note on the first year's rent.

The building had two rooms, with a double fireplace at the dividing wall. Thus the front room would serve as an office, while the back room could be used as living quarters. The site was a prime location in early Bristol.

The place had no furnishings, and the nearly destitute Mosby could not buy them. Again Mrs. Keys rose to the need and gave him a small, hand-crafted walnut table, which had also served as her deceased husband's first desk. She took a ladder-back, cane-bottom chair from her front hall to go with the desk. Alas, Mrs. Keys had not a bedstead to spare from her home.

Out back was a slave cabin where one of her slaves, Big Elbert, usually lived. At that time he was rented out. In the cabin was a straw mattress which Big Elbert used for a bed. Mrs. Keys had the mattress brought over and placed on the floor of the room that Mosby would call home. The table and chair and the straw mattress on the floor comprised the sole furnishings of this office and home.

Shortly Mosby's wife arrived from her father's home. (She had gone there to wait until her husband became established in Memphis. As it was, she had to reverse directions and come to Bristol instead.) Perhaps Pauline Clarke Mosby, who had been reared in relative affluence, had such a strong love for her husband that the deprivation that faced her in this new home could be borne with grace. There came with her a slave named Aaron, who had been a wedding gift from her parents. He was soon rented to Col.

John Preston of Walnut Grove at an annual stipulation that equaled the rent on Mosby's first office and home. Indeed, the note to Mrs. Keys was paid by the hire of this slave.

John Mosby sat in the little office for weeks before he had his first client. At that time the town had two other capable and well-respected lawyers (Joseph B. Palmer and Gideon Burkhart), and it seems that they were taking care of about all the legal matters of the local citizenry.

Then came Austin M. Appling. He was a pioneer settler of Bristol, an early merchant, and had served as the first elected mayor of Goodson (better known as Bristol, Virginia). He too had a heart of gold. He had heard that the Mosbys were sleeping on the floor and were otherwise deprived of the common comforts of life. He remembered an old bed stored in the woodshed back of his store. Actually, he had meant to cut it up and burn it in the store fireplace. It had belonged to his father, and perhaps his grandfather, and had been brought with him when he moved to Bristol.

After using the old four-post, rope-type canopy bed for a while, he had hired a local craftsman to make modern beds for his home. Thus the old family bed had been discarded and marked for firewood. (Many a fine antique has perished in this manner.)

Now, upon hearing of the sleeping arrangements of the new lawyer and his wife, Appling firmly decided to do something about it. He searched among his papers until he found a past-due note that he knew could be easily collected. Pocketing the note, he briskly walked the two blocks or so to Mosby's office. There he soon had a deal made with Mosby to give him the old family bed if he would collect the past-due note. The note (it was for only ten dollars or so) was soon collected. This was Mosby's first case in Bristol, and the old Appling bed was his first earned fee.

Ann Bachelor, who lived in Bristol at the time, later wrote of seeing Mr. and Mrs. Mosby carrying the bed from Appling's store to their new home. She stated that they seemed to be happy as children with new toys. The addition of so grand a piece of furniture to such a bare house must have been of great satisfaction to the struggling young couple.

This early Bristol lawyer later became the famous Col. John S. Mosby of Civil War fame. He went the way of all flesh well over eighty years ago, but his table, chair, and bed, which came to him because golden-hearted Bristolians were kind to him as a stranger, yet exist. They are all prized articles in the home of this author at Pleasant Hill, in Bristol, Virginia.

The Totin' Woman

Old Hulda "Hulley" Seneker, a black woman, had grown older as the town of Bristol grew up. As a slave she had belonged to the pioneer Seneker family of Sullivan County. In the late 1850s, she was brought to the new town on the border by E. H. "Lige" Seneker to do domestic work in his home.

After the Civil War she married Big Tom Seneker, another of her former master's ex-slaves. The two then lived in various rental properties and eked out a living any way they could. Big Tom sickened and died, leaving Hulley to fend for herself.

For years she earned her living by making deliveries for the merchants of the town. Every business day morning she could be seen in her long black dress and red bandana walking slowly along Front Street or down Main Street, stopping at the store doors and calling to the merchants to see if they had deliveries to be made. At the door of Valentine Keebler, she might call out, "Mr. Val, have you stuff for Old Hulley to tote today?" Or, at the W. W. James door she might pause and call into the merchant, "Mr. Will, I feel pretty good and can tote stuff a fer piece today." To her former master, E. H. Seneker, she often offered her services, perhaps saying, "Mr. Lige, I be ready to take stuff around today."

Often her pay was a little cut of side meat, perhaps a few apples, or maybe a little bag of flour; occasionally a coin was placed in her work-worn hand. When it looked like clothes were needed, some kind merchant might give her a few yards of cloth.

Many were the Bristol homes where a knock at the back door and the call of "Old Hulley's done come with yore stuff" meant that ordered goods were being delivered. In time she came to know about every home and every person in the growing town. She was commonly called "the totin' woman." She endeared herself to many whom she faithfully served. It was not uncommon for some kind housewife to give her a little container of soup, perhaps a bit of cake, or sometimes leftover biscuits from breakfast for her to carry home after deliveries were made.

Ever so gradually, the passing years began to wear her down. Slower and slower she padded along the dusty or muddy streets. She bent lower and lower as her eighty-five or so years began to press down upon her. Then one day there was no call of "Hulley's ready to tote for you" at the store doors.

Someone went to her little hut and found her still in bed. "I just can't seem to get a-goin' today," she said. "I's jist too stiff to tote fer ye but hopin' I can soon."

It was clear that not only was Hulley sick but that her hut was unfit for human habitation. The floor was falling through, daylight could be seen through the roof, and cold air was whistling through wide cracks. Most of the windowpanes were broken or had fallen out.

At the north end of James Row (along present Piedmont, between Sycamore and Goode streets), W. W. James had what he called "the left-over house." It was small and had been built just of what materials had been left over from the building of his long row of cheap rental houses. He moved Old Hulley there, charging her no rent and promising to help supply her needs. He asked the other merchants to join in his charitable effort, and all agreed to do so.

It should be remembered that this was long before the days of government assistance to the poor, and Social Security and Medicare had never been heard of. Dr. M. M. Butler agreed to provide her with free medical services, and Jeremiah Bunting would see that she had any drugs that she might need. Thus, the totin' woman was kindly cared for through the remaining two or three years of her life.

When Hulley's final days came, during which she needed constant care, the ladies of elite Solar Hill, back of her home, rose to the occasion. It was a common sight to see the stately Harriet Moorman Johnson, the humbly dignified Mrs. J. H. Wood, the old but able Mrs. Thomas C. Lancaster, and others trekking down the hillside with baskets of provisions, prepared to take their turn caring for Old Hulley. The totin' woman was totally dependent upon Bristolians with hearts of gold, and they were many.

When the end finally came, local undertaker Hiram Bickley bore all costs of her burial. Such was the great kindness of many of the pioneer settlers of Bristol. This writer will add that there are many like them in the city today.

Golden Heart/Brave Heart

Sometimes, the hearts of gold that were so evident in early Bristolians were also brave hearts. Dr. John J. Ensor, who began his medical practice early in life, was among the physicians of the new town of Bristol. He soon endeared himself to the local citizenry and thus greatly prospered here in his chosen profession.

In 1871, Dr. Ensor built a fine brick home that still stands on the southeast corner of Cherry and Seventh streets. (It is now the Sesco building.) By then he was married and had a small family.

Not long after he moved his family into the new house, an epidemic of cholera broke out in Jonesborough, Tennessee. There were many deaths, sometimes several within a day. Indeed, the mortality rate was so high that several graves were dug every day in anticipation of the impending need for them. It is interesting to note that a man of the town dug graves all afternoon and was himself buried in one of them before sunset the next day. There was panic in the town. Many of the residents fled to other places, including Bristol.

There was a pressing need for more doctors, and, because of his well-known success in treating cholera in the past, Dr. Ensor was sent for. Though he knew the great danger to himself—there was a real possibility that he might become a victim of the dread disease—he allowed duty to overcome fear and bravely agreed to go.

The plea had come by messenger during the night. At daylight the next morning Dr. Ensor left his home for the local train depot. Years later he would tell how, when he was leaving home that morning, he had stood for a few moments, holding on to the front gate, looking back at the house and wondering if he would ever see it or his family again. Then he turned and walked toward the depot.

Dr. Ensor had much success in treating the desperately ill patients in Jonesborough. He knew that dehydration was the big danger, so he required all his patients to drink copious amounts of water—just about poured it down them, it was later told. Once during the epidemic, he went sixty hours without going to bed; he just napped a bit as he sat by the bedsides of the deathly ill.

Dr. Ensor was fortunate; he did not contract the awful scourge. He survived to come home and indeed lived until well after the turn of the century.

Need Overcomes Hatred

Bristol's many hearts of gold have often forgotten old hatreds and grudges and have unhesitatingly gone to the aid of enemies in times of extreme distress. In the late autumn of 1882, the legendary Maj. Z. L. Burson was in the midst of a bitter lawsuit with a fellow townsman. The depositions in this case were being taken in the home of Philip Rohr, a notary public who lived on Scott Street near the present Hayes Plumbing shop. The rancor between the two was so great that it could be felt in Rohr's tiny living room. The opposing lawyers were not so amicable either. Indeed, one of them detested Major Burson and was very eager to win the case against him.

In the midst of this strained proceeding, the town fire bell began to ring out its message of impending disaster. At about the same moment, a young man who lived up on Moore Street burst through the door and, though almost breathless from his hard run, managed to yell out that Major Burson's smokehouse was on fire.

Instantly, old animosities were forgotten, as lawyers, witnesses, the defendant in the case, and hostile onlookers joined the major in his mad race down Scott Street and up to 342 Moore Street. There, all joined in the frantic effort to save the meat-filled smokehouse.

In a day or two afterward, Burson and his enemy, along with their hostile lawyers, might have again flashed fiery eyes at one another in the courtroom. For that moment, however, stony hearts had become hearts of gold, as need overcame hatred.

How Alabama Street Got Its Name

In 1867, John G. King, youngest son of Rev. James King, inherited a large tract of land from his deceased father. This land extended southward from the old Bristol, Tennessee, town limits to beyond Cedar Creek. The tract included the fine old mansion known as Oakland, which was already occupied by Mr. King and his family. Oakland stood on a hill west of the large King spring and immediately north of what is now Defriece Park. There were several tenant houses scattered over the plantation, one of which was in a little hollow off Cedar Creek, near what became the Tennessee Colored Cemetery.

Soon after the close of the Civil War, the house and a portion of nearby land was let to a family of ex-slaves from Baldwin County, Alabama. The family had formerly been owned by John G. King's brother-in-law, Col. John G. English. The family name was Cane (probably originally Kane or Kain). Soon after moving onto King's plantation, a baby girl was born. They named her Alabama in honor of their former location. She became a bright, plump, pretty little girl, much adored by her family.

Mr. Cane, as head of the ex-slave family, not only tilled his allotted acres but also helped his landlord in the latter's vast farming operation. However, in midsummer, there might be a lapse of several days without contact between the Kings and the Canes.

In the summer of 1872, Mr. Cane had worked on a Saturday in the Oakland garden and upon leaving was told to return one week from that day, when there would be more work. The following Saturday came, but Mr. Cane did not appear. This seemed rather strange, for the faithful tenant had always been dependable and punctual when expected to fulfill his duties. Sunday passed and still there was no word from him. When he did not come early Monday morning, Mr. King decided to saddle a horse and ride down to the Cane house. When he arrived there, everything was deathly silent, except for the faint sound of a child crying out back of the barn.

Having no answer to his repeated calls at the gate, Mr. King dismounted and walked to the barn lot. There he found little Alabama Cane, then five years old, with tin cup in hand, trying to milk a cow. Doubtless, she had seen her mother do this many times and, being very hungry, was trying to do likewise. The cow's udder was greatly distended, which was likely painful for the bovine, so the little girl's efforts were being resisted, though she was valiantly trying.

When she saw Mr. King, Alabama came running with empty cup in hand and blurted out that Papa and Mama were asleep and wouldn't get up and cook breakfast. She added that they had been asleep a long time. Indeed, they were asleep—eternally so. Some type of lethal sickness had taken both Mr. and Mrs. Cane and the other three children. Little Alabama Cane alone had escaped the scourge.

John G. King apprised neighbors of the situation, then took the little orphan girl to his home. The late Hattie King Taylor, then about twelve years old, remembered her mother, Harriet Netherland King, holding the hungry little girl on her lap and feeding her gingerbread and milk. Mrs. Taylor also remembered that her father and others buried the rest of the family on a high hill back of the tenant house. Some say that this was the beginning of what is now known as the Tennessee Colored Cemetery.

The Kings took little Alabama Cane into their home to raise. Perhaps because he had rescued her, she became very attached to Mr. King—so much so that she would hardly allow him out of her sight. At that time he was laying off a portion of his land for a new addition to the fast-growing town of Bristol. Each morning as he rode away to supervise his surveyors, the little orphan cried piteously and begged to be taken along with him.

Finally, one bright, balmy morning, the kind Mr. King gave in. He picked Alabama up, placed her in his lap, and took the happy child with him. On that day his men were surveying what was meant to be the grandest street in his new addition. It was to be broad and long, and would connect to the road leading to King's beloved Oakland. Before he went about his work that day, King put little Alabama Cane under a huge oak tree that stood at the crest of the hill on the lot where Dr. J. M. King later built his home (west side of the 500 block of Alabama Street). There she contentedly played for hours, happy just to be near Papa King.

John G. King had planned to name the grand thoroughfare leading toward his home "King Avenue." It would seem that such a name would have been fitting and certainly would have been an expected choice of this Bristol developer, but it seems that on the way home that afternoon he had a change of mind.

Perhaps the story is best told in a letter King wrote to his respected brother-in-law, Col. John G. English. Writing on August 25, 1871, he stated:

> I had placed the little orphan in the saddle with me and we had started toward home when suddenly there came a feeling to me that this poor, unfortunate child ought to be honored in some way—a way that would be lasting. She had suffered the loss of so much I felt that she should be given something more than kind care. And the firm conviction seized me that the best way was to name a street for her. In a moment of supreme unselfishness—which you know is uncommon for me—I decided to give her the best. When we reached home I took out my maps and where King Avenue had been written I struck it out and replaced it with Alabama Street. She sleeps gently in the trundle from under Harriett's bed as I write this, not knowing that she has been immortalized.

One hundred and thirty-one summers have come and gone since Alabama Cane played under the great oak near her beloved Papa King, but the street that was surveyed that day still proudly bears her name. Certainly, John G. King must be numbered among those who truly had a heart of gold.

The Abandoned Baby

On a cold, snowy, sleety day in February 1878, a young woman carrying a beautiful, plump little baby boy boarded the train at Greeneville, Ten-

This kind lady raised an abandoned baby left on a train.

nessee. The train was crowded, causing the young woman to have some difficulty finding a seat. At last she came to share a seat with a kind lady who was formerly from Knoxville but who had recently moved into the thriving town of Bristol. The lady had been back to Knoxville to bring home her own three small children, who had been left there in the care of her mother.

In facing seats, the two mothers and their children had a comfortable little nest for the ride through the beautiful, snow-covered valleys and hills of Upper East Tennessee. Though the two women enjoyed an amicable visit as they traveled, the younger mother never revealed her name or where she was going.

When the train stopped in Johnson City, the younger mother asked the woman from Bristol if she would hold her baby while she made a quick visit to an acquaintance who was riding in the next coach back. Her request was gladly granted, and the Bristol lady and her children enjoyed the smiling baby as the train lurched forward and steamed on toward Union Depot (present Bluff City). Union Depot was reached and passed, but still the mother had not returned. As the miles clipped away, with Bristol not far ahead, the woman became concerned. As the conductor came through, calling out the upcoming Bristol stop, the lady expressed her concern to him.

"Why, I remember that young lady leaving the train in Johnson City and she seemed to be nervous and in a great hurry," the conductor replied. He then added, "I venture to say that baby has been abandoned in your arms."

The kind woman hugged the baby closer to her heart of gold as she, filled with pity and compassion, begged for the privilege of keeping and caring for him until there could be further action by the concerned authorities. Actually, the conductor and later the town officials in Johnson City, where the abandonment had occurred, were glad to have so easy a solution to what could have been a real problem for them.

Finally, the train came to a halt at the Bristol depot. The woman's husband, waiting there for the return of his wife and family, was much surprised to see four children instead of the expected three. Once he was made aware of the situation, he too showed that he had a heart of gold by agreeing with his wife as to the care of the abandoned baby. That baby, pressed close to a loving heart while the cold wind and snow swirled around him, was, though he then knew it not, at home in Bristol.

No trace of the natural mother was ever found. She seems to have just disappeared. The baby was tenderly cared for by the kind lady with whom he had been left. She and her entire family accepted and loved him as if he were one of their own.

He grew to manhood in Bristol and in time became a respected citizen of the city. He became an employee of the Norfolk and Western Railway and eventually was required to move to Lynchburg. He married and had a family there and still has descendants living in that city.

Kindness Triumphs Over Obedience

Among the more prominent residents of early Bristol was William Philip Brewer. He sprang from a respected family of Carter County, Tennessee, and came to Bristol sometime before the Civil War. He soon became rather prosperous, engaging in a commission-house business (where produce and other items were sold on consignment) and a hardware. At the beginning of the Civil War, he and his family occupied a fine home on Third Street, then considered to be a desirable residential section of the new town.

In 1864, Mrs. Brewer, the former Lizzie Rhea Netherland, was having a difficult birth. Dr. R. M. Coleman, thought to be the best-educated and most-skillful doctor in town, was called in. He soon saw that he needed additional assistance. Instead of calling in another doctor, he sent one of the Brewer servants for "Aunt" Polly Taylor, a noted midwife. She was often called in to aid the regular Bristol medical men when a case proved to be difficult. Some considered her to be more skilled than those whom she assisted.

According to informants of long ago, Aunt Polly and her husband, Dawson Taylor, had moved here from "somewhere way up in Virginia." They lived on the southernmost section of Russell Street. The midwife soon endeared herself to a town that was grateful for her often-needed services.

At the beginning of the Civil War, it became known that the Taylors were strong supporters of the Union, especially Dawson Taylor, who soon had the reputation of being a radical Unionist.

"Aunt" Polly Taylor

Naturally, tensions developed between Mr. Taylor and the Confederates, who constituted a vast majority of the local residents. Finally, he delivered an ultimatum to his wife that she would deliver no more "little rebels." For a time, but with much remorse of conscience, she obeyed her husband.

Indeed, her obedience was with protest. She had been aiding the Confederate mothers as well as those of her own persuasion. She knew that several Confederate women in town would soon need her help. She considered her work to be a calling, and she silently determined to find some way to fulfill that calling.

Then came that day when the very nervous Brewer servant came to her door, earnestly beseeching Aunt Polly to come quickly. It was apparent that there was much fear and apprehension in the Brewer home. Alas, the Brewers were strong Confederates.

Dawson heard the plea and immediately forbade his wife to go. "Let the damn little rebel die, there's too many of them being born around here," he bellowed out. Even as the servant sorrowfully turned to go, a plan was forming in Aunt Polly's cunning mind. For a few minutes she pretended to be resigned to the wifely duty of obeying her husband's command.

Next door to the Taylors lived John Bosang and his wife. Mr. Bosang was a saloonkeeper (the first in Bristol) and always kept plenty of strong drink at home for his own consumption. Dawson Taylor would drink anything that smelled like whiskey. Aunt Polly put the two facts together and—eureka!—she had her plan. She told her husband that she believed she would go over and visit with Mrs. Bosang for a few minutes.

Shortly, she was back home carrying a full bottle. She told her husband that Mr. Bosang had concocted a new blend of choice liquor and wanted Dawson to be the first to sample it. She added that it was extra mild and that he would have to drink a lot in order to "get any kick out of it." The truth is that it was extra strong, containing some Holston Mountain moonshine that would "take the hair off a hog's back." Gladly, Dawson Taylor agreed to be a sampler, and he downed about half the contents of the bottle. It was called Bosang's Formula Number Five. Apparently it was well named, for within five minutes Dawson Taylor didn't know he was in the world.

Aunt Polly then grabbed her bag and headed through the fast-darkening streets to the Brewer home. Within two hours she had delivered not one but two "little rebels." (Having twins had caused this difficult birth.) She gathered up her equipment and was back home several hours before Dawson recovered from his bout with Formula Number Five.

Kindness had triumphed over obedience in the golden heart of this early Bristol midwife. She and Dawson Taylor sleep in unmarked graves somewhere in Bristol's historic East Hill Cemetery.

The twins born that night were James King Brewer, longtime Bristol businessman who built the house that still stands at 220 Johnson Street, Bristol, Virginia, and Harriet "Hattie" Brewer, who became the wife of Dr. Joseph Bachman. She and Dr. Bachman long maintained a home at 940 Anderson Street in Bristol, Tennessee.

Golden Choice

In early Bristol there were several doctors who could easily have been accepted into the Order of the Golden Heart. Among them was Dr. Matthew Moore Butler. Dr. Butler was born and reared on Steele Creek but early came to the new town of Bristol as a clerk in his father's hotel (The Famous). Later he went away to study medicine.

At the outbreak of the Civil War, Butler entered into the service of the Confederate States of America and served as a surgeon. While serving in that capacity he had the distinction of having assisted in removing the arm of Gen. Thomas J. (Stonewall) Jackson. Soon after the end of the war he established what became a flourishing medical practice in Bristol. For some unknown reason he moved to Verona, Kentucky, and practiced medicine there for a few years. While living in Kentucky, he began sending money to his father for the purpose of having a fine brick house erected at 848 Anderson Street. He soon moved back to Bristol, and the house, known as Butler's Hill, served as his home for the rest of his life. (It was demolished when the Volunteer Parkway was constructed.)

One day in the mid-1880s, Dr. Butler returned from making a house call at Paperville only to find two urgent calls awaiting him at home. Both were maternity cases and needed immediate attention. One was to attend a lady on Solar Hill, then a rather elite section of Bristol. The other was from a poor black teenage mother-to-be who lived in a notorious slum known as Burson's Row (between Scott and Quarry streets, along what is now Piedmont Street).

The ever kind Dr. Butler did not take long to decide which woman to attend to. He knew that the well-to-do woman on Solar Hill could easily obtain help from any doctor in town. With her the pay was certain. The poor first-time mother on Burson's Row would likely not be so fortunate. Doubtless, there would never be pay from her, but there he chose to go.

It was good that he did, for his services were desperately needed. His presence was of great comfort and help to a frightened and suffering young girl. Not only did he deliver her baby, but he also made arrangements for the new mother's penniless family to have some necessary provisions from a local store. It is true that he never received pay for his work, but he was always thankful and glad that he had been of service to a girl and her family who so greatly needed his help. Dr. Butler was like that. He truly had a heart of gold.

The golden heart that so long beat within the breast of one of early Bristol's most beloved and respected doctors was forever stilled on August 12, 1913. He rests in the old section of East Hill Cemetery, in the city he so long served.

Regular Journeys of Mercy

A woman who long lived near the corner of Spencer and Lee streets used to say that she could have set the clock by the regular passing of a young lawyer carrying a set of twin babies in his arms. It was both a sad and glad sight; sad if one knew of his situation and glad if one knew the solution. This sad and glad sight went on for months and months, as regularly as the coming of night and day.

Something like a century ago, a young and promising Bristol lawyer made a trip to Dallas, Texas, to visit close relatives. The relatives had previously lived in Bristol but had moved to Dallas, where they were prospering. Indeed, their prosperity had become so great that they were prominent in the high society of that city.

While there, the young lawyer met a young lady of the upper strata of the Dallas citizenry. There followed a whirlwind romance. (Some said it was more like a tornado!) When he returned home he had a promise from the lady that she would come to Bristol and marry him. She kept her promise. There soon followed what was said to have been the grandest wedding ever seen, up to that time, in Bristol's First Presbyterian Church. The happy couple then settled in with his mother and lawyer father, who lived on Spencer Street.

Barely a year had passed when this young wife gave birth to twin girls. Evidently, increase in the family was against her wishes. Much to the shock of her husband and others who knew the situation, she flatly refused to nurse the babies, saying that such would ruin her figure. (She is said to have been vainly proud of her beauty.)

The husband was devastated. In desperation he went up on Lee Street to the home of a close friend, J. Cloyd Byars, then a prominent and respected lawyer of Bristol. In the Byars parlor he poured out his tale of woe to his friend, bitterly weeping as he did so.

Mrs. Byars (formerly Jane Bailey, a daughter of the noted Bristol lawyer Col. D. F. Bailey), who just a few days before had given birth to a baby son, was in an adjoining room and heard his tearful lament. Her big heart of gold swelled with deep sympathy and compassion. She stepped to the parlor door and, addressing her husband, she offered her solution to the problem.

"Cloyd," she began, "you know when I am nursing a baby, I'm just like a Jersey cow. I'm right now producing enough milk to feed three or four babies. If the young man will bring his twins up here every time they are hungry, I'll take care of them."

So the young lawyer did. No matter where he was when feeding time came, he rushed home, picked up the twins, and carried them up to be nursed by Jane Bailey Byars. Indeed, one could have "about set the clock" by his regular "little journeys of mercy." Those journeys took place both night and day. The kind Mrs. Byars kept an oil lamp burning in her front hall for him, and her door was always unlocked.

In less than a year after the birth of the twins, the young lawyer's wife ran away with a railroad man. Though little was ever known of her after that, it was thought that she finally returned to her people in Dallas. The lawyer and his mother reared the twin girls to adulthood. Both of them finally married and settled in Richmond, Virginia. On every occasion when they came back to Bristol for a visit, they always spent much time with the golden-hearted Jane Bailey Byars, who had been a mother-in-practice to them.

The lawyer, Mrs. Byars, and the twin daughters have long gone the way of all flesh. The memory of the goodness, kindness, and compassion that affected them all still lives on.

Labor of Love

It was a common sight back in the spring of 1897 to see young Clifton Peake working in neighborhood gardens, trimming lawns, or perhaps cleaning porches—just whatever work he could find. Cliff, as he was commonly called, was earning money for a purpose and earning for himself a place among those who are remembered as having hearts of gold. Indeed, his work was truly a labor of love. As hard as his labors sometimes were, he looked beyond that burdensome toil to a noble goal ahead.

The Peakes lived in a modest cottage on Broad Street. Cliff was the oldest of five children in the family. Next to him was a daughter, Dorcas, then about sixteen years old. Dorcas had been a bright, energetic, vivacious girl until late 1896, when she developed the dreaded tuberculosis, which felled so many Bristolians in those days. Her rosy cheeks paled, her energy drained away, and her breathing became difficult. By the spring of 1897, she was spending most of her pain-filled hours in bed.

Up the street from the Peakes lived a German family. In this family was a son who was about the age of seventeen-year-old Cliff. The two became good friends. In this home was a windup music box which had been brought from their native land. It played several melodious tunes in deep, resonant tones; it was cheerful and soothing to hear. Seeing that Cliff was enthralled by the music box, the family told him that they had been thinking of selling it.

Immediately, Cliff thought of how the music produced by this wonderful box might be comforting to his slowly dying sister. Though the price seemed prohibitive to him—all of twenty-five dollars—he then and there firmly determined to do whatever he had to do in order to get that box, hopefully to brighten the final days for Dorcas. It was then that he began to go far and near, seeking any jobs that were available.

In late spring, Cliff, after much labor and saving of earnings, had enough money to buy the music box. Indeed, it did bring a little sunshine into the life, fast fading though it was, of the sickened Dorcas Peake. Time and again the lovely, soothing tunes of that box sounded in the sickroom. Many times it lulled her into a peaceful sleep, in which she was, hopefully, briefly freed from her acute awareness of ever-present pain.

Summer had barely arrived when Dorcas breathed her last. The golden-hearted Cliff was comforted to know that he had done what he could to brighten her final days. Over a century has passed, but that music box still remains in a Bristol, Tennessee, home. It is one of many reminders that over the years our city has been blessed with many persons who indeed had hearts of gold.

Good Samaritans All

King's Cut was on the railroad a short distance below the present Mitchell-Powers Hardware building (near the end of Fifth Street). John G. King's vast fields and pastures lay along the tracks in that vicinity. One day in the summer of 1879, a crew of workers stopped for lunch under the shade of a large tree that stood in a fencerow near the tracks.

There were heavy weeds just back of the tree. The men of the crew were hardly settled under the tree, when they were startled by the sound of low moans coming from that weed patch. Upon investigation they found a young man lying prostrate on the ground with a small suitcase under his head.

At first thinking him to be drunk, they soon determined that he was deathly ill. Evidently he had been walking the railroad when illness ended his weary journey. The crew loaded him onto the work car and brought him to the Bristol depot. Isaac Nickels, who then operated the Nickels House Hotel, was at the depot when the crew arrived. He immediately offered the use of a room for the sick man, while others went for medical help.

The man, who was perhaps in his late twenties, was in a state of delirium brought on by a bad case of typhoid fever. He was never able to give his name or address and carried not a scrap of identification. As Isaac

Nickels supplied the sickroom for this unknown man, Dr. M. M. Butler and Dr. H. T. Berry gave freely of their medical services, with Dr. J. J. Ensor later joining them. The drugstore of Bunting and Dickey supplied the medicines. All these men knew that they would likely never receive a cent for their services, but, golden hearted as they were, they let kindness triumph over any hope for or need of monetary gain.

The poor man died on the third day after being brought to the Nickels House. A. H. Bickley, the legendary local undertaker, supplied a nice coffin (again no pay), and up East Main (State), ahead of the hearse, he did his usual grand march, with black silk hat held over his heart of gold. He was followed by a surprising number of local citizens, who turned out for the funeral as if a well-known local person had died. At the cemetery, Rev. George A. Caldwell held forth for over an hour in an eloquent funeral oration. Presbyterian that he was, he postulated that perhaps in the great providence of God, this young man may have been the instrument used to test the Christian charity of local citizens. Divinely used or not, the sick and dying man certainly became the beneficiary of a band of local Good Samaritans, who truly had hearts of gold.

A Standing Reminder

For many years Isaac Chapman Fowler was editor and publisher of *The Bristol News*. For the first few years, he was assisted by his brother, Elbert Fowler. Then Elbert found a more promising future in West Virginia. Soon after his departure, A.C. Smith came to assist in the publication of the widely read paper.

A.C. Smith was an honest, hardworking man, but there was little profit in newspaper publishing at that time, so his salary might be best described as meager. Within a few years he was able to save enough to buy a lot that is now numbered 413 Fifth Street. (It was then known as College Street or College Avenue). On this lot he erected a modest cottage. It was actually a choice property. It overlooked Anderson Park, was near King College, and the street upon which it was located seemed destined to become one of the best in the town. Smith had earlier married, and by the time his cottage was erected he had a small family.

On a bitterly cold February night in the late 1870s, Dr. J. J. Ensor was returning from a late sick call. His route home lay on the opposite side of Anderson Park from the Smith home, although the house could easily be seen from that route. Coming in sight, Dr. Ensor saw that the kitchen wing was engulfed in flames. He ran to the front door of the cottage and awakened the soundly sleeping family. Had he not been passing by at just the right time, the tragedy likely would have been greater. As it is, the family escaped, but with barely the night clothing that they wore. All else was lost.

The Smiths were taken in by the William Dixon family, neighbors who lived on Fourth Street where the S. P. Rutherford building is now located. The Dixons and other kind neighbors found clothing for them. Within a few days, Editor I. C. Fowler published a story concerning the tragedy and told that a move was under way to raise funds to build the Smiths another cottage.

Later, *The Bristol News* reported that local citizens were responding well to the appeal, making donations from as little as a quarter up to fifty dollars. There were also some out-of-town donations. Several local carpenters offered their services. "Uncle" Will Smith, a local contractor, offered free brick from his plant for the foundation and chimneys. Windows would be supplied from the G. H. Mattox furniture works. (Mr. Mattox was Bristol's first undertaker, and he later operated a furniture shop on Buford Street.) J. P. Rader offered to paint the cottage, free of charge. Most of the building materials came from the local Hoffman lumberyard, and all were donated.

The work progressed swiftly. In late April, Mr. Fowler reported that the Smiths had just moved into their new cottage. Later, when Fowler received an appointment as clerk of the federal court in Abingdon, Virginia, A. C. Smith became editor and publisher of the paper. He continued as such for several years.

Though much remodeled, the Smith cottage still stands at 413 Fifth Street in Bristol, Tennessee. In a sense it is a monument to those citizens who long ago demonstrated that they truly had hearts of gold.

A Parting Word

This is merely a small sampling of what the author has been told of the kind deeds of those early pioneers in Paradise. He is happy to state that he personally knows that this marked kindness and helpfulness of Bristolians flows on unabated today.

Morals of the Masses

In this section, a candid and fearless look will be taken at the moral situation in early Bristol. "Morals, why, they didn't have any!" exclaimed one old-timer when queried about the matter. With only a cursory look at the record, one might tend to agree with him. Indeed, moral conditions here were about as black as they can get, but in the midst of it all there were moralists who hated even the garment spotted by sin. They may have been—at least for the time—in the minority, but nevertheless, their purity of life sharply contrasted with the moral depravity that was all around them.

In matters of moral laxity it may be truly said that if it can be done, it has been done here. One can name anything—any type of moral transgression—and somewhere within Bristol, at some time, it has occurred. Now, true to man's nature, the lewd actions of the many were longer and more clearly remembered and told than were the good deeds of the few. Blatant incestuous practices, rapes of every description (even the rape of a cow!), unlawful cohabitation, love triangles, polygamy, bigamy, wide-open brothels, street prostitutes—all of these conditions and more were part of daily life in the then wild and wooly railroad town on the border of Tennessee and Virginia.

An indication of what life was like in Bristol after sundown may be had from an old, yet on file, complaint made by young Stephen Davis to the constable of Bristol (Goodson), Virginia, on September 5, 1879. Mr. Davis, a devout member of what is now State Street United Methodist Church, was a clerk in his father's store, and stores closed long after dark in those days.

He complained: "I cannot walk from my job to my home after dark without being hailed from every side by women of ill repute, some of them even taking hold of me and opening their clothes and trying to open mine and they attempt to draw me down in the street with them. Time and again I have had to shake them off and flee." Wow! It was a wild town, wasn't it!

Not all the immorality was confined to local citizens. The fame (or should one say ill repute) of this vice-ridden town spread abroad. People (mostly men) from distant places came for the express purpose of "tasting the unique pleasures" that were so easy to find here. Many travelers on the railroad arranged for a layover in Bristol so that they might make the rounds of the local vice dens.

That era passed, even though it was a long time passing, and was replaced by a tamer version of immorality. Of course, there are those who contend that Bristol is very immoral today. Certainly, that element yet exists. To those who have made an in-depth study of the situation that early existed here, today's moral laxity is a Sunday school picnic when compared to what it used to be.

Col. James King and the Double Standard

For a view of the double standard that prevailed during the slaveholding era, we will go back before Bristol to the time of Col. James King. Though not affiliated with any church until shortly before his death (he finally became a Presbyterian), he was, nevertheless, a strong moralist of a puritan-esque persuasion. His own family was under constant admonition to maintain "purity of mind and body." However, it is evident that, with the exception of his only daughter, his admonition was not always heeded.

It seems that Colonel King's puritanical views did not extend to the slave population on his noted Holly Bend plantation. Their morals did not matter to King. In the early 1800s (about 1815), Colonel King and his two sons made a trip to the Cranberry Iron Works in Shady Valley, and there they dined with a prosperous farmer named Blevins.

While on Blevins's farm, Colonel King became impressed with a male slave whom the Blevinses called Big Richard. He was half white, stood well over six feet in height, and weighed over two hundred pounds, all muscle. He was noted for his great strength, and it seems that he could not be exhausted. His age was then reckoned at about twenty-four years. Colonel King desired to have this slave so much that he offered Blevins a far greater sum than was the current going price of a sound male slave. The offer was accepted and Big Richard was brought to Holly Bend on Beaver Creek.

It was noted that Big Richard possessed a superior intelligence as well as physical strength, so Colonel King put him in training as a carpenter and brick mason. Almost daily, King saw some characteristic in Big Richard that greatly increased his admiration for him. Gradually, Colonel King began to contemplate another purpose for which this rare specimen of humanity could serve. Realizing that much of his wealth consisted of the slaves he owned, King had, from time to time, thought about selective breeding. Thus, he became convinced that Big Richard's greatest value would be to improve the slave force, so he made this superior slave the "official breeder" on the Holly Bend plantation.

According to Clora, one of the numerous offspring of Big Richard, Colonel King set up what was considered, in this area, to be a unique system of selective breeding. When a female slave reached the age of fifteen, she was put in the cabin with Big Richard for a stay of at least two weeks. When the babies of these girls turned a year old, the mothers were sent back for another stay with the "official breeder." The older mothers were also brought into this same system. Other male slaves were strictly forbidden from associating with the females until it was certain that a pregnancy had occurred. Then, "to keep them pacified," they were allowed to consort with the pregnant slave women. Through the years, the master of Holly Bend became convinced that superior slaves were being produced by this unique system.

Now, Colonel King, always attuned to the idea of making more money, eventually began to sell the services of Big Richard to neighboring slave owners. From time to time, those slave owners brought female slaves to Holly Bend for a stay in the "special cabin." The stay usually produced the desired result.

Among the estate papers of Col. John Preston of Walnut Grove (near Bristol) was found a bill from Colonel King (marked paid in full) for the services of Big Richard. It gives insight into the workings of this selective breeding process:

BILL FOR THE USE OF RICHARD BLEVINS

Fourteen days in cabin—$1.00 per day $14.00

For lost work of Richard while consorting
with Caroline—.50 per day 7.00

For Richard's regaining [recuperating?]
period, five days—.50 per day 2.50

Total due $23.50

Thus, for less than twenty-five dollars, Col. John Preston was likely to get a superior slave.

It is said that Big Richard sired well over one hundred babies in the ten-year period before Colonel King's death. The Colonel remained very concerned about adultery and fornication in his own family, but that concern did not extend to the slave population at Holly Bend, nor to those female slaves who were brought there to breed.

At Colonel King's death (August 17, 1825), Big Richard was taken back to Shady Valley to live at the iron works, which was under the supervision of the colonel's bachelor son, William King. It is said that this superior slave was used for the same purpose at the iron works. Perhaps he even got outside his "harem" a few times. Rumors persisted in the highland valley that several white women bore one or more children by him.

When William King died in the winter of 1844, Big Richard became the property of Rev. James King, who then lived on what is now Solar Hill in Bristol, Virginia. Being the pious Presbyterian minister that he was, James King did not wish to carry on the family tradition of selective breeding. He sold the prized slave of his father and brother to a plantation owner in Strawberry Plains, Tennessee. After the end of the Civil War, Big Richard, then an old man about seventy-five years old, was taken into the home of his daughter Clora. He died there in 1875, aged about eighty-five years. He is buried somewhere around Strawberry Plains. Doubtless, he has thousands of descendants living today.

Since skeletons are being rattled in the closets of the then local elite, perhaps it is good to rattle another. Col. Samuel E. Goodson, a nephew of the wife of Col. James King, was a lifelong bachelor and the aristocratic master of West Point, a fine plantation located on Beaver Creek, near present Bristol. It was commonly believed and long told by those who lived in the area at the time that Colonel Goodson served in the same capacity for his slave force as did Big Richard at Holly Bend. It is known that most of the slaves born on his plantation were half-breeds. One female slave, who did the work of a maid in his home, was said to have borne eleven children by him. Such was the case on many Southern plantations at the time, including the Lawrence County, Tennessee, plantation of this writer's great-great-great-grandfather.

The Unholy Line of William King

The noted Rev. James King of Bristol fame honestly acknowledged that his never-married brother, William King, did indeed have many descendants. He always referred to these descendants as the "unholy" line of brother William. Actually, this line of illegitimate children numbered more (twelve—some say thirteen) than did the legitimate line of Rev. King (seven). Interestingly enough, all of William's children had the same mother.

In 1804, William King, then nineteen years old, helped deliver a flatboat load of iron to New Orleans. While there, on instruction by his father, he bought four young slaves—three males and a female mulatto named Daisy, who was then about fifteen.

As was the common practice, the delivery crew bought horses for the long trip back to East Tennessee. The slaves had to walk ahead of the horses. Well, the male slaves had to, anyway. Hardly had the trip begun, when young William King had Daisy on the horse with him. A major link in the journey home was the famed Natchez Trace. One of the crew later revealed that when camp was made along this road through the Mississippi wilderness, William would lead Daisy into the dense brush and remain there for hours.

On the King plantation at Holly Bend (near present Bristol), it was the practice to see that the female slaves were impregnated when they reached the age of fifteen. Perhaps William King was tending to this duty before home was reached. Anyhow, it seems that those long hours spent in the brush produced results. Barely nine months passed before Daisy became the mother of a nearly white child, a daughter who was to be known as

Little Daisy.

After arriving back at Holly Bend, William King continued to keep Daisy close to him. Indeed, this was so for the rest of his life (he died in 1844). He loved to fish, and sometimes he would camp on the nearby Holston River for as much as a week at a time. At such times he would always take Daisy with him, ostensibly as the camp cook. If he had to travel about to his father's far-flung properties, Daisy was always taken along, again as his cook. When William briefly settled on newly acquired

This beautiful woman was a granddaughter of William King.

lands in Northern Alabama, Daisy was there with him. When he lived for a time on his sister's plantation at Strawberry Plains, Tennessee, this favorite female slave was kept in a little cabin near the Big House. When he came back to Holly Bend, Daisy was brought with him. When he finally settled permanently at the Cranberry Iron Works in Shady Valley, Tennessee, Daisy stayed with him as his cook and housekeeper.

Daisy continued to regularly bear light-skinned babies, until there were twelve or thirteen of them. (Two or three older members of the King family told that the thirteenth child was born dead, or died soon after birth.) Clora, long a slave and later a hired servant in the King family, always said that no one doubted that the children born to Daisy were King's. Si Goodson, a slave who worked for William King, said his master always called Daisy's ever-increasing family "our children." Though born to the master, they all remained slaves until freed during the Civil War.

William King died during the long cold winter of 1844. Honoring his request, slaves and several neighbors carried his coffin through deep snow, on a dark and freezing night, down the high mountain from Shady Valley and on to what is now the Ordway Cemetery. Daisy followed along behind

This son of William King married five times and was the father of thirty-eight children. He lived well past the century mark, dying at the age of 109.

them. The next day, she stood weeping under a snow-covered cedar tree as his body was lowered into the ground.

Soon after William King died, Daisy and her younger children were brought to Rev. James King's place, at what is now Bristol. After being freed, she worked on briefly as a hired servant in the King home. After Rev. King's death (1867), she became a servant in the Joseph Anderson home. (Mrs. Anderson was a daughter of Rev. James King.) Daisy died in the Anderson home in 1888, aged about ninety-eight years. She had often begged to be buried at William King's feet in the Ordway Cemetery. The Andersons, defying criticism from several Bristolians, honored her request. Her grave is unmarked. (The grave of William King was covered with an iron slab, which disappeared about one hundred years after it was placed.)

Now a word on the descendants of William King. Little Daisy married Job Wisdom at an early age. A son of theirs, Shadrack Wisdom, became a valued slave of Rev. James King—so valued that he was remembered in King's will. It is interesting to note that Shadrack's son Sedrick (or Cedric) Wisdom married into the Gillispie line of Greeneville, Tennessee, a line that descends from the second daughter of William King by Daisy the slave girl. Thus, there are descendants who have a double line to William King. One of them, a fine lady who died in May of 2000, was a close and valued friend of this author.

Doubtless, the "unholy" line of William King will continue on as long as the world stands.

Unique Method of Pre-Civil War Birth Control

Two old letters yet exist, brought together by a family historian, that reveal a unique form of pre-Civil War birth control. One was written by a distressed new mother then living in Green County, Arkansas, but formerly of Sullivan County, Tennessee. Dated September 1, 1859, it is addressed to her sister, then a new resident of the thriving border town of Bristol, Tennessee/Virginia. Both sisters were in slave-owning families. The husband of the sister living in Green County, Arkansas, apparently had a large cotton plantation. The husband of the sister living in Bristol owned a large farm just outside the town limits and kept a few slaves there. Among them was a female slave named Molly. We will meet her again soon.

This story is best told by quoting portions of the existing letters. The following was written from Green County, Arkansas:

Sister, I hardly know what to do. In August [the 11th] I gave birth to our sixth child, and that in a little over ten years. It was an awfully hard birth, and in the dreadful heat of these lowland summers. I was as wet with sticky sweat as if I had been doused in a river, and came out so weak that I could hardly lift a finger or barely speak. You know my health has always been delicate, and it gets much worse every time I am kept in. ["Kept in" was a common expression in those days—pregnant women seldom were outside the home.] This time was worse than ever. All the time I was frequently deathly sick—did not think I would live until the time. I know I just barely made it. I am still so weak as to have to be in bed much of the time and still have my doctor's attention. You can see I hardly can write. I feel certain the next time will take me from this earth. While prepared to go I do not want to leave my dear children motherless when they are so young and need me so much. I have pled with Richard [her husband] about this, but he will not relent on his rights to me. I would love to see you and dear old mother and the rest of the family back there, but if I am this way again I know it shall never be.

The answer to this letter is headed Bristol, Tennessee, and is dated

September 13, 1859. In it the concerned sister gets right to the point—and that in a frank manner:

> Sister, I have agonized over you ever since your letter came. I feel I know of a way that will save your health and life, and about release you from the dread of Richard's loathsome night burdens. Now, I tell you what to do. Give Richard one of the slave girls. I know you have several. Pick out one that will stir his lasciviousness, and make her entice him if necessary. I feel it will be no problem to settle him in this way once he knows you are not going to be contrary about it. I speak on experience, as I did my Marion [evidently her husband] this way—I gave him Molly when she came seventeen—and you know I have not been kept in for nearly eight years.

Perhaps this unique form of birth control worked for this Green County, Arkansas, woman. Further research revealed that she was living eighteen years later and had no children at home. Desperation can create some strange remedies!

Prostitution in Early Bristol

It is true that the world's oldest profession was one of the earliest institutions in Bristol—at least in the immediate Bristol vicinity. In the summer of 1856, the first work crews of the Virginia and Tennessee Railroad began to approach this area. The workers were engaged in the clearing of the right-of-way and grading the roadbed. A camp was set up by these workers on the knoll where now stands the Janie Hammitt Home.

Almost immediately, another camp was set up on the slope of the hill behind it, but the inhabitants of that camp were not construction workers. Rather they catered to the "needs" of those workers. That camp was home to a half dozen or more prostitutes who had followed the crew all the way from Lynchburg, Virginia. When the railroad crews broke up camp in Lynchburg and moved on, the girls did likewise. Indication is that these traveling prostitutes had a thriving business.

Marion Madison Thomas (the father of Old Daddy Thomas, who supplied a wealth of information for this and other books) was a member of that work crew. He passed some information on to his son, who much later shared it with this author, an excerpt from which is given here:

Pap said them wild women from Lynchburg were bossed by a big old nearly blind gal, who they all called "Lazy" Lucy. But I guess she didn't move around much because she was so big and couldn't see much good. But she could see enough to tell the difference in money. She done the takin'-in of the pay. She stayed in the tent and done that. The girls did their part of the work in the brush and weeds all over that hill back of the tent. The only time Lazy Lucy ever tuck on a feller was when all the girls were busy, and that didn't happen often.

For a quarter a girl would go to the brush with a feller. Pap said they were just strips of gals, most of them under twenty, he thought. But old Lucy were older. Most of the brush work was done at night. One of the men that worked with Pap got up in the brush one night, and him and that gal got down on a snake. That gal took out of that thicket lack a hant were aholt of her, and he never could get Lazy Lucy to give him his quarter back. And that girl wouldn't go back up there that night, and they had a time of ever gettin' her to go back up there after that. I never could get Pap to tell whether he ever took to the brush er not. Guess he were afeared that Ma would skin him alive, even if that were years ago.

That tent house of ill repute did not move on into Bristol. (The knoll where it was located was then considered to be far out in the country.) Possibly the reason that the girls did not move into town was because Bristol was then under the iron hand of Joseph R. Anderson, a noted moralist.

While there were a few lewd women in early Bristol who may have received paying guests in their homes, the first real public house of prostitution did not open in Bristol until the autumn of 1859. Strangely, it was operated by a seventeen-year-old girl. For a picture of that young madam we shall have to back up a bit.

The Saga of Ann Bachelor

In the spring of 1855, Lewis Bachelor (originally Baecheler) came to Bristol from Fredericksburg, Virginia, with his wife, Rosetta, and his orphaned niece, Ann. The growing little town would never be the same after this notable arrival.

Lewis became an important businessman. Rosetta became a legendary figure in her own time and so remained for nearly fifty years. And Ann gained the distinction, dubious though it may be, of operating Bristol's first brothel.

Ann was only twelve when the family arrived in the town (she turned thirteen on October 28 of that year). She was outgoing, vivacious, and sweet in spirit and attitude. She soon became a favorite of the local citizens. Lewis Bachelor (as the name soon came to be called here) was the town's first drayman. Ann, always an industrious person, helped her uncle in his work. This brought much admiration from the people they served, as well as others.

One of the stores to which she helped her father deliver goods was the James and Seneker mercantile, located at the corner of what is now Randall Street Expressway and State Street (then Fourth and Main—later Front and Main). W. W. James, the principal partner in this firm, had not yet moved to Bristol. He had placed a relative (some say a nephew) as manager of his part of the business.

This relative was young Joseph William James (called Joe Bill), then only eighteen years old. In spite of his youth, he made a capable manager of the large store. In her memoirs, written about eighty years later, Ann Bachelor comments at length on his remarkable intelligence, good nature, charm, and handsome demeanor.

Mutual attraction soon flared between the young merchant and the drayman's assistant. Young Mr. James soon began to call at the Bachelor home. The senior Bachelors made no objections—indeed, they were rather pleased that the neice they were raising might land so promising a young man. However, when marriage began to loom as a real possibility, the Bachelors, for some reason, insisted that the young couple wait until Ann reached her sixteenth birthday.

Now we will quote from Ann's memoirs, in which she is surprisingly open and honest about every matter: "We [she and Joe Bill] were bitterly disappointed that we could not marry, and somehow became much closer in our disappointment."

They indeed did become much closer on the night of October 1, 1856. Hundreds had gathered in the town to celebrate the arrival of the first passenger train. There was much excitement as the train came creeping into the station, but young Joe Bill James seems to have had other things on his mind.

Again, let Ann tell the story: "In all the excitement no one noticed when Joe Bill took me by the hand and led me farther and farther into the darkness and farther and farther from the crowd, even into a willow thicket on the bank of Beaver Creek, and there he made me a woman, and we began to practice marriage." Ann was four weeks short of her fourteenth birthday at the time.

It seems that this "practicing marriage" continued for nearly two years, but apparently the "wife" did not think it had to be monogamous.

In early spring of 1858, J. Austin Sperry of Knoxville came to Bristol to take over operation of *The Bristol News*. His coming here would bring a great change in the life of Ann Bachelor. Indeed, for her, life would never be the same again.

There was not much income from *The Bristol News*, so, in order to fare a little better, Sperry set up a subscription school in the newspaper office. This was done soon after he moved the newspaper into a building he had rented on the east side of Fourth Street, not far from Main (now State) Street.

Ann Bachelor was one of his first students. She was then a beautiful, vivacious girl of fifteen and was eager to learn. Perhaps the rest of the story is best left to Ann, as she wrote it in her memoirs over eighty years later. As she is in everything else she wrote, Ann is honest and forthright in revealing her involvement with J. Austin Sperry:

Austin was a young, strong, handsome man and a very good, patient, and kind teacher. I learned more under him in four months than I had for two years with another teacher. There was a strong feeling between Austin and myself from the beginning. He soon asked me to work a little after classes in his newspaper shop. I then suspected that he did this so we could be alone together, and later was made sure of it. I was very glad to do so, for I had come to the place where I wanted to be near him as much as I could. And I was aware that he had the same feeling about me. I confess I thought of him almost constantly and had sweet dreams about him at night though I was still practicing marriage with Joe Bill James as often as we could find the opportunity. We became more and more at ease with one another and stronger feelings were exchanged.

Mama [Rosetta Bachelor—actually her aunt] had always dressed me cheap and plain, but in mid-spring, Austin began to have beautiful clothes made for me, and he bought fine jewelry to go with them. I told Mama that I had bought them with my earnings at the newspaper office, but I doubt that she believed me.

It was about that time that we became very close. I made no objection, indeed gladly went with him late one afternoon, when he took me by the hand and led me up the back stairs to his bedroom. We there became as close as one can get, and many a time we went up those stairs afterward.

Then came that afternoon in which my life would be changed forever. We were folding papers on a big table that was kept in the back room of the shop for that purpose. Somehow we both got in great excitement. Neither he nor I thought of the unlocked, indeed, open, front door. We were in such haste that we did not go upstairs. A few minutes later, Mama, who become very suspicious about me and Austin, slipped through the door. She eased into the back room, where she discovered us at the edge of the table, clinging together in great delight.

Mama exploded in great fury. She jerked us apart and knocked Austin to the floor and kicked him several times. She then grabbed me and dragged me through the shop, all the while calling me a two-bit street whore and other bad names. Without giving me time to get my clothes back in place, she shoved me out into the street. Her anger boiling hotter by the moment, she told me to go from her and not to come home ever again, not even to get my clothes.

In a daze and not knowing what to do, I wandered on and across Main [State] Street, weeping all the while. As I was passing by the Dr. R. M. Coleman home, Mrs. Mary Coleman, who knew me well, saw me from the parlor window. She came running out and kindly led me into the house, inquiring all the while as to what my troubles were. Once inside, I told her everything leading up to that moment. Now, in my tale of woe, Mrs. Coleman saw a ray of hope.

Though married to Dr. Coleman for several years, only one child had been born to them, and I was told why. It seems that Mrs. Coleman had a mortal fear of pregnancy and childbirth. She was very fearful of becoming pregnant again, indeed, was terrified at the thought. This had caused much trouble in their marriage, because Dr. Coleman was a romantic man and often insisted upon his rights to her.

Before supper was set she had arranged with me to stay in the home, and for an unusual purpose. She would be the housewife of

Dr. Coleman and I would be his bed wife. She was so relieved by my agreeing to do so that she moved into the little bedroom behind the kitchen that very evening. I was put in the big bedroom across from the parlor with the doctor. For a little over a year we lived in a dream world of mutual great delight. I soon actually fell in love with Richard [Dr. Richard M. Coleman], and wish that I could have ever continued there.

Mrs. Coleman never seemed to be the least concerned or troubled by the situation. We all lived in sweet

Mrs. R. M. Coleman

harmony. To the town people I was a maid in the home, and no one ever seemed to suspect otherwise. Had this been known it would have been the scandal of the century for Bristol. The doctor, while not much liked because he was supposedly an atheist, was highly respected because of his great skill. Mrs. Coleman was strong in the Baptist faith and later became a leading member of the Bristol Baptist Church. So you see what a stir it could have caused, and Richard would likely have been jailed, for I was not yet sixteen at the time.

Dr. Coleman died the year I left Bristol [1870] and his secret died with him. His wife soon married a Mr. Head and left Bristol, though she returned a little later. Of course, she would never tell the matter.

About a year after I came to the Coleman place, there was a great revival in the Methodist church. Much to the town's surprise and joy Dr. Coleman became honestly, completely, and fully converted to religion. That meant our time together had to end, but he did not force me out destitute. He was kind to me and rented a little house for my home, near where he lived. [The little house stood on present Lee Street about where the law offices of Herbert G. Peters are now located.] He paid my rent for a year and saw that I had food until I began the work which will shortly be told.

I soon found two other girls of the town who were already wise to the ways of men and who badly needed a home. Soon that little house became the first public brothel in Bristol. I had just become seventeen [October 1859] when I became the madam of that brothel. It went over big, so much so that I soon rented a larger house and put on three more girls. By the time the war [Civil War] started [April 1861] we had moved to a much larger place on Water Street. By then there were a dozen of us.

The war greatly enriched us. Once, when an army of soldiers was stranded in Bristol, I had to take the girls and flee to hiding. Hordes of those men came there until all of us were exhausted and feared for our lives. J. Austin Sperry was in Bristol for a while during the war and often came to see me.

During all those years I kept a great supply of powdered cotton-wood bark on hand, which we all partook of greatly to keep from getting in a family way [pregnant]. I ordered it in large quantities from somewhere in Alabama and sold some to other madams who had opened places in the town.

Ann Bachelor continued her operation in Bristol until 1870. Years before that time she had become selective, and personally catered only to the elite who came to her door. The common trade was left to the "common" girls.

In late 1869, a gentleman from Philadelphia spent about six weeks in Bristol, seeing to land matters. He more or less rented Ann for the time he was in Bristol. She entertained him exclusively.

Perhaps her then supply of powdered cottonwood bark was not as strong as usual, for during that six-week period she became pregnant. It was her first pregnancy in a long career of constant "exposure."

Now, this Philadelphia gentleman had a relatively good marriage with a high-bred wife and a stainless personal reputation—at least up to that time. He felt that these must be protected and preserved at all costs, thus a strange deal was struck. Much detail could be given, but suffice it to say that he persuaded his widowed son to marry Ann and take her away from Bristol. Ann was very willing. She knew the son well. Indeed, he had also been a visitor to her brothel, and she was rather fond of him. The father owned a 926-acre plantation in central Georgia, and this he gave to his son as part of the arrangement. In February of 1870, Ann began her new life as mistress of this fine Georgia plantation, known as Mt. Holly.

Over the years that followed, Ann became one of the most respected and beloved women of her county. Two years after moving to Mt. Holly, she embraced the Methodist faith and joined the church of that denomination in the county seat, four miles from her home. She remained a faithful member of that church for the rest of her life. When a grand new building was erected for that church soon after the turn of the century, she donated one-third of the total cost. She also had a little chapel built on the plantation, for the use of the many tenants on the place. (Most of them were former slaves.) It still stands, is in current use, and is called Ann's Chapel.

During the summer of 1900, Ann made her only trip back to Bristol, to "again view the scenes of her younger days." Almost everything had changed; hardly anything was recognizable. She had so changed that no one recognized the refined and prosperous lady visitor from Georgia, and she did not reveal her identity. While in Bristol she arranged to visit her mother, the legendary Rosetta Bachelor, then an old, sick, embittered, and near-senile woman and a dope addict as well. Ann simply sat quietly in the room with her for a long while, unrecognized and never revealing who she was.

Ann wrote in her memoirs that, sitting in that room, she recalled how after the Sperry affair in 1858, her mother ever after held her in contempt, even turning her head and spitting in the opposite direction when they met on the street. Ann wrote that while sitting there in that room she finally and fully forgave her mother and thus increased her own sanctification (a strong Methodist doctrine at the time).

In her nineties Ann began to write her memoirs, finally producing well over four hundred handwritten pages. (She had hired a tutor soon after moving to Holly Hill, and was thus able to express herself in a clear manner.) The family (she had borne five more children) was instructed that the memoirs were to remain unread for five years after her death.

What a shock that family must have had when those memoirs were read! They had not the least inkling that their refined, proper, and dedicated Christian mother had once been a prostitute and the madam of the first brothel in Bristol, Tennessee/Virginia. According to her own confession in those memoirs, she had enjoyed (that is the word she used) carnal connection with close to six hundred men.

Ann Bachelor died on a bright and mild autumn afternoon while sitting on the spacious porch of her palatial, late-Victorian home and reading (without glasses) the county paper. The date was October 28, 1944, her 102nd birthday.

The madam of Bristol's first house of prostitution sleeps in the family cemetery on the Mt. Holly plantation. Her grave is marked by a large, chalk-white, Georgia-marble monument. Other than the usual vital statistics, the only engraving on the monument is a quotation from the Bible, said to have been done by her special request. It reads:

> For the grace of God that bringeth salvation hath appeared to all men, teaching us that, denying ungodliness and worldly lusts, we should live soberly, righteously, and godly, in this present world. (Titus 2:11-12)

Perhaps, for her, it is most fitting.

The Prostitutes

Just who were the women who staffed Bristol's brothels, and where did they come from? Information along that line is rather scarce. However, from a few pioneer settlers and from a court case here and there, a little light can be shed on the matter. By far the majority of the shady ladies came from other cities, particularly Lynchburg, Virginia, and Knoxville, Tennessee. Rumors circulated in the fraternity that the robust young town on the border of Tennessee and Virginia was fertile ground for the trade. One reason they came to Bristol was the fact that those larger population centers were becoming a bit too well supplied with common prostitutes, thus profits were down. It is well-known that the more notorious madams who operated in Bristol were from other localities.

There are at least two divorce cases on file in the Washington County, Virginia, courthouse wherein the aggrieved husbands reveal that their wives have taken up a life of prostitution in Bristol.

One husband states it thus: "She has left my home, bed, and board, has gone into the town of Bristol and there has entered a life of prostitution and is regularly employed in the Black Shawl, a notorious house of such, where for pay she offers carnal knowledge of her body to any who will have her."

Another abandoned husband charges: "Without cause she has departed completely from my house and moved to Bristol, Virginia, and there openly, flagrantly, and without shame has become a common whore. She now stays in the home of one Mag Worden, a lady of like character, and the two receive men, both white and black, at any time, night or day."

He got his divorce! Doubtless, other women were recruited from broken homes.

Some local recruits were women who were simply seeking a way of making a living. Old Daddy Thomas once told this writer that as a youth he had a neighbor lady who was a widow with three young children. She earned her living as a part-time prostitute, and in that manner supported not only her children but also her widowed mother, who kindly kept the children while the widow worked!

It was not uncommon for daughters of broken homes to take up a life of prostitution, and some of the girls were barely into their mid-teens. Pocahontas Hale, a notorious madam who long operated the Black Shawl (site of the present Cameo Theatre), was once charged with the modern-day equivalent of contributing to the delinquency of a minor. This happened because a girl of barely fifteen had been on her staff for over three months. Madam Hale swore that the girl had claimed to be twenty-two years old, and the jury agreed that she could pass as such. Madam Hale was cleared of the charge and agreed to send the precocious girl back to her parents.

In less than a year, the girl was employed in another house. Strangely, two members of the jury from Hale's trial were later caught visiting the girl in her new location. Perhaps they were trying to see if she really was as wayward as formerly charged!

One local young lady is known to have joined the staff of a local brothel (the Happiness Hotel) to spite her ex-boyfriend. They had broken up, and she thought a good way to get back at him was to become a prostitute.

There were many "one-" and "two-stall" operations scattered all over Bristol. Sometimes a single prostitute operated in her home. This was called a *one-stall* operation. Occasionally, two went together in a home, and this would become known as a *two-stall* setup. The common and well-known mark of a house where male visitors could be received was a red light in a window (kerosene lamp with dark red shade).

The story is told of a naïve young merchant here who went to Baltimore to buy stock for his store. While there he bought a quantity of red lamps, not knowing what they generally indicated back home in Bristol. Months later, he was still wondering why they wouldn't sell! Of course, no decent family would use such lights. It was also suspected that he was catering to the prostitutes of the town, and that almost ruined his business. What did he do with his lamps? Well, he finally did sell them to the local one- and two-stall houses of ill repute.

Rosetta Bachelor, a legendary local moralist, hated prostitutes. Once, when her righteous indignation reached fever pitch, she roamed through the dark streets of Bristol, shattering red lampshades with well-aimed shots from the two pistols she always carried. A very old man, yet living here in 1953, remembered that night. He candidly admitted that he was visiting in a one-stall operation on old James Row. (A row of cheap rental houses along the west side of what is now Piedmont Street, between Sycamore and Goode streets.) It seems that the highlight of his visit was suddenly interrupted by a shot from just outside the window and the explosive shattering of the red light. According to him, he was soon alone in the room, where the floor was covered by shattered glass. It seems that his lewd lady had bolted out the back door and fled at this unexpected interruption of her business.

Some of the women who eventually wound up as prostitutes in this rip-roaring town on the border were poor girls from the surrounding countryside who were seeking employment. There was always a madam ready to employ them if they were willing to lay their inhibitions aside, and many of them did. Old Daddy Thomas told of one of this category with whom he became "well acquainted." He once made the statement that she had learned she could make a better living flat on her back than she could hoeing corn!

Many want to know if these "easy ladies" were street walkers; that is, did they go out and actively solicit business. Largely, no, although it did happen extensively at a later period. For the most part, these women stayed in the brothels or in their homes and waited for visitors to come to them. It is said that some who were employed in the local houses might have gone for years and never leave the building. The truth is, they didn't need to solicit. Word soon got around, and after that they had all the business they needed.

And what became of this near army of lewd women who used to work within early Bristol? Well, like old soldiers, most of them seem to have just faded away, but not all. Several took local men for husbands, often their former customers. Some of them did well in such situations. Others returned to their families. Some became servants in Bristol homes. A few turned to that last resort of near-destitute women—taking in washings. More than a few did indeed become destitute in their older years, becoming wards of the county poor farms. More than one are known to have ended their days in state mental hospitals.

Two veterans of the oldest profession were still living in Bristol less than fifty years ago. This writer was fortunate to have interviewed both of them. Information about them and their early days as prostitutes follows.

Old Ti

Her name was Vashti Hays, but most older Bristolians referred to her simply as "Old Ti." When this author interviewed Old Ti, she lived in two small side rooms of a dilapidated house on Second Taylor Street. The people from whom she rented were as desperately poor as she was, but the rent received from the two drafty side rooms (six dollars per month) was a welcome addition to their meager, always uncertain, income. Old Ti's heat source was a small coal grate, for which there was not always coal. Sometimes sticks and leaves gathered from the hill behind the house had to suffice for fuel. A few feet from the back door was the communal outhouse, but on frigid winter days and in times of heavy rain, a hole in the floor behind the kitchen stove served as her "indoor plumbing."

The furnishings were sparse and rather crude. A twin-size iron bedstead, brown from rust; two cane-bottom, straight-back chairs; and a broken-down lamp table made up the inventory of the living room. Holes in the seats of the chairs were covered with pieces of cardboard. There was some type of battered stove (this writer thinks it was a wood burner) in the small kitchen. A small, uncovered table and a backless chair were the other principal articles in this room. A wooden fruit crate served as a stand for the water bucket. (A yard spigot supplied water for Old Ti and the landlord's family.) Such was the condition of her humble living quarters when this writer first saw them back in late October of 1953.

Old Ti had once been a noted Bristol prostitute, but ceased working in the Black Shawl brothel when she was about forty years old. She carried on a one-stall operation in her home for perhaps another twenty years after leaving the regular circuit.

The following years were very hard for her. She had no local relatives and seemingly never more than a half dozen persons she could call friends. Her poverty had increased as she gradually became unable to do menial tasks for others. Finally she became totally dependent upon a small welfare check from the state. "I get so little it is hard to keep soul and body together," she often said. She thought she was then (1953) about ninety-two years old, but her age could be approximated only by calculating from the time she was brought to Bristol.

In the fall of 1953, this writer was employed in the welfare department of the local Salvation Army. Part of the work consisted of passing out government commodities (food products) to the needy of the city. One day as this was being done, an old man who always came on "give-out" day tarried long so he could talk a bit in private. It was then that he told of the impoverished Vashti Hays. He was open and frank, admitting that "far back he had used her for a wife when his own dear Nellie had been ailing for a long time." (This was after Old Ti had set up her one-stall operation and was doing her business at home). He added that Old Ti wasn't so young and pretty then, but went on to admit that he wasn't so young and good looking at the time either! "But she'd do in a tight," he explained. His plea was that some food be delivered to the needy woman. "She shore could use some of that government stuff but just ain't able to hobble off down here for it."

After he left, much thought was given to his plea, and sympathy reached out to the suffering ex-prostitute. The regulation then was that no food could be delivered to anyone, but this writer was never one to believe

Vashti Hays

that charity should ever be governed by endless and oftentimes uncharitable regulations. So, on the afternoon of the next day (a Saturday), he sacked up a run of commodities and hoofed it up to Old Ti's humble abode on Second Taylor Street.

The old lady eyed with undisguised suspicion the stranger standing at her door on that bright and clear, but rather cold, late October day. Once his mission was made known, she welcomed him in. She was very grateful for the food he brought. (He suspected that there was little, if any, other food in the house that day.) After the commodities were placed on the tiny table in the kitchen, she invited him to one of the broken-down chairs by the fireplace. Thus began a series of visits that extended through that long cold winter and into the following spring.

It was noticed during that initial visit that there was little cover on Old Ti's bed. Actually, it appeared that her only bedcover was a ragged quilt, which had so many splits and holes in it that it could have provided little comfort in that frigid room on long winter nights. On the next visit (actually the next morning before church), two wool blankets and a good comforter from the Salvation Army rummage room were delivered to her door. No fortunate child inundated with toys on a Christmas morning would have been happier and more delighted than was Old Ti that Sunday morning so long ago.

After this writer gained her confidence and after a promise was made to reveal nothing until after her death, Old Ti opened up and talked freely of her coming to Bristol and the work that followed:

> I was born up somewhere in Shady Valley, Tennessee. Must have been about the starting of the war [Civil War]. I reckon I was the only child, never knowed of any more being around. Pap went off to the war about the time it started, I think. When I can first begin to recollect, he came back home late that winter. A big snow was on the ground. Near night I think it was, some of them mean fellers [likely bushwhackers] came to our house and got hold of Pap and led him off in the woods. That made a dent in my mind that I can remember. I can recollect Maw screaming and crying as he was led away. Then I remember hearing the shot over in the woods.
>
> About daylight next morning Maw took me up and started with me to her sister's home in Bristol. I must have walked some, for my feet were froze when we took lodging in a big house out in Holston Valley. A woman there spent a long spell trying to thaw me out. I reckon it was the next day when we come to Aunt Dessie's in Bristol.

Then she made a startling statement:

> You know that's been way over ninety years ago and I ain't been out of Bristol since. We stayed at Aunt Dessie's through the rest of the war then moved out on our own. Maw worked at all kinds of jobs

in order for us to live. I was just past fifteen when she took bad sick and soon died. I was taken into the home of two old people by the name of Simpson, who needed help. Within two years both of them had sickened and died. It was then that Pocahontas sought me to work in her place on lower Main Street.

I really knowed what the Black Shawl was, but at first I did think that she just wanted me to work as a maid. In no time she put me in a regular room upstairs and told me I must let any man that came in to do what he wanted with me. I reckon I just couldn't think of any way out so I just stayed on.

I well recollect that the first man who came in to see me was the constable on the Tennessee side of the town. I think that was the first night in my room upstairs. I was scared and attempted to run, but as big and strong as he was he didn't have any problem holding me down and having his way with me. Pocahontas Hale—we called her Old Pokey behind her back—said I must not resist the men anymore.

I was there fifteen years I think, maybe twenty. Well, I guess more than that. I was seventeen when I went there and about forty when I came out. By that time Old Pokey were long dead, but another woman who worked there took it over.

Now I can't say that I ever did like my doings there, but it got to where it was every day and night business, so I got used to it and worked on. Ordinary men I never thought much about—didn't bother me—but I was troubled that some local men brought their teenage sons to break them into the "joys of life" as they said it. Being in my teens myself I was usually the one chosen to do those jobs. I think the youngest I ever saw brought to me was just four-teen, but he had become a man early. He kept right on coming till he married six or seven years later.

Old Pokey was a hard boss. She made us bathe every day in an old washtub she kept in the kitchen. She watched over us while we bathed and then sprinkled us with rose water, which she made her-self. Some folks in town made good selling her roses from their yards.

We might have been clean, but some of our men visitors were not, especially them loggers and lumber men from Holston Moun-tain. They always seemed to come to our place when in town. Some of them shore didn't have rose water on them. Seemed more the products of a hog pen.

After this writer gained her confidence, he became bold and asked her specific questions, ones that are common to all researchers of life "beyond the tracks."

She pertly responded to a question about the going price in those days:

Oh, yes. I well remember that. Pokey always collected the pay down in the hall. At first a time with one of the girls cost fifty cents, but there were places that charged less—some as low as twenty-five cents. Later, I would say about seven or eight years after I come there to work, the price went up to a dollar, and not long after that she set up two prices. One dollar and fifty cents for the girls upstairs and two dollars for the girls on the first floor. Just before she set it up that way she had moved me downstairs, saying I had got popular with the trade and was frequently being requested.

Did she have a time limit on visits?

Oh, yes, Pokey wore a watch on a long chain around her neck, and she worked both floors through the night. About twenty minutes was the time of a visit. If the door didn't open by then she would stand in the hall and sing a strange song. That was the signal that the man must come out. It were this strange song that a feller hears her singing up in the Flat Hollow Cemetery a few years after she died. I can hear it yet in my sleep and dreams.

Was there any form of birth control practiced in the Black Shawl?

Well, yes and no. They was lots of those things that was then called French novelties [condoms] sold in the drugstores and pool halls here. They cost Old Pokey a nickel apiece and she tried to sell every man that come one for a dime—made some money that way. Some men refused to bargain further, and some of them might wrap themselves in a silk handkerchief. With some it was a rough cotton handkerchief—I always dreaded them. Some of the men had nothing.

Old Pokey kept a pot of slippery elm bark on the kitchen stove. If a girl took some of the broth from this it was supposed to help. And, yes, some of the girls did get in the family way, but for some reason not many. The babies seemed to disappear right after being born, and the girl would be back to work in a few weeks. There wasn't a doctor in town who would come to the Black Shawl. Some did serve other places, for why I don't know. Pokey was a good midwife, so she took care of things. There was rumors later that she buried the babies in a big garden behind her building, but I really don't know about that. You know, she often let those bigged [pregnant] girls work close to the time they were due. She once told me that there were men in town who would pay extra for a bigged girl.

Soon after coming to Bristol, this writer had more than once been told the story of a mob attack at the Black Shawl. It seems that Rosetta Bachelor, the town's resident moralist, had become enraged when a young man was killed at the back of Pokey Hale's establishment. On a Sunday morning she had, as usual, attended services at the First Presbyterian Church. There, Rev. George A. Caldwell preached a fiery sermon on the evils of prostitution. That caused the already smoldering anger of Mrs. Bachelor to burst into flame. She could hardly wait to leave the church and go out looking for recruits in the "holy" cause. She had no trouble in finding them. There were many women in the town who had good reasons to hate Old Pokey's place of business. These women received their instructions and eagerly waited for the coming night.

When asked about this, Old Ti's eyes lit up:

Land, yes. I was right there when the house was attacked. Never can forget it. Why, I reckon I'm the last veteran of that battle.

It were on a Sunday night about ten, I think. Business was good; it seems that Sunday nights always were—almost equal to Saturdays. I don't think there was a room but that had a man in it. We were all just taking care of business, when all of a sudden old Rosetta Bachelor ramrodded the front door down with a big beam of some kind. The other women were sent to knock out windows, and once inside they began to yell like Indians and began battering the room doors down.

Well, now, most of the girls and their men on the lower floor jumped out the windows and fled into the darkness. My man that night were a well-known businessman of the town, and I recollect him yelling out, "Oh, hell, I can't be caught in here," and he jumped through the window and I was left alone. I ran into the hall, which by that time was filled with the shouting mob.

Now, folks on the up floor couldn't use the windows. Land, those girls, most of them naked as jaybirds, came running right down the stairs. Their men were among them, and most of them were naked or just partly dressed, and most of them were still in that peculiar shape as when they left the bed.

The sight of all this enraged Rosetta, and she and the other women began striking at them. Most wildly tore through the hall and escaped, but a few were knocked down in the floor and roughly handled by that mob.

Old Rosetta kept shouting, "Now get out of town and stay out. Don't you dare show up here again."

Most didn't obey her, though some did. I reckon Old Pokey dashed out the back door at the first attack on the front one. I don't remember seeing her at all. She got the owner to repair the place, and we were at it again in two weeks or so.

Rosetta once emptied that place again, but not by open attack. In the darkness of night she carried two beehives from her yard and placed them at either side of the narrow trail that led up to the back door. This entry was for those who had to make sure that they were never seen entering the Black Shawl.

Just as she had anticipated, at about ten that night a young man came hurrying along the back trail. Suddenly his feet encountered a rope, and he fell flat forward, emitting a loud and surprised groan as he hit the ground.

The sudden jerk of that rope threw the hives over. Angry bees swarmed out and into the open windows of Old Pokey's notorious establishment. In moments the same kind of stampede that had followed the open attack on the place was on. Pedestrians out on the street were shocked when nude men and women raced out among them, yelling and slapping at the little tormentors. It is said that Mrs. Bachelor, who seldom laughed, sat back on the hill above the backyard of the Black Shawl and had herself a merry old time.

This writer's visits to Old Ti extended through that winter. She was always glad to see her "boy from the Salvation Army," as she came to call him. It is certain that the government commodities which he always brought formed most of her meager diet. January became exceedingly cold—too cold to go out and gather sticks from the hillside. Strangely and unexpectedly, a load of coal was delivered to her door. Another followed in February and again in early March. It is almost certain that she had the warmest winter she had ever known in the drafty rooms that she called home.

When the colorful glories of early May began to spread over Bristol, word came that Old Ti was very sick. Some hot soup was simmering on the Salvation Army kitchen stove when the word came. Some was being dipped into a container to carry to her, when another message arrived that she had just died.

Not a relative or close friend could be found. She had been almost completely alone in the world, and that for years past.

Only the kindness of a local undertaker kept her from receiving a pauper's burial. She was buried in Potter's Field, at East Hill Cemetery. A local minister delivered a short funeral sermon and tried to lead the six or so persons present in the singing of "In the Sweet Bye and Bye." Mrs. Osborne, then living on Highview Hill (Second High Street), sent over a dozen or so pink roses from her yard. These formed the only floral piece on Old Ti's grave.

And so sleeps in an unmarked grave in East Hill Cemetery one who, for this writer, painted a vivid picture from life's "other side." Her contribution to a complete history of Bristol is gratefully acknowledged.

Mattie Dixon and the Happiness Hotel

Of all the old veteran prostitutes interviewed, Mattie Dixon was the most talkative. Indeed, she talked so freely of her career days that simple discretion does not permit recording here many vivid details that she gave this author. At the time she was interviewed, in early 1954, she was careful to make it clear that she had "done got religion and then got plumb sanctified," and that her past life had lost its power to condemn her. Actually, it appeared that she got a certain satisfaction, and perhaps felt an inner cleansing, by telling it all—and that like it truly was. Whatever the cause of her complete confessions, she certainly painted a vivid picture of life's "other side."

The only way Mattie could date her birth was that she had always been told that she was born the day Abraham Lincoln was shot (April 14, 1865). She was an illegitimate child of a woman who also had been born to an unwed mother. Mattie's father supposedly was a well-known Bristol businessman, but, because it is a case of supposition, his name will not be given here. (He still has descendants living in this city.) It was clear, though, that Mattie Dixon remained a bit proud of her distinguished ancestry all her life. Indeed, she often spoke of her locally prominent half brothers and half sisters, two of whom were still living in 1954. Of course, it is certain that they were not proud of her! Mattie had four or five siblings, supposedly all with different fathers.

Mattie Dixon told of many hardships endured by her mother and the baseborn children that made up her family. They lived, more or less, as squatters in a miserable shack in the vicinity of what became Second High Street (across the tracks behind the present King Pharmaceuticals Plant). There was no government aid for impoverished children in those days, and local charity did not often extend to "unrespectable" families. Their principal support came from certain men of the town who often visited the little shack. Even this support was meager.

Mattie remembered that when she was a small child, the man who was supposed to be her father came with a small amount of meal and a piece of side meat from his downtown store. She and her siblings were made to stay in the small kitchen while this man was "entertained" in the front room.

Mattie Dixon never attended school. She could neither read nor write, and most figures meant nothing to her. When she was between fourteen and fifteen years old—closer to fifteen, she thought—her mother sent her to pick up apples from under a gnarled tree that stood near the present First Christian Church. It was not uncommon for Mattie to be sent out to find whatever bits of food she could—often from local garbage cans. That fall day was rather cold, so the shivering girl (she had no coat) hoped to find a few apples and then hasten home. As it happened, she never reached the tree, nor was she ever home again.

Mattie Dixon's path to the apple tree passed along notorious Front Street. On the left side of this street, a short distance south of the Beaver Creek crossing, stood what was supposedly a large boardinghouse principally catering to railroad workers. Secretly, and somewhat facetiously, it was known as the Happiness Hotel. In reality, it was a thriving brothel owned and operated by an unusual and eccentric woman who had the fitting name of Sweet Charity Love. She had moved to Bristol from Lynchburg around 1876. Soon after arriving in the wide-open border town, she divorced her husband, and it was then that she opened her boardinghouse, which quickly became more than that. Indeed, she did continue to keep boarders, and those boarders soon learned that more was available in her establishment than just food and a simple room.

Sweet Charity Love had known about the blossoming young Mattie Dixon for some time and had been seeking a chance to talk to her. When

Sweet Charity Love operated the Happiness Hotel.

she saw the girl hastening along in front of her place, Charity quickly went out and invited her to come in and warm a while. This was the opportunity Mrs. Love had been waiting for, and she would make the most of it.

Once inside, Mattie was taken to the kitchen and given a bowl of hot soup, the most food she had eaten in several days. While the hungry girl devoured the food, Mrs. Love offered her work, "perhaps in the kitchen." She told Mattie, "I'll buy you some pretty clothes, and you'll have a nice warm room and a good clean bed." As a further inducement, Mattie was told that she might make as much as a dollar every day if she did as she was told.

Then, in a moment of what was likely genuine charity, Mrs. Love told Mattie that she need not bother with picking up half-rotten and sour apples. "Why, I'll send your mother a bushel of perfectly good apples from Buckner's store." Later that day she took Mattie to the Buckner store, bought the pretty clothes she had promised, and ordered a bushel of apples to be sent to the Dixon shack.

After a nice warm supper, the best she had ever eaten in her nearly fifteen years, Mattie Dixon was shown to the room she was to occupy. It was back of the kitchen, had a cheery, open fireplace, and was well furnished. It was then that this cunning madam became more open about what Mattie was to do. Let us hear it in Mattie's own words, as told to this author nearly fifty years ago:

Mrs. Love told me she didn't want me to be afraid or lonely my first night there. She had arranged for a nice young man to come to my room later that night. He was an engineer on the Virginia and Tennessee Railroad, and would not be in town until about ten o'clock, but he would come right over and be with me the rest of the night. She assured me that he was very handsome, was kind and gentle, and that I would be very pleased with him, and would want to see him every time he was in town. She made it clear that he would make me feel safe and keep me from being lonely by sleeping with me.

I confess I really knew what I was getting into, but the thought of spending another cold and hungry winter in that drafty old shack was unbearable. I also confess that I really knew what to expect, as once or twice I had watched through a crack as Mama had connected with the man who was supposed to be my daddy. Really, as the night wore on, I began to thrill at the thought of what was to come.

This man did come into my room around ten that night. I liked him from the first. He did come into my bed, and I don't think either of us slept a wink until he had to go away soon after daylight the next morning. I had liked him at first, and I loved him before the night ended. Yes, I went to bed as a girl but I got up a woman. My long life of sin began that night. I later learned that this young engineer had a standing call with Mrs. Love for a young girl that had never been touched, and he paid her, maybe thirty dollars, when she found me.

From that night I began to do regular work at Mrs. Love's. I took anyone she sent to my room, but I always was happy when the young engineer came back to my bed. I finally learned he was married and had two or three children. You know, that bothered me a sight when I began to think on religion a few years back. Yes, it bothered me awful bad, but now since I'm saved and plumb sanctified I reckon it won't be held against me. Of course, there were lots of other married men, but somehow I always felt worse about him.

When asked about the men who came to the Happiness Hotel, she replied:

Now, there was a sight of different men, but a lot of our trade came from the railroad men. There were others, from the lowest in town to some up and well-shined men. When peddlers came to town—you know, men from the country that had stuff to sell—they often came to our place. Drummers [salesmen] were a good bet. Seems we got lots of the local officials of the town too. Mrs. Love always told us to be extra good to them, that it would help to keep us from getting lawed [raided by law enforcement]. Now, men whose wives were late in the family way would come to us.

Our men were young and old and all the way in between. We had some teenagers and some in their eighties. Old Jim Stutts, who lived just outside of town, was like eighty-five, and he usually showed up once a week. He always said he had "run through" with three wives and was out again. He took a special liking to me, and would leave me extra money. Well, to put it short, we had all kinds of men from the town and country and from off the railroad.

It was only logical that this author would inquire about the then going price (1880 and later):

When I commenced working there they charged fifty cents for a run [visit]. From that I got a dime. For $1.50 a man could stay in my bed all night. Later, she raised the price to $1.00, and $2.50 for all night. I got a quarter out of the dollar and seventy-five cents out of the all-night cost.

When Mattie Dixon was asked about birth control, she revealed the strange practice of what many Bristolians in the know called the "pepper dance." Instead of using Mattie's description of this unique form of contraception, let us hear it from one of her customers. That customer was none other than Old Daddy Thomas, who told this author so much about early Bristol history:

When I was about twenty-four and fresh married, my woman got bigged [pregnant], and on late I got to hurting for female comfort. I had heard of this new gal at the Happiness Hotel. Men told me I sure ought to get with her. I went down and I soon got with Mattie Dixon—she was just a strip of a gal, about sixteen, I think. Well, now, when the curtain fell, that gal leaped out of the bed and swooped her hand through a plate that was settin' on a table, and then swiped it under her nose. Then she started a leaping dance around that room, a-sneezin' fast all the while. I thought at first that she had really got happy, but I later learned that she had put pepper under her nose and then went to dancing as she sneezed. Us men called it the "pepper dance." They thought that it would keep them from getting in the family way. That started at old lady Love's, but finally I think they did it down at the Black Shawl.

At night in the Happiness Hotel the whole building would shake when girls all over the place got to doing that quare dance. I never went back there no more.

At the Black Shawl, French novelties (condoms) were available. They were probably more effective than the strange pepper dance. One strong girl, who incidentally did not last long in the Happiness Hotel, had the "unholy" habit of shoving her visitor from the bed and into the floor at the crucial moment. Sweet Charity Love quickly dismissed the girl when several customers demanded their money back. It is likely that her method of birth control was a surer bet than that "quare dance," as Old Daddy Thomas called it.

Mattie Dixon told much of daily life inside Mrs. Love's brothel. This unusually kind madam boarded the girls and did most of the cooking herself. The girls ate at a long table in the kitchen. For the most part, the girls looked forward to the times of fellowship at this common table. Food was abundant and well prepared. When business was slow, the girls often gathered in the front parlor for games or small talk. Sometimes the talk was of experiences had with the male visitors during the previous night. Usually there had been one to three visitors for each girl—seldom more than three. When there were large gatherings in town, the numbers might run higher. Mattie told that the most men she ever entertained during one night numbered either five or six; she could not remember for sure about the matter.

If a girl became ill, she was well cared for. If a doctor seemed to be needed, they sent for one. Dr. H. T. Berry seems to have been the house physician for the Happiness Hotel. Mattie remembered that two girls died during her time there. One of them had no known relatives. Mrs. Love gave her a decent burial, but it had to be in the black cemetery in Flat Hollow. Shady ladies were not allowed to be buried in the town's main cemetery (what is now East Hill).

One thing this author quickly noticed was that Mattie Dixon would never speak an unkind word about Mrs. Love. This madam had been very kind to Mattie, as she was to all her employees. Mattie had enjoyed her company for a few years, as well as her genuine compassionate care. Mattie had been helped on several occasions by good advice from Mrs. Love. "She was more like a mother to me than a boss," Mattie once said.

After Mattie had worked in the Happiness Hotel for about six years, she began to tire of it and looked for a way out. An eighty-five-year-old customer has previously been mentioned. Mattie was his favorite at the brothel. Finally, he proposed that she come out

Mattie Dixon began a life of prostitution in early Bristol when only fourteen years old.

to his farm and work for him. Of course, she well knew what a part of that work would be, but from experience in the brothel she knew that such a particular job would be done only about once per week. She could endure that. So she left the brothel and went to live on the man's farm, not far from Paperville, Tennessee. They were married, and about six months later the old man suffered a severe stroke and died.

Mattie then went to live in the home of her dead husband's son, whose wife was ill. Mattie's job was to cook and keep house as well as tend to the ailing wife. Soon her employer was having her work in the barn with him, shelling corn, feeding the livestock, and so on. Well, you can guess what happened next. She soon found herself serving as his wife. (He was even more romantically inclined than his father had been.) He and Mattie were married less than a week after his ailing wife died.

It was a profitable marriage. By it Mattie gained a fairly prosperous farm. Four years and two children later, her second husband died. Then Mattie set somewhat of a record by marrying her deceased husband's son from his first marriage. She had been married to the grandfather, the son, and now the grandson, in a descending scale. (By being married to her stepgrandson, was she her own grandma? You figure it out!) For the first time she had a husband who was about her age.

Mattie and her third husband had many years together. Five or six children were born to them. When this author first met her, in late 1953, she had been a widow for several years. Her family had scattered. The farm had been sold, and she had moved to a small apartment on Third Street in Bristol, Tennessee, where she was living in dire poverty. (Money received from the sale of the farm had long before been depleted.)

As he did for Vashti Hayes, this writer supplied the aged Mattie with government commodities, and she was grateful. Because she was too feeble to walk the short distance to the local Salvation Army for her dole of food, it was taken to her, even though it was against the regulations at the time. The attitude of the deliverer was that the hungry must be fed, and regulations be hanged.

On a mild October evening in 1955, this author strolled over to the local depot to watch Number Forty-Two come in. He was a lover of trains, and this was a common practice of his. By the time he reached the depot, the whistle of the incoming train could be heard from far down the track. The platform lights came on, and the express and mail wagons were rolled into place.

In the midst of all the commotion was a faint call. "Mr. Bud, oh, Mr. Bud," came from the shadows near the waiting-room door. It was Mattie Dixon, leaning on a cane with a small satchel in her hand. "My daughter, Betsey, that lives up in Lynchburg, has sent for me to come live with her," she explained. "I'm going, for I don't have nothing here. I'll miss here but I reckon I'll be better off up there. I'm getting mighty feeble, and I don't guess I'll be able to take care of myself much longer," she said, just as Number Forty-Two came to a halt by the long platform. It was later learned that she simply walked out and left what few personal possessions she had in the little apartment on Third Street.

The conductor practically lifted Mattie onto the train. She turned in the vestibule of her coach and waved to this author. He stood transfixed as the train slowly pulled away. Indeed, he watched until it disappeared at the upper end of the railroad yards, and he listened to the moaning whistle until it became ever fainter on the rapidly cooling night air. The last of the old veteran prostitutes was gone—an era had ended.

The House of the Rising Sun—A Black Brothel in Bristol

A black brothel once operated on Second Taylor Street in Bristol, Virginia. The madam, known only as Miss Ethel, was a mulatto from Atlanta, Georgia. She came to Bristol with a man, who soon dumped her. Alone in this city, she turned to her former trade of operating a house of ill repute. If she had family or near-relatives, no one in Bristol ever knew it. She is said to have been markedly refined and graceful and to have spoken near perfect English. She always presented a youthful and cheerful expression, even into extreme old age. She dressed in the latest fashion and wore much jewelry, including rather large earrings, and her fingers dripped with diamonds. It was evident that she had been reared well and apparently had prospered in her former Atlanta operation.

Soon after Miss Ethel was abandoned in Bristol, she rented the largest house on Second Taylor Street (eight rooms), and then went out to recruit black girls and women who were willing to work in her kind of business. She was more than successful in her quest. She staffed all her rooms, and there were several more who wanted to become part of the operation. The latter she put on hold, sometimes calling them in when the house overflowed with waiting customers. At such times she turned her kitchen and basement into receiving rooms.

Her brothel became a smashing success from the very beginning. Soon after it opened, someone who was well traveled facetiously called it "The House of the Rising Sun," likely after the much larger brothel of that name in New Orleans. The name stuck. Miss Ethel's place was so known all through its several years of operation.

Though set up as a brothel to serve the black population, a vast majority of the customers were white. Occasionally, a black man called for a white woman. Ever ready to accommodate the trade, Miss Ethel had arrangements made along that line. Next door lived a young white widow who had agreed to entertain black men. When a black man came to The House of the Rising Sun with such a request, he was sent to the widow's home. She made her living in this manner over the next two decades.

Old Daddy Thomas used to tell of a neighbor of his who regularly went to Miss Ethel's place "when his wife was contrary," as he put it. It seems that this contrary wife found out about his visits to the brothel. One night the man told his wife that he was going to visit a friend. She became suspicious, put a pistol in her pocket, and followed him. Sure enough, his journey ended at the notorious house on Second Taylor Street.

His enraged wife waited until one of the girls led him into her room, then she entered the brothel, without bothering to knock. With pistol in hand, the man's wife stormed into the room where her husband, by then completely nude, was, shall we say, just "getting down to business."

To say that the business was suddenly interrupted is putting it mildly. Giving him only enough time to snatch up his clothes from the floor, she, at gunpoint, marched him out into the snowy night. Nude and carrying the clothes under his arm, he was marched home. Along the way, his wife decided to add to his punishment by making him use the icy waters of Beaver Creek as his path. She walked along the bank with the "persuader" still pointed at him. Perhaps that midstream march helped to cool him down a bit. It is near certain that he never ventured back to Miss Ethel's place.

Nightly, for a little over thirty years, eager men found their way through the darkness (no streetlights at that time) to the famous, or shall we say infamous, house where a red light was always kept burning in a front window. During those years, the fame of The House of the Rising Sun spread abroad. Traveling men often stopped off for a night in this place of reputed unique pleasures.

Miss Ethel finally made a crucial mistake. Ever attuned to ways to increase business, she began to recruit very young black girls—some of them were in their early teens. She hoped they would attract teenage boys, which would open up a new and large group of the town's male population. She even lowered the going price so that these largely unemployed boys could afford to finance their young lust. As it turned out, not many boys came, but the girls were much patronized by thrill-seeking older men.

Somehow the town authorities learned of Miss Ethel's young workers. They made a sweeping raid and closed down the entire operation. Miss Ethel was tried in the Washington County Circuit Court, heavily fined, and given three years of probation.

During her probationary period, she opened a restaurant in downtown Bristol. There she kept far more waitresses than she needed. They were housed in rooms over the restaurant, and it was said that their real purpose was to wait on men in a special way.

When she was probably in her early sixties, Miss Ethel became the so-called housekeeper for a rather wealthy local businessman. There she spent the rest of her long life. She died during the flu epidemic of 1918 and was buried in the Citizen's Cemetery, near the end of Piedmont Street.

At least in one instance, the effect of this local black brothel was felt many years after it closed. Around 1925, two local men sat conversing on a shady porch of a house that stood on Lottie Street, near its intersection with Second Taylor Street. The wife of one of these men, a big, rough, Amazon of a woman, sat nearby.

The visitor asked the husband of this woman if he remembered Miss Ethel's House of the Rising Sun.

"Land, yes," the man replied. "How could I ever forget it. I went there lots of times!"

That big old wife heard what her husband had said and instantly flew into a rage. She sprang on him like a panther on its prey, gave him a good slapping, then shoved his rocker off the end of the high porch, causing him to sprawl out in the yard. You can bet he never mentioned Miss Ethel's place again!

Prostitute Lottery

Early Bristol prostitutes were poorly paid. Those working in the regular houses received only a small percentage of what the male customers paid for a visit. For years the cost to the customer was one dollar. Of this, the girl who did the entertaining received only a quarter. It is likely that the madams of these houses wanted to keep the girls poor, so they would be less tempted to leave the establishments.

One of the more enterprising girls—a beautiful blonde named Lorena, who had formerly worked in the Happiness Hotel on Bristol's notorious Front Street—devised a rather unique plan to increase her earnings. She made a deal with Isaac Nickels, who operated the palatial Nickel Plate Saloon on the northwest corner of Cumberland and Front streets, to sell chances on herself. She also rented a room over the back of his saloon, where she could deliver the prize to the winner of this rather unusual lottery.

The tickets—little pieces of paper with numbers handwritten thereon—were sold to customers of the Nickel Plate for twenty-five cents each. At nine o'clock each

Lorena offered herself in a Bristol lottery.

evening, hopefuls and interested onlookers gathered around Nickels's bar for the drawing. Whoever held the lucky number was immediately sent up the back stairs for a stay of several hours with Lorena. If Lorena was especially pleased with her man of the evening, she might invite him to spend the night.

It became a common occurrence at the Nickel Plate for a customer to walk up to the bar and call out, "Give me a dram of your best whiskey and a chance on Lorena." Sometimes they would buy several chances. Indeed, there were men so desperate for a night with the reputed best prostitute in town that they bought all the available tickets—usually forty, at a cost of ten dollars. Not many could afford such a lavish bid.

What was Isaac Nickels's commission on lottery ticket sales? Well, he had the privilege of visiting with Lorena during the day, the time when she was not busy paying off a winning ticket holder.

Lorena soon became the best paid shady lady in town. She carried on the lucrative lottery for perhaps four years or so. Then, a rather wealthy man from Montgomery, Alabama, bought all the tickets for three or four nights straight. During what must have been highly enjoyable times for both, he persuaded her to return to Montgomery with him. There were likely many men in Bristol who regretted to see her go.

As far as this writer can determine, this was the only prostitute lottery that ever operated in Bristol.

A Male Prostitute

Most readers will find it almost impossible to believe that Bristol, as small as she was in the 1880s, actually had a male prostitute, who reportedly had a thriving business. According to many old-timers, such was actually the case.

Stephen Overstreet was perhaps twenty or twenty-one years old when he became one of those many persons who seemed to appear in Bristol for no known reason. It generally came to be believed that he was from Baltimore, Maryland, and that he was of French parentage. There was some indication that he carried an assumed name. Some said this somewhat unusual name was chosen because he once lived in a Baltimore townhouse, in a room that overhung the sidewalk—thus came the name Overstreet.

Somewhere he had learned to be a watchmaker. Indeed, he soon proved that he was an expert in this field. Archibald "Arch" Pickens, a prominent local jeweler, employed Overstreet in his establishment, which was then located in the 400 block of Main (State) Street, on the Virginia side. A little upstairs room at the back of Pickens's jewelry store became Overstreet's home. It was reached by an outside stairway.

Overstreet was readily accepted by the people of Bristol. He was a warm, kind, friendly, and outgoing person. He was described as being of tall, muscular build, with a dark complexion, thick black hair, and a heavy mustache. Locals, especially the young ladies, considered him to be quite handsome, and doubtless some of them dreamed of someday becoming his wife.

He soon became a regular attendant in one of the local churches, a move which would have far-reaching consequences. He also became a frequently invited guest to the social activities of the town. This happened in spite of the often heard rumor that he was a frequent visitor to the Black Shawl, a large brothel located about three blocks down Main Street from Overstreet's room.

There came to Pickens's shop late one afternoon a wealthy young widow of the town. It seems that she had inherited a fine grandfather clock from her late husband's estate, and that clock had recently quit running. Mr. Pickens promised to send Overstreet to her home in the early afternoon of the next day. This skilled repairman filled the appointment and soon had the clock running. The fee was five dollars, which the widow gladly paid.

Then the widow, who apparently had become rather attracted to her repairman, candidly told him that he was welcome to come back to see her "when the rest of the town had gone to bed." Of course, young Overstreet got the message. He gladly accepted her invitation. When he was leaving her home just before daylight the next morning, she put five dollars in his pocket, explaining that such was a

Stephen Overstreet was Bristol's only known professional male prostitute.

token of her deep gratitude for his enjoyable visit.

Many times after that he slipped across town to her comfortable home, and always he was rewarded with a five-dollar gold piece. He was saving the two dollars that a visit to the Black Shawl would have cost him, and was being paid more than double that by his grateful and close friend. That caused him to do some serious thinking. If one woman was willing to pay him for services rendered, might not others also be willing to do the same? In that way he could make far more money than he could working for Pickens, even when combined with his regular gift from the pleased young widow.

In some way Stephen Overstreet let it be known that he was available for a fee. He may have been surprised that a male prostitute in so small a town would soon have a sizeable clientele. Certainly this clientele was not made up of lewd women. Indeed, most of his visitors were women from the "right" side of the tracks. Likely most of them had secretly longed for an extramarital affair but had been prevented from doing so by fear of discovery and resultant scandal. Whatever their motives, they were willing to pay for a little extra male attention.

The little room Overstreet occupied over the back room of Pickens's jewelry store seems to have served as his business office, and it appears that he made house calls whenever the coast was clear. He did find early in his unusual career that most women could not or would not pay as much as did the wealthy young widow. So he lowered his price to equate with that of the females at the Black Shawl brothel—two dollars per session. It later came out that not all of his clients were frustrated housewives. Some were young, unmarried women who were seemingly most anxious to know what awaited them when they did finally marry.

By the end of this first year of operation, he was getting more business than he could handle. It seems that his fame had become so widespread that he was having a sizeable number of out-of-town visitors. At that point, he simply became more selective of whom he would receive, and he upped the price to three dollars.

For about three years he enjoyed a flourishing business. He was then tripped up by a rather unusual circumstance. The pastor of the church he attended was in his second marriage, but no children had been born to either union. To those in the know, these barren marriages were no surprise, for, as one old-timer told it, "the mumps had gone south" on the pastor when he was a teenager.

The pastor's second wife, an attractive, much younger woman, desperately wanted to be a mother. After three years of marriage she had just about given up hope. Then came a teenage member of the church who had visited Stephen Overstreet several times but was now repentant. She confessed her dark sins to the young wife of her minister.

Now, in those dark confessions, the long disappointed wife saw a bright ray of hope. She knew Overstreet well. After all, he was one of the most faithful attendants of her husband's church. He had visited in their home, had meals with them, and had fixed their clocks and watches. Yes, in her later court depositions, she acknowledged that she had "felt a carnal attraction to him, long before they ever actually came together."

Soon after her talk with the teenage church member, she communicated her plight to the young man. Doubtless, he was happy to aid in her effort to become a mother, but she could not be seen slipping into his downtown office. No problem—he made house calls. In back of the parsonage where she and her husband lived was a yard kitchen, which was common in Bristol at that time. In that kitchen was a bed, near the alley door. Enough said!

Over the following weeks, it seems she needed to spend long late hours in that kitchen. She was perhaps preparing special food for the next day's meals—or so her husband may have thought.

It was a great surprise to the pastor, the church members, and fellow townsmen when, a few months later, it became obvious that the young wife was pregnant. Not only was the pastor-husband surprised, he was also suspicious. He seriously doubted that his long-lost fertility had returned, as did most of the others. A few days later his suspicions became shock when he found a note from Overstreet tucked away in his wife's clothes drawer, telling what night and hour the gigolo would be at the alley door of the outside kitchen.

Of course Stephen Overstreet soon learned that he had been tripped up. Though he did not really fear for his head as far as the man of the cloth was concerned, there were two or three other wives in town whose pregnancies were under suspicion, and their husbands were known not to be so civil. Also, there were three or more unmarried teenage girls in town who were also pregnant, and Overstreet had every reason to believe that he was the cause of their condition. Now, their fathers might be more uncivil than the feared husbands. Figuring that discretion might be the better part of valor, Overstreet decided to quickly flee, and flee he did.

Doubtless, there were many women in town who lamented losing him, but the worst lamentation seems to have come from an old man whose prized gold watch seemed to have fled with the young man. Perhaps an hour before Overstreet learned of his impending peril, he met the old man on the street, and the man handed him his watch for repairs. Overstreet slipped it into his pocket, promising to have it ready within a few days. But, alas, within a few days he was far to the west.

The shocked and mortified pastor soon filed for divorce. The depositions for that case tell the whole story, including the cost of obtaining the pregnancy this young wife so desperately desired. She estimated that it had taken twenty-seven carnal connections with Stephen before the desired result was obtained, but, not knowing she was pregnant, the connections had reached a total of forty-two before ceasing. The cost had been eighty-four dollars, and it must have been galling to the husband to learn that she had taken money from his pants pockets as he slept in order to pay the bill. That baby was rather expensive for that day and time.

What of her future and that of the baby? Well, she soon married a widower, a local businessman who was a prominent member of her husband's church. Needless to say, that membership was soon terminated! The baby son was reared in Bristol, graduated from a local college, and became a noted businessman in a nearby city. Much of this story came from him, but, because of a special promise, his identity cannot be revealed.

Then what of Stephen Overstreet, the noted Bristol male prostitute? Actually, little is known. It was later discovered that he was living in Bentonville, Arkansas, and that is just about all that was ever learned of him. In the late summer of 1949, this writer spent some time in that small Arkansas city. Downtown, there was a thriving jewelry business operated by a Mr. Overstreet. Could this handsome and personable young man have been a son of the male prostitute who, in the 1890s, gained a bit of fame (or shall we say infamy) in Bristol, Tennessee/Virginia?

Stephen Overstreet's son became a noted businessman.

Brothel Barter

During the nineteenth century, barter was far more common than cash exchanges in most Bristol businesses. Produce was brought into town by the wagonload and exchanged for goods and services. To a lesser degree, barter was sometimes resorted to in the local brothels.

The late Tom Faidley used to tell that a peck of potatoes could be traded at the Black Shawl for a session with one of the girls in that notorious establishment. The potatoes were used in the common kitchen there.

Old Daddy Thomas once told of a bachelor living on Broad Street who traded vegetables from his garden to the local brothels for services rendered. This bachelor used to boast that as long as his garden stuff held out he could get into any brothel in town. When the garden season ended he resorted to canned foods for the same purpose.

One unemployed young man, who had recently learned what a brothel was, got caught stealing his own mother's chickens, which he was using as barter at the Happiness Hotel. It took two chickens for each visit, and any man's destination was suspected when he was seen carrying two live chickens, one under each arm. A gallon of molasses would also be accepted at the same brothel.

Whiskey was sure to be accepted in trade at any local brothel. Usually it was sold to customers, which brought in more money than if the patron had paid in cash. A local merchant always traded dress material for favors in the Black Shawl. Three yards per visit was the going rate.

One traveler, who may have been a bit desperate, traded a fine gold watch for a short, between-trains visit with a prostitute in the Happiness Hotel. The value of that watch would have paid for many visits there.

A local painter who did a job for a three-stall operation on what is now Piedmont Avenue boasted in the Nickel Plate Saloon that in a day's time he had worked out four sessions with the girls there.

Old Love Apple Flat, an area extending along the north side of Ninth Street (now Volunteer Parkway) from near Main (State) street to Broad Street, got its name because of brothel barter in early Bristol. Along this section of Ninth Street was a row of cheap rental houses that were mainly occupied by common prostitutes. It was also in this area that out-of-town produce peddlers often set up their portable operations.

Those peddlers who came from distant points often camped for two or three days on the nearby banks of Beaver Creek. It was not uncommon for some of them to dispose of a little produce at night by trading it for the favors of the nearby prostitutes.

In autumn there often came apple peddlers from the mountains of North Carolina. It seems that they were the most lusty of the lot. Any of the prostitutes could lay in a winter's supply of apples by being a bit "kind" to those wild and wooly mountaineers.

Ordinarily, a peck of apples would admit a peddler to a prostitute's shack. (Four cabbage heads would also suffice.) There was one shady lady living in that area who claimed to be superior to the others. She always required two pecks of apples from any would-be visitor. Thus she came to be known as "Two Peck" Belle. Perhaps there might have been some grounds for her claim of superiority—at least she never seemed to want for apples!

Two Peck Belle was still living when this writer came to Bristol. Though her days of bartering were long over, the woman who had helped to give Love Apple Flat its name still lived within sight of it. Belle then occupied a cheap apartment in a ramshackle house at the mouth of Crumley's Alley, just across Ninth Street from her former place of business. This writer could obtain only a small amount of information from her.

There is an interesting divorce case on file in the Washington County, Virginia, courthouse which touches on barter in a Bristol brothel. It seems that a young wife had an extended visit with her mother, who lived in a distant town. Upon returning home, she found that her husband had traded virtually all of her clothing for favors at the Black Shawl, and he had also traded most of her kitchen wares for the same purpose. Her divorce was granted.

Most of the madams then operating in Bristol would extend credit to trusted patrons. Unfortunately, there were no MasterCard or Visa cards in those days! Sometimes the madams were a bit too trusting and allowed clients to incur bad debts.

The credit book that Ann Bachelor kept is still extant. In it are the names of many men who had to "court on credit," as the current owner of the book expressed it. Many bills were marked unpaid. By one, Ann made this notation: "found out to be a drunk—do not admit again."

Well, business was business—even in the Bristol brothels.

Won't You Come Into My Parlor?

Joe and Annis Bevins lived on the 800 block of Main (State) Street (Tennessee side) with their only son, Ernest. At the time of this story

Ernest was almost seventeen. Even at that young age he was nearly full grown.

Joe and Annis had brought up their son as a regular church and Sunday school attendant. They were proud of him and always boasted that he was a good, morally upright, clean-minded boy. Perhaps he was, but he was also a fast maturing boy, and certain biological pressures were becoming very strong, as we shall later see.

All might have continued as before if Joe Bevins's brother Harvey had not moved back to Bristol. (He had been living in Knoxville for some time.) Unlike Joe, Harvey was rather rowdy. He did not attend church, and he made no effort to raise his children in an upright manner.

One of those children, Bandy, was a lad of about the same age as his first cousin Ernest. Bandy and Ernest soon became close, nearly inseparable friends. Harvey Bevins often took them to the old swimming hole on Beaver Creek or on long hikes in the knobs west of town, and he joined them in sandlot ball games.

Soon after moving back to Bristol, Harvey, true to his lascivious nature, made the acquaintance of Vera Hibermonn, a young widow of about twenty-five years of age and a former employee in Pocahontas Hale's notorious Black Shawl brothel. She had left the Black Shawl and had rented a small cottage on James Row, where she began the operation of a one-stall brothel. Harvey Bevins became one of her most frequent visitors.

Early in the fast-warming spring of 1882, Harvey decided it was time that his overgrown son, Bandy, and his equally mature nephew, Ernest, were introduced to the pleasures of young manhood. It seems that the boys were most eager for such an introduction. Harvey made a deal with Vera Hibermonn to entertain Bandy one night and Ernest the next. Harvey paid her, rather generously, in advance to provide the boys with several hours of close female companionship. He provided some type of excuses for the boys to be away from home on the nights when they were to be guests of Vera, the one-stall prostitute.

As shocking as this may seem to the reader, the desire to have teenage sons introduced to the "joys of mature manhood" was fairly common among early Bristol fathers. This writer has been told of numerous instances similar to that which has just been described.

Now, Ernest stayed quiet about his experience with Vera Hibermonn, but Bandy did not. He boasted of it to many friends, and told it for Ernest too. Such talk has a way of getting around.

Meanwhile, in a strange twist of developments, Vera Hibermonn was planning a move. Indeed, she had commenced negotiations with the owners of a small rental house on Seventh Street. The owners were Joe and Annis Bevins! The Bevinses then knew nothing about her business. Vera was scheduled to come to the Bevins place to close the rent deal just a few days after her encounter with their son, Ernest. But before time for her to come, word somehow got to them about what had happened. Though very angry, they said nothing to Ernest or anyone else. Privately they plotted their strategy for severe retribution.

In a day or two, Vera showed up at the Bevins door, with due expectation that her business would soon be finished. Some business was finished that day—but not the type she had expected!

Mrs. Bevins met Vera at the door with a cheerful greeting. Once in the little hall, Vera was cordially invited to come into the parlor, where Mr. Bevins sat, calmly reading a newspaper.

Let Vera Hibermonn tell the rest of the story as it has been recorded in an old civil court case:

> I knowed something was wrong when Mr. Bevins quickly jumped up and ran to the back door, locking it. At the same moment, Mrs. Bevins did likewise at the front door, locking it also. Then Mrs. Harvey Bevins suddenly appeared from the room across the hall. I tried to escape through a window, but could not get it to rise. By then they all had grabbed me, and they throwed me down in the floor. They then raised my dress and jerked down my drawers, grossly exposing my person. From somewhere they brought out a popcorn cob that had been soaked in turpentine. That they forced into me, and vigorously churned me with it until I was in the worst of pain. All the while they were shouting hateful things at me, in the most obscene use of wicked words. When they finally let me go with the soaked cob in place, I fled, but continued to be in horrible pain for a great while, even three or four days, and milder pain for sometime beyond that.

Vera Hibermonn received a few dollars in damages, but not near the amount for which she had sued. Perhaps the amount was sufficient to pay her traveling expenses to wherever she went. Not more than two days after she had the money in hand, she left Bristol, never to return.

Incest

Though court cases concerning incest are relatively rare in this area, a few do exist. Handed-down tales of such are far more common. It is clear that there were many suspected cases of incest that were never brought to court, and of these, few details are available. Usually, informants of long ago simply stated a supposition such as, "Well, it is said that old Mr. (whoever) had children by his own daughter, or daughters." Or, perhaps, "I knew of a brother and sister who were left alone up here on such and such a street, and folks thought they were living like man and wife. Anyway she had several young'uns by someone, and they sure looked like her brother."

Only one instance was mentioned where it was thought that there was an "unholy" relationship between a mother and son. (The taboo has always been much stronger in such cases.) There were two or three instances where rumors of incestuous relationships between grandfathers and their granddaughters came to light.

An unusual and rare case was found in the author's quest into the dark area of local morals. The case involves a young, happily married couple who were half brother and half sister, but did not know it, and seemed to have never known it.

The father of the young man in this case was a noted womanizer of Bristol during the last decade of the 19th century. True, he had a wife and family, including the son mentioned above, but that did not stop his seemingly compulsive roaming. A young woman who lived across town from his home became pregnant by him. Her child, a daughter, grew up in Bristol; indeed, she attended school and church with the children of the unaccepting father.

When in her late teens, she began to date a son of this father. They fell in love and made plans to marry. The father knew that these two were half brother and half sister but, fearing the wrath of his wife, was afraid to tell it. This fear was so strong that he let them marry without interference from him. The girl's mother must have felt the same way, for it is evident that she did nothing to stop the marriage.

The young couple settled down in Bristol. In time, they produced a sizeable family of healthy and intelligent boys and girls, descendants of whom still live here. It was a good marriage, enduring for over fifty years.

The story might never have been known had not the father finally revealed all to a trusted friend. It was a son of this friend who, fifty years later, told it to this author.

All in the Family

Buried away in old indictments in an area courthouse is the record of a sister-in-law/brother-in-law case of incest that occurred in Bristol-Goodson, Virginia, soon after the Civil War. Indeed, that war seems to have been a causative factor in this case. The indictment tells the story well:

> This Grand Jury on the strength of evidence heard does charge that Fronia Steffner, in the Town of Bristol, Washington County, Virginia, did on the 10th day of May in the year 1866, willfully, cunningly, and by design and directness of purpose, lewdly and by certain lascivious means and methods, seduce one Alden M. Steffner, her brother-in-law, he then being a youth of tender years, that is of the age of sixteen years, and she a mature woman of accountable age, that is of the age of twenty-eight years. That in the same town and on the date afore stated in the home of herself did consummate her devious seduction by causing the said Alden M. Steffner to carnally know her body in the act of fornication. And the same Fronia Steffner has numerous times and in various places seduced the same Alden M. Steffner, and was discovered in the very act in a stable behind her home, by Sarah Steffner, her mother-in-law, and her mother-in-law's sister, Annie C. Obrian. At that said time Alden M. Steffner did confess to numerous acts of fornication with the said Fronia Steffner. Thereby, his morals have been corrupted and have caused him to become lustful, wanton, and rebellious against the restraints of decency and morality.
>
> Therefore, the said, Fronia Steffner is hereby charged with unlawful seduction, contributing to the delinquency of a minor, and further charged with incest, in that, the said, Alden M. Steffner is her brother-in-law, being a brother of her late husband, Matthew J. Steffner, casualty of the late War, and who was in his lifetime, husband to Fronia Steffner, who is hereby charged.

Fronia Steffner was sentenced to six months in the Washington County, Virginia, jail for her little indiscretion. Soon after being confined there she was found to be pregnant, but the authorities did not suppose that Alden M. Steffner was the father, because he was only sixteen years old. (How much they had to learn!) It is said that because of this pregnancy

Alden Steffner   **Mattie Collins**

she was paroled and came back home to Bristol.

What of Alden, who was the supposed victim in this case? Well, maybe he did become rebellious against the restraints of decency and morality. Two years later, when he was eighteen, he was charged with statutory rape. The charge states, "For willfully seducing and carnally knowing by committing fornication at diverse places and numerous times with one Elizabeth Rebecca Gage, a girl of tender years, that is of the age of fifteen years." The record shows that, for some unstated reason, he was completely cleared of the charge. Old-timers told that he eloped with Rebecca soon after being cleared by the court, and that they were never in the Bristol area again.

One of the strangest cases of incest ever found in the area's court records is that of Mattie Collins, who sued her brother-in-law for the support of her unborn child. The case is strange because of the alleged manner in which the impregnation occurred.

When local lawyer D. F. Bailey wrote up her case to file in chancery court, he told the story well. The old and yellowed paper still exists, and reads thus:

> The plaintiff, Mattie Justice Collins, widow of the late Charles L. Collins, complains and charges that on the night of September 23, 1876, she was attending the wake of her late father-in-law, Woodrow C. Collins. That she had cared for him for several weeks

past, and that she was completely exhausted, having been several nights almost completely without repose. That about midnight she could not sit up any longer, and thus retired to a bed in the back wing of the house immediately beyond the kitchen. She instantly fell into a deep sleep. Perhaps three hours later she was having a strange dream of a man hovering over her. The dream became so real that she began to slowly awake, and then jerked fully awake when she saw her brother-in-law, Thomas T. Collins, sliding from her bed. There was a full moon in the west, which lightened the room to the point that she saw that the said Thomas T. Collins wore only a shirt, being nude from the waist downward, and that she clearly saw that he was still partly carnally excited. She was further horrified to find that her dress had been lifted to around her waist, and her drawers had been fully removed. The said Mattie J. Collins avers and fully believes that her brother-in-law had carnal connection with her as she slept. The said Mattie J. Collins further states that she is now about six months pregnant and is certain the pregnancy came of the contact made by her brother-in-law as she slept, she having had no carnal connection with any other man. And so she sues both for a name for her unborn child and for a support of three dollars per month and for whatever medical costs she may incur.

The reader may be tempted, as was the author, to exclaim, "Well of all excuses, haven't we now heard them all!" Apparently, that was not the attitude of the presiding judge. Her entire petition was well-taken, and her requests granted. An old-timer living here nearly fifty years ago who knew all those connected to this case said, "You know, when that little boy baby was born, it did look just like Tom Collins!"

Bristol's First Divorce Case

Patrick Medford came to Bristol from Rockingham County, Virginia, in 1856. This was soon after his marriage to Anna Holmonn. He was some ten years older than Anna and had been previously married. It was told that this new bride had been a nurse for his first wife, and he had married her soon after he became a widower.

Mr. Medford had accumulated more than an average holding of worldly goods. He had hoped to increase his wealth in the flourishing new town of Bristol, but two or so years later, he decided he was not prospering in the degree he had hoped. Consequently, he decided to make a tour of the Deep South, hoping there to find a better prospect for future prosperity.

He left his wife in Bristol, promising he would send for her when settled in a new location. His wanderings took him to Southern Louisiana, where he became a guest on the plantation of Dr. Ulys Sampson Hill.

Finally, having decided that it was best to remain in Bristol, he returned to his wife. All went well until a letter of inquiry came from Dr. Hill to Mrs. Medford's brother, who also lived in Bristol. It seems that a letter from this brother to Mr. Medford had been left in Dr. Hill's guest cottage, and from it the address was secured. The letter from Dr. Hill proved to be the undoing of Patrick Medford. The entire story came out in the divorce case as filed in Abingdon, Virginia, by local attorney Joseph B. Palmer.

It came to be known that while Medford was at Dr. Hill's plantation, he had been "overly friendly" with a fourteen-year-old slave girl. The result was an early pregnancy. Now, ordinarily, Dr. Hill did not mind when his slaves got pregnant, but his rule was that the girls must be at least sixteen years old before such occurred. The general rule on most plantations was that the girls should be fifteen, but Dr. Hill, medical man that he was, felt

that they should be a little more mature. However, he apparently did not become aware of the young slave girl's pregnancy until after Mr. Medford had departed. Once her condition became apparent, she named the recent plantation guest as the father.

But that was not all. Even as Medford was being overly friendly with the fourteen-year-old, he was also carrying on a close relationship with an older female slave. Finally, he stole this slave and fled with her. Using a forged bill of sale, he managed to bring her back to Sullivan County, Tennessee. Before coming home to Bristol, he rented her to a pros-

Patrick Medford was the first husband to be divorced in the new town of Bristol.

perous farmer who lived near Paperville. Medford evidently reserved the right to visit this slave often, and those visits seem to have been of the overnight variety.

This slave woman was pregnant by the time the suit was filed, and so was Mrs. Medford. As if that were not enough, Mrs. Medford's niece also became pregnant, and she named Patrick Medford as the father. The divorce was granted (the first involving citizens of Bristol), and in the decree Mr. Medford was forbidden to remarry.

That was not the end of his troubles. Dr. Hill of Louisiana had the law on Mr. Medford's trail because of the stolen slave. Soon the farmer at Paperville was pressing charges of fraud. It was then that Patrick Medford took the "GTT" solution to his troubles. (GTT was facetiously applied to those who had "Gone To Texas" to avoid the law.)

Some twenty-five years later it was learned that he had settled near Clifton, Bosque County, Texas. By then, he was a rather prosperous rancher, had become a devout Baptist, and was serving as a deacon in his church. The defendant in Bristol's first divorce case now sleeps in the town cemetery of Clifton, Texas.

My Daddy is a Railroad Man

It was almost a status symbol among the many illegitimate offspring in early Bristol to claim that "my daddy is a railroad man." Doubtless, in many cases that claim was well-founded. A clue to why such claims may have been justified can be found in the following little rhyme. It is said that it was composed and often sung by a local saloon musician:

> Oh, where did you get those pretty blue shoes,
> The silver purse in your hand;
> I got them, sir, from my own true love,
> My lover is a railroad man.

One old and rather frank Bristol citizen once said, "I tell ye, this way of living like stock in this here town was brung in here by them railroad people." Though certainly not wholly correct, there is a degree of truth in the charge. It is well-known that the first "mass" prostitution in the Bristol area was done by a group of women who were following the builders of the Virginia and Tennessee Railroad in the late summer of 1856.

Bristol was the terminal point of two (finally three) railroads. Crews on these railroads usually ran into Bristol one day, then reversed their runs the next day. From near the beginning, many of these railroad men, most of whom were married, began the practice of having a "wife" on both ends of the line. In fact, wives might live in Lynchburg, while "wives-in-practice" were housed in Bristol.

Such was still common when this writer came to Bristol nearly fifty years ago. In one case, well-known to this writer, a wife-in-practice became the wife-in-fact after her railroad man's legal wife died in Lynchburg. In some—perhaps in many—cases, there were gifts of "blue shoes and silver purses," followed by illegitimate offspring.

Some of the railroad men who did not have wives-in-practice in Bristol were frequent patrons of the local brothels that stood near the depot, especially the Happiness Hotel. There were several freelance prostitutes who regularly met incoming trains, hoping to entice crew members or male passengers to their one- or two-stall houses of ill fame, or to brush thickets a little way up the tracks. Often they were successful.

Sometimes a desperate prostitute worked the railroad yards at night, hoping to pick up a little money from the men who worked there. Even in the large Bristol yards, these men were not hard to find. The bobbing lanterns they carried clearly marked their locations. A lantern might even be set down by the tracks for a few minutes while the worker and his visitor retired to the grassy spots at the side of the yard, for a friendly visit.

A mother/daughter team that operated in town for several years often walked for miles up and down the tracks, hoping to find a work crew that might be willing to take a recess from their labors for a little "refreshment" in a trackside brush thicket or hay field.

One such episode came to light in a divorce case involving a crew member. It seems that Hanner Hall and her daughter, Bertha, came up on a crew of six men working on a bridge near the old Goodson place (West Point—about a mile and a half beyond the upper end of the Bristol railroad yard).

According to later court testimony, "Hanner and her daughter serviced all our crew except me." The "except me" was a laborer who, as he put it, "had recently got religion and did not go in for such sinful doings." According to this laborer, he "worked on as Hanner and Bertha took the rest of the men into a nearby hay field and without shame had carnal connection with them."

This new religious convert became the chief witness in the divorce case that followed. It seems that Bert Cole, the defendant in the divorce case, had "connected" with both Hanner and Bertha while in the hay field. Divorce was not the only result. Hanner and Bertha were charged with "gross immorality and open lewdness." The men involved were charged with "willful and open fornication by carnally knowing the bodies of Hanner Hall or her daughter, Bertha Hall."

Alas, those who admitted to having carnally known the body of Bertha Hall were further charged with contributing to the delinquency of a minor, because the girl was only fifteen years old. All this did not keep the mother and daughter from eventually again engaging in walking the tracks.

It seems that one not-long-married railroad worker from Bristol had a considerable difficulty with a fellow worker who had no legal wife or wife-in-practice.

Benjamin "Benny" Solomon arrived in 1874 from Bedford County, Virginia, as a brakeman with the Virginia and Tennessee Railroad. Soon after moving to Bristol, he met and married Bonita "Bonnie" Merman, a recently divorced woman of whom he knew very little. Just how little will soon be shown. The couple rented a modest cottage on Railroad Street (later known as Spencer Street and now the Randall Street Expressway).

Not long after moving there, a fellow railroad worker, a young man with the unusual name of Hercules McCaddon, took a room in a nearby house. Though Hercules had a room, he still needed a place to eat. His good friend, Benny Solomon, offered Hercules board in his newly established home. The offer was gladly accepted and the situation worked well—for a while.

Sometimes Benny had to go out on a night train to Lynchburg. In the late afternoon of October 27, 1874, Benny, Hercules, and Bonnie had an early supper together. Hercules soon returned to his room, and Benny walked over to the freight-yard office to catch his run. After waiting there about three hours, Benny was informed by the yard master that the run would not leave until well after midnight. Contemplating a good rest in his home while he waited, he returned there.

The rest of the story is told in his divorce case deposition, still on file in an area courthouse. The reader should bear in mind that this deposition is an exact record of his statements made at the time.

When I was released for a time from my run, I hastily returned home, expecting to have a little rest. When I got in my yard I was puzzled that the lamp was not burning in the house. Bonnie usually did not go to bed until ten o'clock or after. Before going to the front door, I started around the house to the woodpile to bring in some for the fire. When I passed the bedroom window, I first noticed that a bright fire was burning in the little fireplace, and I then saw more. I was quickly jolted when I saw a man near that fireplace who appeared to be undressing in great haste. I was jolted more when I looked at our bed and there lie Bonnie just as naked as a jaybird, and a-laying all spraddled out like a common huzzie. She had her head reared up a-watching that man take his clothes off. By then I saw that it was Hercules in there with her. He had done flung his shirt off and was taking his britches down. It was plain to see that he was already carnally excited. I'm just as sure as I am sitting here that he was a-fixing to lunge onto Bonnie, and that young huzzie was a-laying there eager for him to top her. I'm fully sure that if I had been a minute later I would have found them a-doing the devil's wrestle.

Now, I flew into a mad rage when I saw what was going on and I lunged against that window and yelled out at them. Land, at that, Bonnie leapt out of that bed and squalled out that they were done caught. She grabbed a sheet and wrapped it around herself, and he jerked his britches up, and in seconds they tore out the back door. I started to tear after them but run into a clothesline and got knocked down. When I could get up they had done run plumb out of sight.

I had to go on my run to keep my job with the railroad. When I got back her clothes were gone. I reckon he left town, and she may have gone with him for a while. Some of the neighbors got bold and told me that she had once worked in Old Pokey Hale's house of ill fame and I don't doubt it now. They also told me that soon after Hercules got to boarding with us they'd see him come back there after I left on a run. And soon the lamp would be blowed out. Now, she finally come back to her mother's, and now has a young-un—a boy that she named Benjamin Hercules. I don't know, and I doubt if she knows which one of us is the real daddy.

The divorce was granted. That little boy could be sure that, whether Benjamin or Hercules, his daddy was a railroad man.

Bristol's First Shotgun Wedding

It is amazing how many men tried to be successful Bristol merchants during the first decade of the town's existence. Only a few succeeded. Most of them had to close their establishments within a relatively short time and move on to other locations or turn to other means of making a living here.

Among those early aspiring merchants was Frank Stutts, formerly of Campbell County, Virginia, who came here in the late winter of 1857. He was actually a fireman on the Virginia and Tennessee Railroad, but he had a plan to operate a store and keep his regular job as well. He rented a residence on Third Street and a store building on Fourth Street within sight of, and an easy walk from, his home.

Before opening this store, Frank made a deal with Jonathan Jennings, also formerly of Campbell County, to come and assist in the operation of his new business. Jonathan, then twenty-eight years old, had been married to Frank's niece. She died young, leaving him with two small children. He temporarily left the children in the care of his parents and sisters when he came to Bristol. His home consisted of one room at the back of the Stutts store, and he took most of his meals with the Stutts family.

Frank's family, other than his wife, Sabrina, consisted of his daughters, Robena and Katherine, and his only son, Thomas Jefferson Stutts. Robena, then seventeen, would play a leading role in the events that were soon to follow.

Robena, already mature, was rather beautiful, and folks considered her to be a bit fast. Certainly, it was plain to see that she was overly interested in men. It seems that this strong interest was not in those of or near her own age. Instead, she let it be known that she was drawn to older men; indeed, she actively pursued her interest in them and without regard as to their marital status. This caused some nervous wives in the neighborhood to keep a closer watch on their husbands—and that with good cause.

In late April 1857, Robena became infatuated with Wendell Stout, a carpenter from Carter County, Tennessee, who was doing repair work on the store building that her father rented. Wendell was about thirty years old and recently divorced. Evidently the infatuation was mutual. Robena and Wendell eloped during the night of April 30, 1857.

Indeed, they eloped, but they did not get married. Nevertheless, they were living together as man and wife in Wendell's Carter County home when they were found about a week later. An angry father brought his

Jonathan Jennings figured in Bristol's first shotgun wedding.

daughter back home, but not before giving Wendell Stout the beating of his life.

After this little episode, it became evident that Robena's interest in men had intensified. Her next target was Jonathan Jennings, her father's store manager and chief clerk. Her first blatant move was to change her position at the family table so she could sit by Jonathan when he came for his meals. Then she started spending long hours at the store with him, but only on those days when her father was out on his railroad run. It was plain to see that Jonathan Jennings was equally interested in her.

Though Frank Stutts was rather perturbed by the fast-budding romance between his right-hand man and Robena, his wife did not seem to mind in the least. Thus, when Frank was away, the couple had freedom to carry on as they pleased. Frequently, when supper was over, Jonathan would take Robena by the hand and lead her away for long walks—walks that often extended far into the night. Sometimes they would mount his horse, ostensibly for the purpose of going to a night revival service somewhere in the area around Bristol. They never seemed to arrive at the purported destinations.

In June 1857, a good customer of Stutts's store invited Jonathan to a party in his Paperville home. The party was held on a night when Frank was out on a run, and, of course, Jonathan took Robena with him. About dark, they mounted his horse and rode off toward Paperville just as a full moon peeped over Rooster Hill (now known as East Hill—location of historic East Hill Cemetery). Needless to say, they never arrived. Later, Robena admitted that they had a private party of their own in a moon-bathed meadow not far from Bristol. That is where she thought "it" happened. We shall see what the "it" is a little later.

Jonathan Jennings was always buying pretty clothes and fancy jewelry for young Robena Stout. Somehow, she managed to buy him a fancy friendship ring, which he proudly wore. Soon they began to talk openly of marriage.

Now, Frank Stutts really had nothing against his prized assistant. Indeed, he admired him and was rather fond of him. However, he thought the age difference (about eleven years) between Jonathan and Robena was too great. Too, he wanted Robena to wait until she was eighteen before marrying, and he well knew that the couple meant to tie the knot soon. Consequently, he devised a plan to give them both what he called a "cooling-off period." His expression may have been well chosen.

Frank's mother, a widow, lived alone in a rural area of Campbell County. Frank sent Robena, against her will, to spend the summer with her grandmother. Her stay would actually extend into mid-fall.

Jonathan was distressed by Robena's leaving. True to his pronounced wolfish nature, he began courting a young widow of the town. Local gossips had it that he was slipping into her cottage in the middle of the night. Well, perhaps he was trying to forget Robena. There is no record of what she was doing while in Campbell County.

Mrs. Stutts, Frank's mother, was a skilled midwife with many years of experience at becoming alert to certain signs. Her merchant son in Bristol soon received an urgent letter from her, stating that there were clear signs that Robena had been "bigged" (an old Southern term meaning *made pregnant*), and that she was sending her home.

The day after Robena arrived back in Bristol, Dr. Flavius Hartman was called in to examine her. He soon confirmed what Frank's mother had strongly suspected.

Of course, the prime suspect for the baby's father was Jonathan Jennings. When queried about it, Robena quickly agreed that he had the best chance of being the father because, as she put it, "He got to me more than anyone else." That statement left the way open for other possibilities, an opening Jonathan would soon take advantage of.

It was nearly five o'clock in the afternoon when Frank Stutts and Dr. Hartman called Jonathan Jennings into the backyard of Frank's store, where they confronted him with the situation. Frank delivered the ultimatum that Jonathan was to marry Robena at once and that Jonathan could by no means escape. All the while, Frank had his hand in his coat pocket, and Jonathan knew that Frank always carried a loaded pistol in that pocket.

Now, Jonathan readily admitted that he could be the father of Robena's unborn child. As later recorded in a deposition pertaining to their divorce case, his words to the men were, "Well, you all know that Robena was just like a young heifer in heat and, yes, I was her bull every chance I got— dozens of times." He then added, "I sure wasn't the only bull in the pasture. There were others who could be the daddy."

He really created a stir when he pointed at Dr. Hartman and said, "Right there's one who could be!" He went

Robena Stutts is shown several years after Bristol's first shotgun wedding.

on to tell how Dr. Hartman had gone to the Stutts home when both parents were away. Robena had soon sent her brother and sister over to the store to stay while she and the good doctor spent the better part of an afternoon together, "with doors shut even though it was a warm day." Jonathan further claimed that he knew of times when Robena had gone to the doctor's office late at night, presumably to have a "private meeting" with him.

At this revelation Dr. Hartman became livid with rage. After a few choice words, he jerked a pistol from his pocket and aimed it at Jonathan. Quick as a wink, Jonathan dashed into a root cellar in the railroad embankment at the back of the store. He slammed the door and locked it behind him.

The door had a little square ventilation hole cut near its top, and Dr. Hartman thrust his pistol through that hole and began shooting wildly into the darkened cellar. Jonathan ducked and then grabbed the doctor's arm, nearly breaking it as he wrested the gun from him. Then Jonathan flung the door open and fired the one remaining shot at the doctor, who was then "high heeling" it around the corner of the store and toward Fourth Street.

By then, the town constable, P. A. J. Crockett, alarmed by the pistol shots, had arrived on the scene. He and Frank Stutts took charge of Jonathan Jennings and marched him across the tracks to the Stutts home on

Third Street. Once there, Frank dispatched a neighbor to Blountville, to obtain the marriage license.

Soon after arriving at the home, they found that Robena had produced a letter that Jonathan had sent to her a week or two before. In that letter he expressed regret that "we have made a baby," and asked her to remain there with her grandmother for another month or so. During that time he would wind up his business in Bristol, go there, and take her away somewhere. Both Frank and the constable took the letter to be good evidence that Jonathan was guilty as charged. Frank then became more determined for the marriage to proceed with all due haste.

Before darkness settled over the town, Frank called in an acquaintance or two to help keep watch over the waiting-against-his-will bridegroom. The wait was long. The neighbor who had gone to get the marriage license had some difficulty locating the circuit court clerk. That county official was finally found and the license procured. It was near midnight when the messenger arrived back at the Stutts home. By then, Robena had grown weary and had gone to bed.

Frank sent for Rev. George Miles, who was in town helping to set up what would become the present State Street Methodist Church. He was staying at the home of Jesse Aydlotte, on what is now Scott Street, and had been put on alert that he might be needed sometime during the night. He came, but, sensing that it was a forced marriage, was rather reluctant to proceed. Frank firmly told the reverend that he must proceed, and conspicuously clutched his pistol a little tighter. Perhaps the reverend decided that discretion was the better part of valor, so he halfheartedly agreed to perform the wedding.

The party then proceeded up the stairs to Robena's room. The girl was sound asleep, and Mr. Stutts had a considerable time awakening her for the ceremony. She remained in bed all the while, clearly dozing as the minister went through the wedding ritual. She was sound asleep before it ended. Jonathan stood by the bed but would give no answer to the minister's questions. When it was over, and without further restraint from Frank Stutts, Jonathan quickly left the house and disappeared into the darkness. He went straight to the house of the young widow he was courting at the time, and there spent the rest of the night.

The newly married couple never lived together one day. Within a few days, Jonathan applied for annulment on the grounds that the ceremony was forced, and that neither he nor the bride had in any way participated in it. His petition was denied. A little later he applied for a divorce. After several months of court proceedings, that too was denied.

Meanwhile, both he and the young widow found themselves in trouble with the law. Unable to marry each other because of Jonathan's strange union with Robena, they began to openly live together in her home, as if they were indeed married. Soon they found themselves indicted for unlawful cohabitation. They ended up having to pay heavy fines, and they were put on probation.

It was Robena who finally came to the rescue. About a year later she again became involved with Wendell Stout, with whom she had once eloped. Greatly desiring to marry him, she applied for a divorce from Jonathan. In her deposition she bore heavily on that fact that she had slept through her wedding ceremony. She had only a "dreamlike recollection of only a part of it," she deposed. The divorce was granted.

Jonathan immediately married the young widow—this time he did not need the impetus of armed force. Within a short time this star of Bristol's first shotgun wedding took his new bride and left town. No one in the town ever knew where they went.

The Rape of a Cow

The sexual wantonness seems to have been so great in early Bristol that even Old Pied, a family cow, was not safe! So it appears from an old indictment found in a local courthouse. It reads:

> That William Crockett, on the 19th day of August in the year of our Lord, 1887, did feloniously commit the detestable and abominable crime against nature by then and there, that is to stay in a stable of a barn belonging to Esther Looper, to wit on the day and year aforesaid, did feloniously have carnal intercourse with a beast, that is the milk cow belonging to the said Esther Cooper, she then being away attending church; and the crime is against the peace and dignity of the Commonwealth of Virginia.

Billy Crockett, as he was called by the locals, made the mistake of taking three friends along to see the performance. In fact, they became his allies, in that they held the rather nervous cow as Billy did the crime. But, strangely, all appeared in court as witnesses against him. Alas, they wound up being charged with lewdness!

William Crockett finally settled in the mountains of Eastern Kentucky, where he "tried to preach," as a former neighbor expressed it.

It seems that there was no end to the consequences of this most unusual sex crime. Billy managed to have two other witnesses who swore that the Looper milk cow was not in the barn during the time the alleged incident occurred. They claimed that they had been hired by Mr. Looper to take the cow to Bosang's public bull lot, and that they were there for hours around the time charged. When John Bosang was called to the stand for confirmation of their claim, he refuted it. According to him, his bull had been moved to a dairy farm in Holston Valley "for several likely encounters," as he expressed it, and had remained there for some time. Thus, the two false witnesses were charged with perjury.

At the end of the trial, Billy Crockett was declared guilty and sentenced to two years in prison. When freed, he did not return to Bristol.

Rape on Holy Ground

It appears that women and girls of early Bristol were not safe from rapists, even when on holy ground. In this case the victim was not even safe from a holy brother.

For many years there was a meeting ground in Flat Hollow (present Rice Terrace area). It was officially known as the Methodist Camp Meeting Grounds of Bristol, Virginia. The open-air tabernacle used for the meetings stood near the intersection of present Buckner and Oakview streets and adjacent to the Flat Hollow Cemetery. On the slope behind the tabernacle was a brushy, wooded area that stretched upward, toward, and beyond present Euclid Avenue. During revivals this area was used for group prayer meetings, called "grove meetings" by some local citizens, and was considered holy ground.

The camp meeting of 1878 was unusually well attended and soon got into a high pitch of religious fervor. Before each service in the tabernacle, ever-enlarging numbers of folks retired to the woods for the group prayer meetings. There were four groups—adult men, adult women, teenage girls, and teenage boys. When these groups started to pray, it seems that each one of them tried to outdo the other in the loudness of their impassioned supplications. Along with the prayers, sometimes there was singing, hand clapping, and shouting. When all this got going at full blast, the din could be heard from some distance.

Just before the morning meeting began on Monday, August 12, 1878, a large number of the attendants retired to the woods, for the grove meetings. One of the members of the boys' group was a son of a respected Bristol family, the head of which was a successful merchant. The boy was a big, overgrown lad of seventeen and was said to have been one of the loudest participants in the group.

The boys all knelt down and, within minutes, got going loud and strong. When this big lad opened up his mind to heaven, the devil must have rushed in, as one Bristolian tried to explain it. Certainly, unholy thoughts must have sent him into a reckless, irresponsible frenzy of uncontrollable passion.

As the other boys roared on, he quietly and quickly arose and went to where the teenage girls were engaged in a similar prayer session. Like a hawk swooping down upon a flock of chickens, he lunged into the group. He grabbed a fifteen-year-old girl, and, half dragging, half carrying her, he headed for a dense thicket a short distance away. Her wild shrieks alerted the other girls, who, when they realized what was happening, immediately ceased their prayers and ran toward the adult men's group. Perhaps they decided that running for help was a better solution for the problem at hand than continued prayer. After they told their tale of woe, several of the men jumped up and ran to the thicket where the crime was in progress.

Editor Isaac C. Fowler of *The Bristol News*, writing in his usual graphic and candid manner, reported that when the men ran to the scene they found that the lad had torn most of the clothes from the girl and was rapidly accomplishing his purpose. He went on to state that the young rapist was in such a frenzy of carnal passion that he did not seem to realize that he was under attack, and that it took three of the stronger men to pull him off the shocked and terrified victim. The news article further tells that the girl was immediately placed in the care of Dr. M. M. Butler, who was present at the camp meeting, and the boy was turned over to the constable of Bristol, Virginia, who was also present.

Later, Editor Fowler reported that the boy had been placed in the care of the chief justice of Washington County, Virginia, for further action. A diligent search of the pertinent records failed to find a final deposition of the case.

One may well assume that women and girls praying in the grove meetings after that memorable day heeded the admonition to watch as well as pray!

Unusual Excitement in the Church

In the early days of Bristol, it was not unusual for there to be a little excitement in the Bristol Methodist Church (now known as State Street Methodist). There was often spirited singing, lively preaching, and even a bit of joyous shouting now and then. On a balmy, mid-May Sunday morning in 1878, there was some very unusual excitement in this church, and of a far different kind than was commonly experienced there. It was spirited, but certainly not spiritual.

On that long-ago day, the singing had ended, the prayers were well on their way upward (hopefully), and preaching time had come. The rather overly pious minister had just opened the large pulpit Bible and announced his text, when the front door was swiftly swung open. Was it a late visitor? Yes, and what a visitor!

Through that door came a young woman, who was seemingly in sort of a daze. Her arms were outstretched and waving about, much as if she were trying to fly. She swiftly proceeded right down the aisle, all the while swinging her hips about in the manner of a bawdy dance. What really "blew the stack" was that she was stark naked—she was without a scrap of clothing, not even shoes on her feet!

The men gasped, the women shrieked, and a few actually swooned away or fainted. Some piously hid their eyes, while others stared intently at the strange visitor. By the time the first shockwave swept through and paralyzed the crowd, the naked woman had almost reached the pulpit. The horrified minister, seeing that none of the officials of the church were acting to remove this "emissary of the devil" from their midst, took matters into his own hands. After jumping down from the platform, he seized the naked woman by the shoulders, intending to push her out the side door, which was immediately to the left of the pulpit.

His plan was thwarted a bit. The moment he laid hands on her, the woman pushed forward, pressed her body against his, threw her arms around his neck, and began kissing him. As one of the old-timers gingerly described the situation, "She blatantly with her body began to make the motions of sin. Now, with his hand on her shoulders it looked for the world like he was embracing her."

The shocked-to-the-teeth minister tried to jerk loose. While backing up, he stumbled on the edge of the platform and fell backward, bringing the clinging nude woman down on top, straddling him. According to the informant of long ago, "She there continued to do the motions of sin."

By then the good reverend was yelling for help. "Get this bawdy house huzzie off before she completely unsanctifies me," he begged. She must have been trying to unsanctify him, for by the time two of the stewards rushed to his aid, she had scooted upward and was rubbing his face with her swinging breasts.

The stewards pulled her off the horrified minister and bodily carried her out the side door, into the yard. There they left her and quickly returned to the sanctuary, slamming and bolting the door behind them.

Needless to say, the morning service did not continue. Indeed, the minister was in such a state of shock that he had to be carried to the nearby parsonage and put to bed. The congregation scattered, hardly believing what they had seen.

It is almost certain that the nude woman was one of the workers in the Black Shawl, the notorious brothel that stood almost in the shadow of the Methodist church. Likely, she had been drinking or doping (yes, there was dope in Bristol at the time), or perhaps she might have been deluded by lack of sleep or from sheer exhaustion. In any case, her bare-backed visit to the church had long-lasting repercussions and was much talked of for generations.

The pastor was so shocked and humiliated that he could not resume his duties for well over a month. It is said that he was never a very effective pastor after that strange incident.

The evening service following the naked woman's morning visit was a fervent prayer meeting to cleanse the sanctuary of the "evil" that had been so blatantly carried on there. One old brother prayed long and fervently that "the men and the boys of the congregation might have their minds blinded to the memory of what they had seen that morning, and that no vile and lascivious thoughts might ever arise in their minds because of Satan's effort to, in the form of a wicked woman, corrupt their morals and Christian virtues."

Well, honesty compels us to admit that though there was much righteous indignation because of this display of nudity and lewdness, likely there were men and boys who thoroughly enjoyed the scenery. Doubtless, many "vile and lascivious thoughts" were centered around this scene for years to come. For most of the men, the incident would be the only time in their lives when they would behold a nude woman, even those who were married or would be married in the future.

One of the first repercussions occurred when the wife of the youngest of the two stewards who had ejected the nude woman from the sanctuary accused him of taking a good look as he did so. Indeed, it was remembered by several in the congregation that the older steward had turned his head and looked away as he performed his duty. It was also observed that the younger man had "looked her over good," as his angry wife had charged. The distressed wife further lamented that she could not ever bear for him to touch her again, because his hands had actually been upon that vile woman.

The repercussion that had the most devastating and widespread effect was centered around an elderly—perhaps the oldest—man in the congregation. His life and works were such that most Bristolians considered him to be a saint. Certainly, he was the most esteemed, respected, and beloved member of the Bristol Methodist Church. As his hearing faded, he had gradually moved forward to the front pew, and there he sat when the unclad visitor entered the church. Rumors began on that very day that the old brother had not covered or closed his eyes, as did many of the men present, when the nude woman pranced down the aisle. Instead, it was claimed by some that he quickly threw on his glasses and intently stared at her, even leaning forward to apparently get a better view!

As those rumors spread, the congregation became more and more divided. There were many who said that such could not be, and that the old brother just could not do such a thing. Others vowed they knew it to be so. Some of them said they didn't want to believe it, but they had to believe what they had seen.

Finally, the saintly old brother was asked about it. He humbly replied, "Well, I just don't rightly remember what I did, but I usually put my specs on when there's something I want to see right bad." Now, that statement didn't do much to help his cause!

According to several old-timers, this issue came the nearest to splitting this church wide open as anything that ever became a matter of contention within it. Bristolians, somewhat facetiously, branded the two divisions as the *Specs* Methodists and *No Specs* Methodists. Some of those old brothers and sisters would become right hostile if one dared put them in the wrong category.

In time, the Specs and No Specs Methodists came back together. Today the State Street Methodist Church stands totally unified, and it is one of the strongest congregations in Bristol. It is doubtful if many in the present-day congregation ever heard of the Specs/No Specs division that threatened their church so long ago.

Strange Sunday School

Cleburne "Clebe" Strait was a bit puzzled by his wife's sudden interest in religion. In all of their seven years of married life, Julia Strait had never once shown the least interest in Sunday school, until early August of 1896. It was then that she began to attend regularly, or so she claimed. Clebe had not been inside a church since he was a child, and indeed he was considered to be rather irreligious by all who knew him. He didn't object to his wife's newfound interest in religion, thinking it might sweeten up her somewhat sour disposition. It really did seem that she was happier after starting to attend Sunday school.

Now, Clebe had a brother, George Strait, who really wasn't so straight. He was something of a con man, a shrewd gambler, and an avid womanizer. At that time he was separated from his fourth wife. Somehow Clebe got little bits of information from here and there that seemed to indicate that an affair was budding between Julia and George. Checking a bit, he found that George claimed to be doing a lot of fishing during Sunday school time. Clebe further learned that George's favorite fishing place seemed to be the Willow Hole. Too, Clebe had gained the information that Julia was not showing up for Sunday school, as she had claimed.

The Willow Hole was a deep place in Beaver Creek at about where the Leisure Towers building is now located. It was surrounded by a wide and dense willow thicket. It was well-known that the willow thicket was a favorite nighttime trysting place for local lovers. Even some street prostitutes took their catches there to complete their business transactions. Clebe put two and two together and determined that he would know the truth come the next Sunday.

On that Sunday, as Julia was getting ready for Sunday school, Clebe told her he was going across town to see a friend. Indeed, he did go to see something, but it wasn't a friend. Clebe walked swiftly over to the Brown Brothers Wagon and Buggy Works, and he somehow managed to climb up to the roof of that large building. From there he had an unobstructed view of the main entry to the willow thicket.

Soon, his brother George came walking down Moore Street in a rather hasty manner and disappeared into the thicket. In a short while Clebe saw his Julia do likewise. He waited long enough for their business to begin (he wanted full evidence), and then he slipped into the notorious thicket. He did not slip carefully enough. He stumbled over a downed limb and fell.

His deposition, given in the divorce case that ensued, is here quoted:

Well, now, when I fell down I reckon I made enough racket to alarm them. I heard the commotion in some dense bushes near me. And I heard them go tearin' out of that thicket like deers with hound dogs at their heels. Soon as I could, I jumped up and run over to where I heard the commotion. I could clearly see where they'd been wallerin' around in the sand a-doin' the devil's wrestle. And aside she'd done indicted herself by forgettin' to grab up her green Sunday bloomers. They's a-layin' right where she left them. When she slunk in home after a while, I throwed her down and took a quick look, and she didn't have any on.

The noted Bristol lawyer David F. Bailey (called "Uncle Dave" by virtually everyone who knew him) was the attorney for Julia Strait in the divorce case filed by her husband. When he heard that part of Clebe's deposition, he quickly posed the question, "Now, Clebe, are you fully sure that the bloomers you found in the willow thicket were those of your wife? Couldn't you be wrong about that?"

Clebe quickly retorted, "Why, dog take it, no, Uncle Dave, I'd know them damned bloomers in the middle of hell, for I've seed them many a time!"

The divorce was granted.

The Outhouse War on Burson's Row

Burson's Row, a notorious slum, was made up of a long line of cheaply constructed shacks that extended from near Scott Street to Mary Street, between the back lots of Moore Street and what is now Piedmont Avenue (then commonly known as Graveyard Road). It was built and owned by the legendary Maj. Z. L. Burson, who charged his tenants from fifty cents to two dollars per week for his rental units. People frequently moved in and out of the shacks, and forcible evictions were common. The major made the rounds to collect his rents, usually on horseback, every Saturday afternoon.

The setup on Burson's row was that four houses were served by one well or cistern and one communal outhouse. This situation was the cause of much contention, and tenants occasionally came to blows over the matter, such as in one case in which an old gentleman practiced taking reading material to his section's outhouse. He would go to sleep while reading and thus hold up matters, sometimes for hours. Those who had urgent reason to go there raised much trouble about the problem.

The greatest brawl of all resulted from a moral situation and was an often-told tale around Bristol for years. Many referred to it as the Outhouse War on Burson's Row.

Bert Lampe and his wife never got along very well; indeed, they were considered to be the most contentious couple on the Row. Mrs. Lampe was a jealous wife, and Mr. Lampe's lusty nature was never much restrained by the bonds of matrimony. Soon after the Lampes moved to the Row, a young, rather feisty widow moved in next door to them. This provoked much jealousy on the part of Mrs. Lampe—and with good cause, as was proven by later events.

Upon returning from town one early April afternoon in 1881, Mrs. Lampe found that Bert was not at home, as he had promised to be. Suspicions aroused, she checked next door at the young widow's place. The doors were standing open, but no one was home.

A somewhat nosey neighbor who lived just beyond the widow was standing in the backyard of her shanty. She called to Mrs. Lampe and said, "Why, he's out there in the outhouse with that widow woman. I seed them go out there 'bout an hour ago. I'm a-wantin' to go out there real bad but seems they's takin' their time."

This revelation enraged Mrs. Lampe. Becoming more hostile by the moment, she charged to the outhouse, pounded on the door, and demanded that they open up. There was no response from within. She then grabbed an old keg and jumped up on it so she could see through a wide crack at the top of the door. According to her deposition in the divorce case that soon followed, when she peered through the crack, she got an eyeful!

Her exact words were: "When I got to where I could see, there they were, all locked up on that privy bench, and just a-goin' to it hammer and tongs."

The sight enraged her even more. She grabbed up a three-foot length of two-by-four and began a determined vigil at the outhouse door. She called in to the erring couple that she'd wait there until hell froze over if she had to, and when they opened that door she was going to batter them down.

Knowing that Mrs. Lampe would do what she said—and perhaps worse—the couple stayed put. An hour passed, then two, then starting on three. Of course, by then virtually all of the people in that four-house run were urgently needing the benefit of the communal outhouse.

This included old Granny Colson, who was plagued with chronic diarrhea. She kept poking her head out her back door and calling out, "You'd better get them outta there soon and clear the way, er I'm gonna mess up creation!"

So great was the urgency with some of the tenants that they broke boundary lines and began to make use of the neighbors' "sanitary" facilities. This was strictly taboo on Burson's Row, and it had been the cause of many a fight and continuing feud among some of the Row's more savage inhabitants. And fights were swift in developing that memorable afternoon. At one point there were four, maybe five, sets of tenants engaged in intensive battle over such trespassing. One lad, who had been bodily dragged out of an off-limits outhouse, retaliated by returning with a can of kerosene, which he then threw on an outhouse wall and set it afire.

That infuriated those who had to use that little house. They knew that Major Burson might wait for weeks before replacing the outhouse, and they wondered what they would do in the meantime. They all charged after the boy like a swarm of angry bees. Quick as a chased deer, he leaped over a fence and dashed away from them. The young arsonist didn't see much safety or peace for months after that. For, every time he started across the backyard to his own designated necessary house, there was always someone lying in wait for him, ready to battle.

Finally, the old man who often read and slept in the outhouse that was then under siege decided that he just had to go. He grabbed up an ax, marched right to that door, and chopped it down. Just as he did so, Mrs. Lampe, deciding that an ax would be a far more effective weapon, whammed that two-by-four over his head, knocked him out cold, and seized the ax.

By then Bert Lampe and his woman were lunging by her. Mrs. Lampe tore after them, swinging the ax, but they managed to race away with such frenzied speed that she couldn't overtake them. They must have kept on running, for neither of them ever returned to Burson's Row. Perhaps they found another outhouse somewhere!

But the excitement wasn't over. As soon as it was seen that the door was open to the lately besieged outhouse, seven or eight of the suffering tenants made a dash for it. They crashed together in front of that door, and a free-for-all, dog-style fight ensued. Right in the midst of it was old Granny Colson, who, before it was over, had profusely fulfilled her recent prophecy.

"Nobody's business what I do," Bert Lampe would have said, but that day his "business" started a war on Burson's Row.

Animal Threat to Morality?

In 1877, a citizen of Bristol was fined for allowing a stallion and a mare to mate in an open lot behind his Moore Street home. The case against him stated that he "allowed his stallion to get to a mare in an open lot clearly within the public gaze." It then went on to state that "such an indecent display has greatly injured the moral atmosphere of the town." That the display had many onlookers is beyond question, at least according to another part of the charge, which tells that many men and boys "stood nearby intently watching the lust-arousing scene." Not only was the owner fined, he was also ordered to remove the stallion to a secluded place outside of the town for future sessions with mares.

Another indication of the fear of an animal damaging morality is that an early town law proscribed a heavy fine for "allowing a bitch [female dog] when in heat to run loose on the streets of the town." The reason stated for this law was "that a great possibility exists that they will mate with male dogs clearly within public view, thereby contributing to the moral laxity of the local citizenry."

One woman was fined because she allowed her female house cat "to mate with a tom in her front yard as several children watched, without doing anything to stop the animals from proceeding with their lewd public display."

Though there seems to have been no law concerning the matter, many local homeowners built plank fences around their chicken lots. This was so the public could not see the roosters "tromping the hens," as they called it.

During the late 1860s and through most of the 1870s, John N. Bosang, a local saloonkeeper, supplemented his income by keeping a bull for hire in a lot in Flat Hollow (present Rice Terrace area near the intersection of Oakview Street and Clinton Avenue). Most Bristolians then kept one or more milk cows, so such a service was needed and frequently used.

Just about any time that a local citizen was seen leading a cow up toward the bull lot in Flat Hollow, a crowd of onlookers was almost sure to be seen following. Most of them were men and boys, but occasionally a "brazen" woman followed along with them.

Of course, widows or maiden ladies living alone who had a restless cow on hand always got some man to make the trek to Bosang's bull lot for them—that is, all except one. "Aunt" Dicey Stutts, who was a rebel in more than one way and had been married seven times, always tended to that chore herself. She would boldly march up Flat Hollow with her cow in tow.

Once, an onlooker asked her if she was not embarrassed by the show in which her cow was then one of the principal stars. She exclaimed, "Hell no. That don't dant [daunt?] me a bit. Ain't nothing bein' done to that cow that ain't been done to me hundreds of times! Only I didn't get a calf every time!"

All these goings-on troubled the moralists of the town. Through their relentless pressure, the town council ordered Mr. Bosang to enclose his lot with a high plank fence, to put a lock on the entry, and to allow no one inside while any carnal activity was going on. In this order it was made clear that the council and "many upright citizens of the town feel that public immorality is being encouraged by the open and easily viewed activity that often transpires in the open lot."

Within a few days Mr. Bosang had complied with the order. He built the fence of fresh-from-the-mill planking. Before the summer ended, those green planks had shrunk so much that the activity could easily be viewed through the resultant wide cracks between the boards.

It was generally believed that the sly keeper of the bull had deliberately created this situation to spite the members of the concerned council, most of whom he openly detested. The only problem with that manner of viewing was that fights sometimes resulted from onlookers trying to gain and keep a choice (perhaps extra-wide) crack.

Animal activities a threat to morality? Well, that question is still debatable.

What Old Indictments Tell

In the courthouses of the Bristol area there are recorded thousands of old indictments. This author has sifted through countless numbers of them, selecting several that give a rather vivid picture of the varied aspects of the moral condition of early Bristol. They are copied here exactly as they appear on the public records. The reader, like the author, may draw his or her own conclusions concerning the situation.

• That Sinda Lewis of the Town of Bristol in this county, a woman of mature years, that is of the age of 23 years, is hereby indicted for gross lewdness and indecency, specifically that for months she had been going about engaging in numerous acts of adultery and fornication every day and every night with any man or boy that will yield to her wanton seduction, both strangers and acquaintances, both white and colored and thus has contributed mightily to the moral laxity of said town, and is hereby bound over for trial during the next term of court, beginning Monday next. [Indictment dated June 14, 1857]

• It is here charged that James A. Seldon in the Town of Bristol, did on the 12th day of September, 1857, and at diverse times within the past twelve months, commit fornication with one Catherine McBee, a free woman of color, by having carnal knowledge of the body of the said woman, afore named.

• That Katey Watson, a girl of tender years, that is of the age of 16 years, of the Town of Bristol in this county [Washington County, Virginia] did entice and lead from said town on the night of September 14, 1869, Charles Trayer of the age of 18 years, Weldon Scott of the age of 16 years, Paul Adams of the age of 17 years, Luther Ruble of the age of 17 years, and Ralph Wilkins of the age of 19 years, to the pasture behind the old Twin Elm School building [near intersection of present Piedmont and Sycamore streets] and there did freely and willfully have illicit connection with each and every one of them before midnight of said day. And it is further charged that the said Katey Watson has from time to time and at other places and with other males had illicit connection, and is therefore guilty of contributing to the moral laxity of said town. She is therefore given over to the Chief Justice of this county for necessary correction.

• Joseph Nelson, of the Town of Bristol, Sullivan County, is this day [August 12, 1872], charged and indicted for keeping a house of ill fame in said town, for the purpose of mass lewdness, which house is resorted to both day and night by men and women, it being contrary to good morals of said town.

• Be it known that on the 10th day of July in the year of our Lord 1875, one Ophelia Adams of Bristol (Goodson), Virginia, did at her home in said town contribute greatly to the moral laxity of her cousin, Olina Simpkins, a girl of tender years, that is the age of 16 years, by placing her in a room at about 3:00 P.M. of said day with Marion Adams of the age of 21 years, for the express purpose of introducing her, the said Olina Simpkins, to the so called pleasures of the flesh, and this after the girl and the said Marion Adams, had been allowed to openly and plainly view the said Ophelia Adams copulate with George Adams, a brother of the said Marion Adams, in the kitchen of her home, thus the said Olina Simpkins was that day degraded and had her purity taken by having illicit connection with the said Marion Adams.

• That on Christmas day, 1877, in the Town of Bristol in this county [Sullivan County, Tennessee] Tom Harkness did, after delivering a present to Fayetta South, throw her down upon the floor and lift her dress thereby exposing her person, she having no drawers upon her, and then did proceed to carnally rape and ravish her two or more times before releasing her, all against her will and nature. Therefore we this Grand Jury, sitting, do charge him with forcible rape.

• It is here made known that Carroll Hopkins, a man of mature years that is of the age of 22 years, in the Town of Bristol did on the 3rd day of June 1870, in said town did seduce and fornicate with one Mildred McBarson in the back storage room of Buckner's store, where he is employed, she being of tender years, that is the age of 15 years, and though she confesses that she was fully willing to be thus connected with him, the said Carroll Hopkins, nevertheless he is charged with the seduction of a minor and statutory rape.

• That on the 4th day of July in the year 1881, Billy Croft, an adult male of the age of 28 years did lead and take into the thicket on the north slope of the City Cemetery Hill [now East Hill Cemetery] Vernie Stutts, a girl of tender years, that is of the age of 16 years, and there did seduce and carnally know her by having carnal knowledge of her body, and by this seduction she is now in a delicate condition [pregnant] and thus he, the said

Billy Croft, is charged with contributing to the moral fall of a minor, statutory rape, and paternity of her unborn child.

• It is hereby charged that on the night of August 10, 1881, Hiram Biggs and Stephen Dow, adults over the age of 21 years, were caught in the alley behind Barker's store in Bristol (Goodson), Virginia, openly, clearly, and flagrantly engaged in an act of sodomy [homosexual activity] which is a crime under the statutes of the Commonwealth of Virginia, and are thus charged.

• We this Grand Jury sitting in Blountville, Tennessee, November 11 in the year of 1882, do charge Sheldon Hines of the Town of Bristol [he operated a photography studio here for a short time] in this county with making indecent and lewd photographs of several completely nude persons, some of whom were engaged in actual or simulated copulation, and offering same photographs for sale without regard to age of the prospective buyers.

• That Isaac A. Nickels, operator of the Nickel Plate Saloon in Bristol, Virginia, did on the 19th day of December in the year 1885, sell and convey to Samuel Fugate, over the age of 21 but unmarried, and Steve Dishner, a minor of 19 years of age and unmarried, one dozen French novelties [condoms], and thus has contributed to their moral laxity, and is so charged.

• Be it noted and charged by this Grand Jury now sitting in Abingdon, Virginia, on the 3rd day of May, 1886, that Cheston Croft, an adult of the age of 27 years, and Neona Cornett, an adult of the age of 22 years, did on the afternoon of the 20th day of April past, after drinking freely of ardent spirits retire to a position under an apple tree in the corner of his home yard, and near the corner of two public streets, and there in broad daylight, and clearly open to the public gaze did grossly expose their persons and did fully have illicit connection two or three times before reported to and apprehended by the Town Sergeant [constable] of Bristol (Goodson), Virginia, and thus are so charged, and further charged with fornication, they not being married to one another.

• That on the 13th day of August, in the year 1887, in the town of Bristol, Lucy Reeves, a minor of the age of 18 years, and Rose Ann McKamey, a minor of 17 years, both being females yet did simulate the act of copulation between male and female in a very profane and perverted manner, the said Lucy Reeves assuming the posture of a man, and using a cucumber wrapped in a silk handkerchief in such simulation, all done within the clear sight and observation of Caroline Dettor and Peggy Cleek, who have before this jury witnessed thereto. Therefore we charge said Lucy Reeves and Rose Ann McKamey with gross lewdness, lascivious display before others, and further charge them with a detestable crime against nature, and turn them over to the Chief Justice of this county for necessary and needed correction.

• Be it known that Harry Collins of Bristol, Tennessee, in this county did have in his possession on August 12, 1889, and for weeks prior to that time, and for sometime afterward, a strange and lewd novelty in the form of what appeared to be a short spy glass, and said to be of French origin, but when held to the eye and before light displayed, by turning a portion of that novelty, ten varied and indecent scenes of fully nude men and women in the act of copulating, some in a very low and perverted manner such as would a dog upon a dog, and the said Harry Collins did encourage and allow many men, and some boys of minor age to view said scenes, thus inciting base lusts within them.

• This body [jury] doth now charge that Ballard Wade, an adult of the age of 28 years, and bartender for the Nickel Plate Saloon in Bristol, Virginia, did on the 18th day of June in the year 1892, at about 2:00 P.M. of that day, go into a strange state of mind, likely because of the profuse use of opium, and suddenly removed all his clothes in the presence of all patrons of the Saloon then present, passed out the front door of that Saloon, then calmly, without the least degree of shame and seemingly not aware of his condition, did stroll down the Main Street of Bristol as unconcerned as others would be when fully clothed, said street being heavily populated by Saturday market patrons, and his moral transgression was made much more damaging by the fact that he was in an obvious, and highly pronounced state of carnal arousal. Further his transgression resulted in injury, actual and physical to several ladies, some fainting and falling hard upon the sidewalks, and others while fleeing in horror and fear stumbled or

Ballard Wade shocked Bristol by strolling nude down Main Street.

slipped and fell down much to their injury. Therefore, we charge the said Ballard Wade with gross lewdness and despicable lascivious conduct and prolonged indecent exposure while in a state of carnal excitement, and further of being the cause of injury to several female citizens of the town, all against the peace and dignity of the Commonwealth of Virginia.

• Patsy Webber and William Clarke are hereby charged with unlawful co-habitation, they being unmarried to each other, but openly live together as man and wife.

NOTE: This short and simple indictment is typical of dozens that are on file in area courthouses. It is given here to point out another aspect of the moral condition of early Bristol.

• This jury now sitting [December 3, 1881] charges that at various times and places during the year past, Conrad Denton, an adult of the age of 72 years, did fornicate with one Freda Hudson, a widow of the age of 28 years, who for the past year lived in his home to care for his invalid wife, now deceased, and that by reason of this unlawful fornication, the said Freda Hudson is now with an unborn child. Therefore, the said Conrad Denton is hereby charged with unlawful seduction and fornication, and with the paternity of the unborn child of the said Freda Hudson.

• Be it known and charged that Thomas Lawson did in the Town of Bristol, within this county [Sullivan] marry one Cordelia Southard, said marriage made effective on May 6, 1893, but it has now been discovered that said Thomas Lawson has a lawful wife yet living in Scott County, Virginia, from whom he was never divorced, therefore he is charged with bigamy and is remanded to the court for further action.

Saloons

The almost constant operation of saloons was always considered by many in Bristol to be a moral issue. Such businesses came early to Bristol. The first was set up in 1855 by John N. Bosang in a little board and batten building that stood on the northwest corner of Front and Cumberland streets. (Much later this was the site of the grand General Shelby Hotel.) Bosang later moved his operation to the northwest corner of Main (State) and Moore streets. At the time of this move the new location was considered to be at the western edge of the town. Other saloons were soon to follow. Forty years later there were thirteen located along Main Street, and they continued to operate until long after the name of that street was changed to State.

One of the early saloons in the area was operated by Isaac Nickels in the English basement under the west end of his famous Nickels House Hotel. Old-timers remembered that the saloon stayed open all night, for the convenience of train travelers and hotel guests who might need a little "nerve relaxer" before retiring. At that time virtually every hotel in town featured an inside bar.

A few years later, Mr. Nickels opened an elaborate saloon on Front Street, the finest ever to operate there. It was called the Nickel Plate and was graced by crystal chandeliers, large French mirrors, wall-to-wall carpeting, and a polished rosewood bar.

At that time, even the most lewd of shady ladies did not venture into saloons, though they often loitered just outside the saloon doors, hoping to pick up a little business. Isaac Nickels dared to have floor hostesses and barmaids serving in the Nickel Plate. In time he became infatuated with one of his barmaids, finally marrying her. Alas, within a few months she eloped with his younger brother, "Angel" George Nickels, who was the chief bartender in his high-class saloon. The elopers went to Montgomery, Alabama, and there found work in a saloon.

In a little less than a year, Angel George Nickels wrote his brother, asking if he might return and take up his work at the Nickel Plate. Isaac answered back that he might do so, if "he wouldn't bring that fool woman back here with him." It was no problem, since "that fool woman" had forsaken George and had become the mistress of an Alabama planter. Angel George did return to Bristol, and he continued his work until his death, at an early age, of some type of fever.

Then, as now, the sale of liquor was vehemently opposed by some local citizens and equally defended by others. The "decent" women of the town tried to avoid walking by a saloon, and if it became necessary to do so, they avoided looking in through the windows or doors. There were men who walked by these places with contempt showing on their faces. Rosetta Bachelor, a staunch moralist, always spit toward the saloon doors as she passed, clearly showing her venomous contempt for such places.

All through those years, the Sons of Temperance, long led by the town's founder, Joseph R. Anderson, relentlessly campaigned against the Bristol saloons. The group strongly exhorted its youthful members to abstain from all forms of strong drink. When there was a local election concerning the matter, this group was at the head of the campaign to get out the opposition vote.

Saloonkeepers and those connected with them were generally shunned by the upper crust of the town, and this shunning often extended to members of their families. Their wives were often blackballed when seeking admission to local clubs. In more than one instance, wives of saloonkeepers were refused membership in local churches. In one such case this was done even though the wife strongly opposed her husband's business. She allowed him to have only his meals at home. He had to sleep in a room at the back of his place of business. Five years after her husband's death, the woman was admitted to the membership of Burson's Baptist Church and finally to that of what is now known as First Baptist Church. Even so, she was still looked down upon by the more pious of the congregation.

In spite of much opposition, most Bristol saloons flourished, seeming never to lack for adequate patronage. However, when local prohibition was voted in, some closed, never to reopen, even after the Wets—those who favored the sell of liquor—were able to bring drink to the town again. The Nickel Plate finally fell victim to local prohibition. Mr. Nickels had just bought an enormous quantity of expensive liquors when the temperance element in town won a local election. This so broke him that he was never able to recover financially.

Some saloonkeepers enjoyed moderate financial success. Some became alcoholics and were soon bankrupt. As strange as it seems, one Bristol saloonkeeper had no chance to become a penniless alcoholic. For, though he dispensed gallons of ardent spirits every business day, he had never taken a drink in his life, and he continued to abstain as long as he lived. He made good money for several years in Bristol, then moved to Knoxville, where he became a successful grocer.

Gambling

Another moral issue that was almost a constant source of contention in Bristol was gambling. There is no record that open gambling was ever practiced in the town, but private gambling flourished. From the time of the early rooster fights (on what is now East Hill) until the close of the century, there was always something to bet on, and plenty of bettors. The betting might be on anything of doubtful outcome. A popular subject of betting was the outcome of elections, whether local, state, or national.

According to several old-timers, one of the largest pots ever put together in the town was from bets on a Senate race. Around three thousand dollars made up the pot in this instance. John N. Bosang, a local saloon operator, was the keeper of that pot.

The money was kept in his home, supposedly in an iron box under his bed. This may seem to have been a risky action, unless one is aware of the savage nature of Mr. Bosang and the arsenal that he had at his command. He always slept with two loaded pistols under his pillow and a rifle within hand's reach, as were two swordlike knives. The outlaw element in town knew him too well to try a robbery or theft.

As Old Daddy Thomas used to say, "Why nobody's hide would have held shucks if they'd been fool enough to try and get that bettin' money."

The pot was won by a local merchant, who soon thereafter built one of the finest homes in town. His descendants have been a bit touchy about the matter, so it is likely wise not to reveal his identity.

Of course, there were always the poker games in the closed and locked rooms back of the saloons, or in local hotels and businesses—even in private homes. Sometimes the stakes ran high. It is known that a local saloon was lost in this manner, as was some valuable rental property belonging to another prominent citizen.

There are many indictments in area courthouses for what is termed *illegal gaming* (gambling). The better-known citizens of Bristol who were thus charged include early mayor William L. Rice and Col. Samuel E. Goodson. The latter was charged not only with gaming, but also for having done so on Sunday. Then, as now, many Bristolians loved to gamble, while many others vehemently opposed it.

A Parting Word

Today, there are no flagrant, wide-open brothels operating in Bristol. Neither do numerous, easily identified prostitutes swarm onto the streets at dusk, seeking out customers, as in former days—even as late as fifty years ago. The numerous saloons that used to flourish in downtown Bristol are no more. Open illegal gambling is not winked at by local officials, as was the usual practice a century and more ago. Though it is certain that immorality still exists in Bristol, it does so in less blatant a fashion than was common during the nineteenth century.

In those days when Bristol was a wild and wooly, wide-open border and railroad-terminal town, just about anything could be expected—not only was it expected, it was nearly a day-to-day reality. Today, one can stroll along the peaceful and pleasant streets of the city and not be much reminded of the lewd and grossly immoral place that she once was.

EPILOGUE

Though you have read many tales of varied length and nature, this work is by no means complete. It is merely a sampling of what the author has on file or stored in his memory.

If you are pleased with what you have read and would like more, please inform this author or the publisher. A second volume of *Pioneers in Paradise* could easily be compiled. Meanwhile, if the reader has such tales of early Bristol, the author would like to hear them. Possibly, they too could be included in a future work.

INDEX

Want to know more about Bristol?
Read these first three books in the series by
preeminent historian Bud Phillips.

Covering Bristol's formative years, *Bristol, Tennessee/Virginia: A History—1852-1900* is the story of people and events surrounding the rise of this city between two states. Enhanced with numerous old photographs, this carefully researched and well-written volume is destined to be the standard reference on Bristol for years to come. $27.95

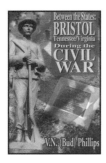

The second book, *Between the States: Bristol, Tennessee/Virginia During the Civil War,* gives a vivid account of Bristol's most trying years—the Civil War period. The book begins with an insight into slave life firsthand from two persons living in the new city just prior to the beginning of the War. However, the story is not one of armies and battles, but rather the effect of the great conflict on the everyday lives of local citizens. $24.95

The Book of Kings follows the King family's contribution to the history of Bristol, Tennessee/Virginia. The history of Bristol would not be complete without including a record of the King family, and it would be difficult to write just of the Kings and not include general Bristol history. From the founder of the clan, Colonel James King, the descendants of the Kings have figured prominently in local history—and continue to do so today. $29.95